BY ALEX BEAM

BROKEN GLASS

RANDOM HOUSE

NEW YORK

BROKEN
GLASS

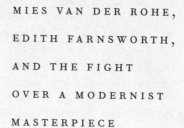

MIES VAN DER ROHE,

EDITH FARNSWORTH,

AND THE FIGHT

OVER A MODERNIST

MASTERPIECE

ALEX BEAM

Published in the United States by Random House, an imprint
and division of Penguin Random House LLC, New York.

RANDOM HOUSE and the HOUSE colophon are
registered trademarks of Penguin Random House LLC.

Photo credits are located on page 322.

LIBRARY OF CONGRESS CATALOGING-IN-PUBLICATION DATA
NAMES: Beam, Alex, author.
TITLE: Broken glass: Mies van der Rohe, Edith Farnsworth, and
the fight over a modernist masterpiece / Alex Beam.
DESCRIPTION: New York: Random House, [2020] | Includes
bibliographical references and index.
IDENTIFIERS: LCCN 2019022841 (print) | LCCN 2019022842
(ebook) | ISBN 9780399592713 (hardcover) | ISBN 9780399592720
(ebook)
SUBJECTS: LCSH: Farnsworth House (Plano, Ill.) |
Mies van der Rohe, Ludwig, 1886–1969. | Farnsworth, Edith. |
Architecture and society—United States—History—20th century.
CLASSIFICATION: LCC NA7238.P53 B43 2020 (print) |
LCC NA7238.P53 (ebook) | DDC 720.9773/0904—dc23
LC record available at https://lccn.loc.gov/2019022841
LC ebook record available at https://lccn.loc.gov/2019022842

Printed in the United States of America on acid-free paper

randomhousebooks.com

987654321

First Edition

Book design by Barbara M. Bachman

TO EDITH

The old Mies friends . . . they didn't want to hear that the house had drawbacks, especially where it was such a milestone in architecture. . . . Then they wound up for the counterpunch, "Do you know what the problem was? It was Edith! Edith wanted Mies. And only because she wanted him did he get the job. And then, later, when he would not marry her, she got mad and hit back."

—ART INSTITUTE OF CHICAGO
ORAL INTERVIEW WITH
WERNER BUCH, ARCHITECT
AND STUDENT OF MIES VAN
DER ROHE, JANUARY 25, 1989

CONTENTS

BROKEN GLASS

"THIS IS MIES, DARLING."

MIES VAN DER ROHE AND EDITH FARNSWORTH met at a small dinner party in Chicago during the winter of 1945. Gallery owner Georgia Lingafelt shared a downtown apartment in the Irving, an elegant low-rise on the North Side, with her friend Ruth Lee. Lingafelt invited three guests who lived nearby on Chicago's affluent Gold Coast: Mies, his girlfriend Lora Marx, and Dr. Farnsworth, a physician, art collector, and poetry aficionado.

While Edith slipped off her overcoat in the foyer, Lingafelt smiled graciously and introduced her to the guest of honor: "This is Mies, darling."[1]

The dinner conversation stumbled forward. Mies, who had immigrated to the United States from Germany seven years before, still hadn't mastered English. (He never would.) Farnsworth later recalled that the women "chatted among ourselves around the granite form of Mies."

When Marx and the hostesses repaired to the kitchen to wash dishes, Farnsworth conversed with Mies. She knew he was a famous architect but knew nothing of his work. Recruited to revamp the architecture department of the Illinois Institute of Technology, Mies had yet to complete a building or residence in the United States.

Mies had no idea who Edith might be, but she was the kind of woman he had been attracted to before: intelligent, stylish, and not a settle downer. The unmarried Farnsworth was forty-two years old and had abandoned a promising career as a violinist to study medicine. Mies, who lived alone, had sampled domesticity, and it didn't agree with him. He'd abandoned his wife and three daughters in wartime Germany. "As a married man, he was a caricature," according to a German friend. "There was something about him that thrived on freedom, required exemption from convention."[2]

Farnsworth told Mies that she had recently bought a parcel of land about an hour southwest of the city, in Plano, Illinois. It was a gorgeous meadow sloping down to the meandering Fox River. She was hoping to build a small weekend cottage there, to escape the demands of her research and clinical work as a kidney specialist at Passavant Memorial Hospital. She wanted to fill her "tired, dull Sundays," as she described her off-call weekends in Chicago. She intended to spend $8,000 to $10,000, the equivalent of about $110,000 today.

"I wonder if there might be some young man in your office who would be willing to design a small studio weekend-house worthy of that lovely shore," she asked.

"I would love to build any kind of house for you," Mies replied. Coming from this taciturn "massive stranger," as she described him later, "the effect was tremendous, like a storm, a flood or other act of God."

Mies had that effect on people. Sixty years old and already feeling the effects of the arthritis that would later cripple him, he still had an oracular presence that particularly appealed to women. Mies was "the epitome of old-fashioned masculinity," according to Farnsworth's contemporary, the curator Katharine Kuh. "His deep, slightly gravelly voice, his slow, accented speech, his elimination of small talk, and his quiet self-assurance all contributed to this image."[3]

Several years later, Mies struggled to recapture details of that fateful conversation. He remembered discussing an unusual, nonstandard project with his prospective client. "She knew that she would get a house that was not normal," Mies said. "When we talked the first time about the house, at that dinner party, I told her I would not be interested in a normal house, but if it could be fine and interesting, then I would do it."[4]

Mies and Edith would soon make architectural history. The Farnsworth House was indeed fine, it wasn't normal, and it was captivating. The house has found its place in the architectural canon, in the slide deck of almost every serious introductory architecture lecture in the world. Architect/critic David Holowka has called the Farnsworth the urtext of modern residential architecture: "Ernest Hemingway famously wrote, 'All modern American literature comes from one book by Mark Twain called *Huckleberry Finn*.' It might as accurately be said that all modern houses come from Mies van der Rohe's Farnsworth House."

Holowka later elaborated: "Icons like Le Corbusier's Villa Savoye are equally famous, but it was Mies's unerring grasp of the irreducible and universal that make his Farnsworth House concept primary and durable," he said.

It plugs into ideas as old as the human impulse toward the primitive hut and as current as [anti-"stuff" crusader] Marie Kondo. It's both groundbreaking and rooted in the fundamental psychological problem of the house: how to resolve our need for shelter with the contradictory human desire for space—to be outside in nature, our evolutionary place where in many ways we still feel most at home.

The critic Paul Goldberger once remarked that "there seems at first to be almost nothing to [the Farnsworth House]—a house so light it might float away." The phrase "nothing to it" invokes Mies's famous dictum of *beinahe nichts*, "almost nothing," his idea that architecture, at its best, should be almost invisible. The Farnsworth House "left other architects little to do except to try to make even more perfect that which was already perfected," according to iconoclastic British architectural critic Reyner Banham.

Invisible; irreproducible, and . . . uninhabitable?

For complicated reasons involving money and a scarcity of materials, the Farnsworth House took forever to build. Conceived in 1945, it wasn't completed until late 1951. For most of that time, Mies and Edith were close friends, intellectual soul mates, and, briefly, lovers, closely attuned to each other's aspiration to create "the most important house in the world."

Then Edith moved in, and Mies moved on. Alienated by cost overruns—she eventually paid $74,000 for the house, almost ten times her original price tag—Farnsworth couldn't abide the myriad problems of her one-of-a-kind architectural gem. The roof leaked. Heating oil smudged the windows. Mies eschewed air conditioning, so the house broiled in the hot Illinois summers.[5]

"Less is more" is the most famous quotation attributed to Mies van der Rohe, a Delphic formula that has been adulated, debated, and inevitably mocked by his revisionist adversaries, e.g., "Less is a bore." The Farnsworth House is, arguably, the least possible house, closer to a Platonic ideal of shelter than a relaxing second home. Perched in its "prairie riparian zone," the house says: Here is a window on nature; what else do you need?

Plenty, was Edith Farnsworth's answer. She quickly decided that less was not enough, and attacked Mies in a lengthy court case intended to besmirch the man whom she once regarded as a genius. She also participated in a very public, and very national, propaganda campaign, eagerly stoked by Frank Lloyd Wright and others, that put modern architecture itself on trial.

AFTER SIX YEARS OF intense amity, the two former intimates ignored each other for the rest of their natural lives. Mies once spotted Edith on a windy Chicago street corner, and remarked that "she looked like a stick in a field—against the birds." He meant she resembled a scarecrow.[6] After immigrating to Italy, Edith spotted "the face of a man in the upper eighties, definite and fearful" in a London newspaper. It was Mies.

This book is the story of their brilliant friendship, their vitriolic breakup, and of the architectural treasure they created along the banks of the Fox River.

"I GIVE YOU MY MIES VAN DER ROHE."

IES VAN DER ROHE, WHO SLAMMED LIKE A gray-suited iceberg into Edith Farnsworth's life on that chilly Chicago night, had traveled a sinuous and improbable path from Aachen, Germany, to the cozy intimacy of a Gold Coast dinner party.

Maria Ludwig Michael Mies was born in 1886 and attended the Aachen Cathedral school, studying in the shadow of one of Europe's most gorgeous cathedrals, a Carolingian-Gothic masterpiece built on the orders of Charlemagne himself. His father ran a masonry business. Mies spent two years in a trade school, then worked as a bricklayer and, ultimately, as a draftsman, after sending his drawings to a Berlin architectural firm that proved eager to hire him. No matter how far Mies traveled, the family business left its stamp. For all his life Mies admired his brother Ewald, a master stonemason who took over the business from their father, and Mies frequently quoted his father, invoking the stonemason's obsession with detail. Why should we toil and sweat over artistic details at the top of a cathedral spire, one might ask, when literally no one can see the work up there? "God can see it" was the axiomatic response of the Aachen tradesmen. It was a lesson Mies never forgot.[1]

Though he would go on to be an academic leader and a successful teacher and mentor to several generations of architects, Mies—like Frank Lloyd Wright and Charles-Édouard Jeanneret (Le Corbusier)—never spent a second in an architecture school.

By age twenty-two, after working as an apprentice for the renowned furniture designer and architect Bruno Paul in Berlin, Mies landed a job as a draftsman in the office of Peter Behrens, one of the most progressive architects in Germany. (Both Le Corbusier and Bauhaus co-founder Walter Gropius cycled through the Behrens office during this time. Mies's tenure overlapped with that of Gropius. Le Corbusier later said he "ran into [Mies] once in the doorway of the office. He was on his way out, I was on my way in.") Mies clearly inspired confidence. Behrens assigned his young assistant to oversee construction of the German embassy in St. Petersburg, Russia.

Like almost all young German men, Mies found his career upended by military service in World War I, as traumatic an experience for the young designer as for everyone around him. Mies never saw combat; an appendectomy put him in the hospital for two months. ("His nerves are in the worst shape," a family member reported.) Assigned first to a headquarters job in Berlin and subsequently to an engineering detail in Romania, he reportedly clashed with a superior officer, had a love affair with a Gypsy, and was generally miserable. His closest friend in the army, the sculptor Wilhelm Lehmbruck, committed suicide shortly after their service.[2]

Rebounding from what has been alternately described as a nervous breakdown or a crisis of professional confidence, Mies embarked on a career as a solo practitioner after the war. Initially, he designed homes for wealthy patrons he met as an up-and-coming young architect. According to his oldest daughter, Georgia, Mies cut a dashing swath through Berlin society:

> My father—tall, quite slender, with an imperial stride, his head always raised high—looked like a Spanish grandee or a Brazilian hacienda owner. An *Arbiter Elegantiarum* [judge of taste and etiquette], always dressed to the nines. He basically lived above his means his entire life.[3]

In that milieu he met his future wife, Adele (Ada) Bruhn, the beautiful brown-haired daughter of a wealthy industrialist. The twenty-five-year-old Mies courted her passionately ("I want to love you with my hot young heart"),[4] fathered three daughters in three years, and just as quickly demonstrated his impatience with domestic life.

The dancer Mary Wigman, who shared a house with Adele before her marriage, testified to intense conflicts during the couple's brief periods of cohabitation. Mies pursued numerous casual out-of-town liaisons, many of the assignations arranged at the couple's weekend property west of Berlin. "He had one girl there," Wigman recalled,

> who was known as "The Horse," because she resembled one. "Yes, I know," he would say to me, "she's no beauty. But she's a dancer, and we are fine together. And it is great fun." He would go on for hours about his Horse.
>
> I could never bring myself to say, "Ludwig, how could you?!" There was something about him that thrived on freedom, required exemption from convention. It was his way, and he blossomed. . . . I do know the whole thing didn't work.[5]

In one of the "Dear Ada" letters chronicling their breakup, Mies returned to the theme of freedom: "Don't adapt your life to mine. Be strong enough that you no longer need me. Then we will belong to a shared freedom; then we will belong to each other."[6]

The marriage lasted barely five years in practice, though the couple never divorced, and Mies never remarried. Marianne Lohan, Mies and Ada's second daughter, remained clear-eyed about her father's life choices. "My mother never stopped being in love with my father," she said. "She would have given Mies a divorce but a no-divorce was convenient for him. It gave him freedom."[7]

Mies launched himself on a life of unconventional relationships, with an emphasis on serial proto-monogamy, coupled with a cool, sometimes cold, indifference to family obligations. As his marriage wound down, Mies began an affair with the talented designer Lilly Reich that would last as long as he stayed in Germany, almost until the beginning of World War II. The self-effacing Reich co-designed the interiors of many of Mies's European masterpieces and co-created much of the famous furniture attributed to him.

Mies, whom we often see in pictures taken at the dawn of middle age, lumbering along in a dark overcoat underneath a nondescript homburg hat, was a handsome young man navigating the waters of the art and architecture avant-garde in Weimar Germany. Lora Marx, his companion in Chicago, recalled that "everything about him was attractive. He was very shy. He never engaged in small talk, except with people who would talk to him about architecture or art. He was innocent, he was not a worldly man."[8]

It was during this period of career advancement and personal change that Mies indulged in a personal reinvention. He abandoned the name Maria Ludwig Michael Mies and rechristened himself Ludwig Mies van der Rohe, tacking his mother's surname *Rohe* onto the Dutch particles suggesting nobility. (To assume the name "von der Rohe" would have been unthinkable in title-conscious Germany.) He also added an umlaut to the "e" of his new surname, making Mies a two-syllable word. Minus the umlaut, the word meant "seedy," "miserable," or "awkward." Mies's first biographer, Franz Schulze, wrote that the Bruhn family's only objection to the ambitious young man their daughter intended

THE YOUNG MIES VAN DER ROHE

to marry was his last name, which may have prompted the change.[9] Later in life he told his daughter Georgia that he was a "self-created" man.*

During the 1920s, Mies primarily designed upper-class

---

* Architect and critic Christian Bjone calls name changes "an overt Freudian tradition for modern architects as shown in the self renaming of Frank Lloyd Wright and Charles Rennie Mackintosh. This continues to current times with the totally invented names of Frank Goldberg changing into Frank Gehry and Jon Nelson Burke into Craig Ellwood." (Gehry's birth name was Ephraim, not Frank.)

residences, although he was simultaneously publishing avant-garde designs in the progressive arts journal *G: Materials for Elemental Form-Creation*, which he supported financially and co-edited. In 1927, he was the chief architect of an ambitious workers' housing complex in Stuttgart that united most of Europe's best-known architects (Le Corbusier, Behrens, Gropius, J.J.P. Oud) to create affordable, attractive worker housing. Allied bombing razed almost half of the twenty-one buildings that comprised the Weissenhofsiedlung (Weissenhof Estate, or Settlement) during World War II, but Mies's low-rise, modernist apartment building still stands. UNESCO added a two-family Weissenhof home designed by Le Corbusier and his cousin, Pierre Jeanneret, to its list of World Heritage sites in 2016.

Also in 1927, despite a pronounced aversion to politics, Mies designed a controversial monument to the martyred German Spartacist revolutionaries Rosa Luxemburg and Karl Liebknecht. Mies cast the stark, gargantuan assemblage in dense, "clinker" brick, one of his favorite materials. The regime shot the Spartacist revolutionaries against a brick wall, he reasoned. That should be their memorial. (In fact, Luxemburg and Liebknecht died in more horrific, sordid circumstances. After torturing both of them, right-wing paramilitaries bludgeoned Luxemburg with a rifle butt, shot her in the head, and tossed her body into a canal. Liebknecht was executed and his unidentified corpse was consigned to a Berlin morgue.)

Two years later Mies designed his first international masterpiece, the German pavilion for the 1929 International Exposition in Barcelona. It was, arguably, a building of no

MIES'S ALL-BRICK LIEBKNECHT-LUXEMBURG MONUMENT

building, a gorgeous pavilion fashioned of the most beautiful materials available. It had almost no purpose whatsoever. Its aim was to display Germany's pre-eminence in post–World War I architecture, and to provide a venue for the king and queen of Spain to sign a guest book to register their presence at the German exhibits. To that end, Mies designed his famous stainless-steel-and-leather "Barcelona chairs" ("monumental objects" he called them) for the monarchs to rest in during their brief visit.

The Barcelona Pavilion was a one-story "open plan" structure slightly elevated from ground level and accessible by a low-slung, travertine marble stairway. There were no rooms, per se, just elegant space flowing from a tranquil outdoor pool through a series of discrete, undefined areas— a new kind of architecture on the world stage. Mies used sumptuous materials, for example, eight thin, electroplated, cruciform columns to support the roof, and a golden marble known as *onyx doré* as a screen to separate open spaces.

"For the first time, Mies was able to build a structure unhampered by functional requirements or insufficient funds," the architect and curator Philip Johnson commented in a famous 1947 monograph. The slender columns and the floating walls contributed to the perceptual sleight of hand: What's holding up those walls? Mies designed glass doors for the pavilion but removed them during the day. Was this an outdoor or an indoor structure? Mies was "letting the outside in," a phrase we will encounter again.

The Barcelona Pavilion "will one day be considered the most beautiful building of the twentieth century," said Mies's mentor and former employer Behrens, who proved to be right. Fritz Neumeyer, a professor of architectural theory at Berlin's Technical University, wrote of the pavilion that "space was no longer defined by limited segments, but rather appeared itself to be set in motion."[10] An austere and bedazzling creation, the pavilion entered the realm of myth when it was torn down along with the other exposition buildings just a year after it was built. Dismantled for shipment back to Germany, the building "was lost" in the chaotic Weimar-era transportation mess, Mies told Peter Blake in 1986. The

INTERIOR OF THE BARCELONA PAVILION,
WITH THE FAMOUS CHAIRS

luxurious marble components were valuable and may have been hijacked en route.

"Did you look for it?" Blake asked.

"We looked for it for years," Mies replied. "No one has ever been able to find it."

For more than fifty years, until Spanish architects mobilized to rebuild it in the early 1980s, the pavilion existed only in Depression-era black-and-white photographs, and in the memories of visitors lucky enough to have ambled through its ethereal spaces.

The very next year, in 1930, Mies designed the Tugendhat House, a spectacular mansion for a wealthy couple in Brno, Czechoslovakia. (Many modern readers have experienced the Tugendhat House in Simon Mawer's novel *The Glass Room*, in which Fritz Tugendhat, a wealthy investor and factory owner, has become car manufacturer Viktor Landauer.)

The Tugendhat had some traits in common with the famous Barcelona Pavilion: Narrow, chromed support columns and a freestanding *onyx doré* wall featured in the "open plan" design. The three-story luxury home flowed down a hillside, with a massive series of second-floor picture windows engineered to disappear into the floor, to open the living spaces to nature on sunny days. If the Barcelona Pavilion was a pure architectural abstraction, the Tugendhat House was abstraction with a purpose: a family of five lived there. The parents' and children's daily lives flowed up and down the three floors, and through the open plan, mostly devoid of corridors, halls, and doorways.

For this project, too, Mies and Reich designed special furniture: the Tugendhat chair, essentially a cantilevered version of the comfortable Barcelona leather loungers, and the Brno, a variation on earlier tubular-steel dining room chairs designed by Mies and his Bauhaus colleague Marcel Breuer. The Tugendhat, Brno, and Barcelona chairs are still sold today.

Mies had now been working as a builder and architect for more than two decades. Famous in Germany, he was suddenly, as his daughter Georgia explained, "in one stroke, world renowned." Barcelona and Brno catapulted him to the top rank of international architects.

It was the young Philip Johnson, after gadding around Europe during a *Wanderjahr* in 1930, who introduced these masterpieces to a broader, if elite, American public. Johnson was the sybaritic scion of a wealthy Midwestern family who savored the decadence of post–World War I Weimar Berlin. The reserved Mies was his antipodal opposite, and yet Johnson developed an admiration and affection for the older architect almost on first acquaintance. On a break from his studies at Harvard—Johnson took seven years to get his undergraduate degree—he was making the grand tour of European architects, and quickly adopted Mies as one of his favorites.

"I was over in Europe with [Museum of Modern Art director] Alfred Barr, and Mrs. Barr and my mother and my sister," Johnson recalled. (Mies called it "the American invasion.")

We descended on him as a guru, but he didn't consider himself to be something like that, he was only in his early forties. . . . Lilly Reich was his mistress at the

time, hovering over him. She was able and practical
and ran the whole studio. She had a definite hold over
Mies, she was a very strong mother woman, and very
able. Mies didn't know from up, he didn't know a steel
beam from a silver watch.

It turned out he was married the whole time, I
never knew about the children. They existed, but they
were in another part of Germany.

We hit it off right away, because I spoke German
and I had heard of Schinkel [Karl Friedrich Schinkel,
the classical German imperial architect], one of Mies's
favorites. Also, I had a car, and nobody had a car. He
liked being taken for rides and he liked good food,
which I could afford.

We would talk, talk, talk until late at night. We
talked about [Johnson imitates a German accent] vat
was important was proportion, vas dedication to the
art of architecture.[11]

Upon returning to the United States, Johnson and his
friend Henry-Russell Hitchcock published *The International
Style,* which introduced Americans to Le Corbusier, Gropius, Oud, Mies, and Richard Neutra, an Austrian who was
starting to make a career in Southern California. The book
accompanied the stripling Johnson's first curated show, in
1932, at the spanking-new Museum of Modern Art in New
York: *Modern Architecture: International Exhibition.* The exhibit featured a model of the Barcelona Pavilion and a photo
of the Villa Tugendhat on the exhibit catalog cover.

Mies, or the idea of Mies, had made its American landfall.

ADOLF HITLER CAME TO power in Germany in 1933. Mies didn't oppose Hitlerism or Hitler, a former art student who fancied himself an expert on architecture. In 1933, Mies submitted a proposal for the high-profile Reichsbank competition, which he did not win. The next year, he offered a design for the German pavilion at the Brussels International Exposition, a blueprint that Hitler personally rejected, decorative swastika and all. Also in 1934, Mies signed a groveling letter of support for the Nazi regime and for "the young Führer of the land. . . . We trust his work, which asks sacrifice beyond all carping sophistry. We place our hope in the man who, beyond man and things, believes in God's providence."

When the Nazis sought to shut down the Bauhaus, where Mies had been director since 1930, he tried to negotiate with Alfred Rosenberg, one of several Third Reich officials who claimed to be Hitler's culture czar. The conversation went badly. Rosenberg all but assured Mies that he had no future in Germany. (Rosenberg was sentenced to death and executed for crimes against humanity at the Nuremberg war crimes trials in 1946.)

Later in life, Mies faced withering criticism for his accommodationist attitudes toward the Nazis. After Mies's death, Johnson—a notorious, *heil*-fellow-well-met Nazi cheerleader during the 1930s—told an interviewer that "if the devil himself offered Mies a job, he would take it." Later, Johnson went further: "Nazis schmatzis, Mies would have built for anyone."[12] This is quite rich, coming from a man who toured wartime Poland in his Ford Lincoln as a correspondent for the

MIES'S DRAWING FOR GERMANY'S BRUSSELS PAVILION

anti-Semitic newspaper *Social Justice*, and reported "the German green uniforms made the place look gay and happy. There were not many Jews to be seen. We saw Warsaw burn and Modlin being bombed. It was a stirring spectacle."[13]

But as *The New Republic*'s architecture critic Martin Filler observed: "To see the photographs and the drawings of . . . the Liebknecht-Luxemburg Monument with its Red Star and its hammer and sickle, the Brussels Pavilion with its swastika—is to realize that the chillingly opportunistic Mies would change party symbols as insouciantly as switching boutonnieres."[14]

Mies's defenders have always maintained that he was apolitical. Even the waspish Johnson allowed that Mies was fundamentally indifferent to politics. "[Mies] wasn't anti-Semitic, he wasn't anti-Nazi," Johnson said in an interview with Peter Eisenman. "He wanted to stay [in Germany.]" That was true, although perhaps not an excuse for cozying up to the Nazis and their outriders. In 1968, his grandson, the architect Dirk Lohan, asked Mies about the left-wing political machinations at the Bauhaus. Mies replied:

> I was not interested in that. I am not someone who wants to improve the world, never have claimed to be that or wanted to be that. I am an architect. I am interested in building and in design in general, and you can interpret "building" in a wider sense.[15]

Those who knew him best pointed to an out-of-worldliness that bordered on extreme naïveté.

For instance, throughout his life he had only the faintest understanding of financial affairs. When informed that ordinary workers could never afford to live in his stylish Stuttgart housing complex, he replied, "Pay them more money!" He almost certainly would have remained in Germany had work been available. But it was not, and it was unlikely to materialize. For the new gauleiters of German culture, Mies's dossier was tainted by his tangency to the great creative minds of his time: Gropius, Paul Klee, Kazimir Malevich, and many others who were left-wing anti-Nazis.

Then, as if by magic, four job offers appeared simultaneously from America. Mies's life was about to change.

THERE WAS AN EASY-TO-DISCERN East Coast establishment in 1930s America, and Philip Johnson's friend Alfred Barr, the first director of the Museum of Modern Art, was at its center. Barr, an aesthete and an aristocrat, was looking for an architect to design MoMA's new building on Forty-eighth Street. Barr approached Mies, who was very interested, although the Rockefellers who ran the board of trustees favored an American architect over a foreigner. In the end, they got two—Philip Goodwin and Edward Durell Stone. Barr quickly pivoted and pitched Mies to Joseph Hudnut, the dean of Harvard's hidebound architecture school, which was looking to Europe for new leadership.

Hudnut admired Mies. He'd spent time with him in Berlin, and spelled out some of his attractions in a memorandum for Harvard president James Conant:

> Mies is perhaps the most original architect among the modernists. He has arrived at his style by a long series of aesthetic experimentations rather than by a philosophical analysis. He is a sensitive artist with an extraordinary feeling for space and for the qualities of the planes which divide space. In his work, he is somewhat extravagant, since he refuses to use any cheap materials. He despises ornament, believing that decorative qualities in work should be achieved by the richness of materials used, and he is especially famous for his successful use of glass.[16]

Because both Gropius and Mies had at different times directed the left-wing Bauhaus, Hudnut felt obliged to explain that "neither Gropius nor Mies have any sympathy with Communism." In his eagerness to whitewash Mies, Hudnut explained he "is now a government architect"—hardly an accolade in Hitler's Germany.

Like the MoMA commission, the prospect of a Harvard architecture chair proved chimerical. Mies had assumed he was the sole candidate. When he learned that he would be competing with Gropius for the position, Mies immediately withdrew his candidacy. This was in part because he was fiercely proud, and also because he had never thought much of Gropius, whom he viewed as a bit of a hustler. There is some question about whether Harvard would have accepted Mies, regardless. Hudnut confided to Barr that Mies's unconventional domestic arrangements might not find favor in cold-roast Boston: "I don't know what to do about Fraulein [Lilly] Reich," Hudnut confided to Barr, "but I suppose that problem, too, can be solved with a little tact—perhaps I should say with considerable tact."[17] What might have been more important was that Gropius spoke English, and Mies did not.

But Barr wasn't done promoting Mies. Barr knew that a fellow MoMA board member, advertising executive Helen Resor, had just fired Philip Goodwin as the architect for her family's ranch home in Jackson Hole, Wyoming. He touted Mies as "the finest architect of the postwar period," adding that if he came to America he could make as great a contribution here as Albert Einstein or the conductor Arturo Toscanini.[18]

Mies seized the Resor commission, which, like so many of his projects of that decade, would never be built. But the Resors paid for him to come to America in 1937. To reach Wyoming, he had to pass through Chicago. There another klatch of would-be Mies suitors lay in wait: the trustees of the Armour Institute of Technology, who wanted to reinvigorate the architecture department at their little-known institution. Armour board chairman Henry Heald admitted to Chicago architect John Holabird, "I don't know Mies van der Rohe, but the Barcelona Pavilion and one or two other things that he has done are outstanding. And after all, even if we don't know too much about this fellow, he's so much better than any of the other people you could get to head a school of architecture: why not take a chance?"[19]

Armour made him an offer and Mies accepted it, with a proviso that he return to Germany to settle his affairs. Mies asked for "a completely free hand, and $10,000 a year." (About $170,000 today.) Heald provided the free hand, and after several years, raised Mies's salary to the desired level.[20]

Even after signing the contract, Mies wasn't certain that he wanted to leave Germany to take the job. By his late forties he was already entropic, reluctant to change, and slow even to face the day. According to Elaine Hochman, who wrote an account of Mies's German years, he rose only after noon on many days and didn't dress until two P.M. "Essentially a solitary man who preferred the lonely certainties of introspection to the capriciousness of daily life" was Hochman's assessment.[21] His daughter Marianne Lohan remembered her father saying, "If I had a dog, that would be a perfect companion! The dog is always here, but never asking questions and making no demands on me!" It was the practical-minded Reich, arguing against her interests as the lawyers say, who browbeat Mies into accepting the Armour offer. More clearly than Mies, she saw that there was no future for him in Hitler's Germany.

One highlight of Mies's first trip to America was an impromptu visit to Taliesin, Frank Lloyd Wright's design headquarters and architectural colony, in Spring Green, Wisconsin. Mies asked for an afternoon with the Master, but stayed for four euphoric days. Wright's hospitality was all the more startling because he was famously prickly. He resented the great European modernists, who he felt (absent much evidence) had pirated many of his ideas and founded reputations on them. Wright had previously rebuffed both Gropius and Le Corbusier when they asked to visit the king in his self-styled castle. But Wright admired Mies's portfolio, paying it the ultimate compliment: He thought Mies's use of open-plan interiors, without doors and walls, was an homage to Wright's own work. The visit may have helped convince Mies that he could find a home in America.

From Mies's perspective, Wright enjoyed a hard-earned privilege available to few people on earth: "Freedom!" he cried when he walked out on Wright's fieldstone terrace overlooking the Wisconsin hillscape. "This is a kingdom!"

Mies left Germany in 1938 under a cloud. The gestapo had seized his passport in an unannounced raid and interrogation at his apartment, so he used his brother's document to slip across the border from Aachen into Holland. Mies's departure had severe consequences for his wife and daughters, whom the regime now considered relations of an "enemy emigrant." The German government froze their bank accounts;[22] and it was Lilly Reich's formidable organizational skills that helped them survive the war years.

"He did not plan to take one of us along or to have us join him later," his daughter Georgia reported. "Except for a postcard from New York, we did not hear from him for seven years. He was not the type of a caring and providing husband and father."[23]

Mies treated Reich as coolly as if she were family. She traveled to America in the summer of 1939 and spent a few bucolic months working with Mies and some of his colleagues, ensconced at a lakeside resort in the Wisconsin woods. World War II was imminent. "Reich wanted to stay with Mies," Schulze wrote, "here, far from the bleak haunts she had left. It is presumed by most of his friends that he did little to persuade her to remain, chiefly because he felt the need to be free of her and her commanding personality." By the time Reich departed for Berlin, German troops had invaded Poland. She and Mies would never meet again.[24]

Allied bombing destroyed Reich's studio in Berlin, and she spent much of the war in Saxony. But not before securing several boxes of Mies's professional effects and safeguarding them in a house in Thuringia. Decades later, these valuable files found their way to MoMA's Mies van der Rohe archive. After the war, Mies sent Reich art supplies to help relaunch her design practice, which did not last long.[25] She died in December 1947.

According to Philip Johnson, Mies told him: "I have only one regret. That I didn't help Lily Reich get out of Germany." Schulze likened his subject to a nautilus that emerges to survey the world and then retreats back into its shell. "[Mies] was not so much lacking in long-standing affection as he was in the ability, even the will, to express it" was the biographer's judgment.[26]

"Immer noch bin ein stille Deutsche" was Mies's famous self-assessment relayed again by Philip Johnson, who liked to drink and speak German, two activities that drew Mies out of his shell. Translation: "I am forever the silent German."

IN NOVEMBER 1938, ARMOUR hosted a banquet at the Palmer House's Red Lacquer Room to present the institute's new architecture director to the world. Mies had asked Frank Lloyd Wright to introduce him to the audience of four hundred architecture mavens and Midwestern grandees, and the Master responded, in imitable Wright fashion. "It was all superficial blah and labored lip service," Wright wrote in his 1943 autobiography, that is, until I—meaning Wright—stepped up to the podium.

> I put my arm across Mies' shoulders . . . and simply said, "Ladies and gentlemen, I give you Mies van der Rohe. But for me there would have been no Mies— certainly none here tonight. I admire him as an architect and respect and love him as a man. Armour Institute, I give you my Mies van der Rohe. You treat him well and love him as I do."

Wright's idiosyncratic account of Mies's remarks, delivered in German, recounted only the moments dedicated to him, again meaning Wright: "For some five minutes he went into the origin of his discipleship and his reverence for me. He told me how much he was indebted to me, frankly and to the point." Wright remembered the talk as "an affectionate tribute such as is rare in the history of the world, the architect's world at least."[27]

Mies's address to the Armour grandees in fact hardly dwelt on Wright, who bolted early from the auditorium. The bulk of Mies's remarks indulged his almost irrepressible urge to philosophize about architecture, a subject on which he quickly became the not-so-silent German. His penchant for "Miesticism" enthralled many and alienated some. Mies appeared to devour—or at least talked about reading— philosophy texts both past and present. In Germany, he had befriended the Jesuit philosopher Romano Guardini and the famous Catholic architect and theologian Rudolf Schwarz, a provocative and successful designer of modern churches. Mies, reared in the Carolingian monumentalism of fin de siècle Aachen, liked to say that architecture represented "the will of the epoch," or *Zeitwille* in German. What did he mean? "Whoever asks the name of the first building master of a medieval cathedral or the name of an Egyptian architect?" he once asked. "And also the cathedrals of the Middle Ages were not the work of individual personalities but the creations of entire epochs."[28]

Alternately explained:

Architecture should only stand in contact with the most significant elements of civilization. Only a relationship that touches on the innermost nature of the epoch is authentic. I call this relationship a truth relationship. Truth in the sense of Thomas Aquinas: as *adaequatio intellectus et rei*, as congruence of thought and thing.[29]

Mies was certainly willing to state incongruent views. He once called Albert Kahn's sprawling assembly plants built for Ford Motor Company and others in Detroit "the cathedrals of the twentieth century."[30] He insisted that his favorite building in New York City was the George Washington Bridge, a manifestation of the "will of an epoch," to be sure. His student and colleague Myron Goldsmith recalled Mies rhapsodizing about a visit to a sprawling plywood storage facility outside of Chicago. "He loved this big, empty warehouse," Goldsmith said. "What a wonderful house it would make, this space where you could just live. How all the problems are solved."[31]

While watching his first skyscraper masterpiece, the twin towers at 860/880 Lake Shore Drive, rise over Lake Michigan, Mies ventured the opinion that they looked better half built. This dovetailed with his view that "Skyscrapers reveal their bold structural pattern during construction. Only then does the gigantic steel web seem impressive. When the outer walls are put in place, the structural system which is the basis for all artistic design is hidden by a chaos of meaningless and trivial forms."[32]

Miesticism had its doubters. Mies's former colleague Joseph Fujikawa thought Mies read philosophy "to confirm ideas which he himself had. . . . I think it reinforced his own convictions. I think he read philosophy primarily for that reason."[33] More of a debunker than a doubter, Reyner Banham observed that Mies's "tendency to quote authorities like Saint Augustine in the original has done much to build up an image of a committed classicist, especially among those who cannot know that this merely means he had a German education instead of an Anglo-Saxon dragging-up."

Philip Johnson, who would, at different times throughout his life, be Mies's disciple, detractor, or promoter, called Mies "a passionate anti-intellectual." Recalling his visits to Mies's Berlin office in the early 1930s, Johnson remembered, "He said, 'I have just read,' so I looked around his library and found that it was not true—he had anyway only three books. Not a one had been taken from the shelf in all these years."

Mies claimed to read, and, especially under the influence of martinis, he could "talk, talk, talk," as Johnson put it, but one thing he almost never did was write. Unlike such prolix and prolific architecture theorists as Gropius and László Moholy-Nagy, to mention only two of the Bauhaus's leading publicists, Mies never published a book or a major theoretical tract. "Convictions are necessary," he once wrote, "but in the realm of one's work they have only limited significance. In the final analysis it is the performance that matters. . . . That is what Goethe meant when he said, 'Create, artist, do not talk.' "[34]

For his Palmer House inaugural address, Mies cobbled together a 1,100-word tour d'horizon of his abstruse views:

> Every decision leads to a specific kind of order.
> Therefore we want to illuminate the possible orders and lay bare their principles.

Let us recognize that the mechanistic principle of order overemphasizes the materialistic and function-alistic factors.

Even Mies's admiring biographers, Franz Schulze and Edward Windhorst, admit that the speech, "like almost all of Mies's published professional expression, [was] aphoristic, proclamatory, and devoid of sustained argument."[35]

By the time Mies reached his stirring peroration—"Nothing can unlock the aim and meaning of our work better than the profound words of St. Augustine: 'Beauty is the radiance of truth'"—Wright and his entourage were holding court in the adjoining hotel bar.

CHAPTER 2

"SHE HAD A VERY SHARP TONGUE."

D R. EDITH FARNSWORTH, THE WOMAN WHOM Georgia Lingafelt placed next to Mies van der Rohe at the intimate dinner party in 1945, navigated the world more or less on her own, and didn't seem cowed by the prospect of continuing that way.

The only account of Edith's childhood springs from her own pen, in an undated memoir written in Italy, where she spent the last years of her life. She described a youth of comfort and privilege, growing up on Astor Street, on Chicago's Near North Side, in a neighborhood of elegant townhouses just north of the city center.

A vivid childhood memory was waiting for her sister, Marion, to return from the Latin School, around the corner on Division Street, to recount her grade school academic adventures.

Edith's mornings would begin "with poppy-seed rolls still hot from the neighboring bakery, eaten at the round table in the dining room." At bedtime, her mother read to her from *A Child's Garden of Verses.* Mother and daughter recited prayers together and sang songs until Edith fell asleep. At holiday dinners, Edith and Marion were encouraged to go downstairs to the kitchen, to thank the two cooks and wish them a Merry Christmas. After the family moved to Chicago's North Shore, Edith recalled watching ships from her bedroom window. "At night, when those black lines with their vanishing smoke were lost in darkness, the long bass notes of their whistles reached me over the water," she wrote. Her father explained that ships everywhere "salute" the lighthouse when they pass. "There was something great, and lovely, about those giant voices in the night, speaking to one another, and saluting the lighthouse."

The Farnsworths were prosperous, and friends reported that Edith never seemed to want for money during her lifetime. Her father's family owned two lumber enterprises north of Chicago: the Oconto Lumber Company in Wisconsin, and the Bay de Noquet Lumber Company in Michigan's Upper Peninsula. Edith visited the operations as a little girl and remembered American Indians on the Upper Peninsula loading lumber onto flatcars for transport southward. She wrote that the mills provided "a detailed model of paternalistic management. The Company owned the land on which the mill and the town were built. The offices, the post office, general store, hotel and churches, schools and residences were built as they were required." Like her sister, Edith attended Latin School, founded in 1888 to teach Latin, Greek,

French, German, and English, as well as math, science, and art, to the sons and daughters of Chicago's first families. It was probably as close as America could come to competing with the venerable cathedral school in Aachen.

Edith spent many childhood summers in the northern timberlands. Remembered from a vantage point fifty years in the future, the logging operations seemed improbably bucolic. "Nobody suffered from want and nobody seemed to be unhappy. Everybody worked at what he knew how to do and everybody was kind and friendly." She remembered an ominous conversation with her father about "outside agitators" pressing for unionization of the workforce, but she provided no further details.

Edith enrolled at the University of Chicago, majoring in English literature and minoring in zoology, but never completed her bachelor's degree. At the same time, she studied violin at the American Conservatory of Music (which no longer exists in Chicago). At age nineteen, she sailed on the SS *Julius Caesar* for Italy, to study violin in Rome with the maestro Mario Corti at the Villa d'Este, a magnificent mansion in Rome's Tivoli gardens. Corti was a famous Italian concert virtuoso, twenty-one years her senior, who later became artistic director of Rome's Philharmonic Academy and superintendent of the La Fenice opera house in Venice.

At the end of the summer program, she reported, "Corti took a furnished room for me in the apartment above the one he occupied by himself" and urged her to stay in Italy as his student. She did stay, apparently as Corti's mistress. In her memoir, she recorded the maestro's *declarazione di amore* ("I love you with all my heart"). She would remain in Italy for almost two more years.

Returning from Italy on board the SS *Berlin*, Farnsworth had a chance encounter that changed her life. She befriended Dr. Elis Berven, a pioneer in cancer radiation therapy from Stockholm's Karolinska Institute. They made a lasting impression on each other. Berven's mesmerizing table talk convinced Edith to pursue a medical degree. Years later, Berven's wife rhapsodized about meeting the young woman from Chicago whom her husband mentioned with such enthusiasm in his daily letters from on board ship.

The die was cast. Edith would pursue medicine.

"Her aim in life was to become a concert violinist," according to her nephew, Fairbank Carpenter. "She worked on the violin for years until she came to the realization that she wasn't going to play at the concert level. That's when she got into medicine." Edith decided to enroll at the Northwestern University School of Medicine.

At age twenty-nine Edith joined the class of 1937 at Northwestern. Mid-twentieth-century medicine was not a woman's world, but neither was the concert stage. Four women entered the class of 140 aspiring doctors with Edith, and five joined the graduating class of freshly minted MDs four years later.

In her fragmentary journals, Edith rarely mentions friends from her younger years. One exception is the writer Katharine Butler Hathaway, whom Edith met in Paris, and again in Maine. We know more about their friendship from

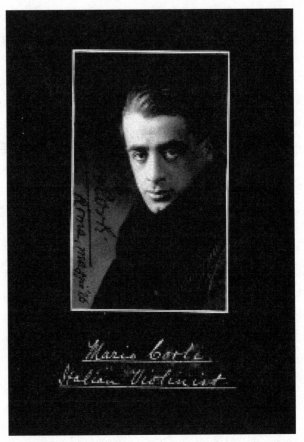

IL MAESTRO CORTI

Hathaway's copious diaries than from Edith's writings. In Paris, the two women vamped at La Coupole, the famous Left Bank café, and called themselves "Miss Furr and Miss Skeene," two unmarried characters from a 1923 Gertrude Stein short story.

Katharine Hathaway was a famous, tragic writer who overcame spinal tuberculosis and its medieval treatment—

she was pinned to a board in her childhood bedroom, her neck and head immobilized by weights—to attend Radcliffe College. Severely crippled, she lived with her husband in a large house in Castine, Maine, wrote poetry, and published a

Canterbury E   Carryer H M   Christie G C

Derlacki E L   Dille R S   Elmore E F

Eyer S W   Fargher R A   Farnsworth E B

ADRIFT IN A SEA OF MEN; A CLIP FROM DR. FARNSWORTH'S MEDICAL SCHOOL YEARBOOK

well-received and bestselling memoir, *The Little Locksmith.*
Serialized in *The Atlantic Monthly,* the book version of *Locksmith* came out shortly after Hathaway's death at age fifty-
two, in 1942.

Edith appears several times in Hathaway's journals,
sometimes playing her violin for her shut-in friend and generally reveling in gossip:

> Edith has written me. . . . There was a guarded
> secret—a love affair. Heavens—I *hope* she will be dis-
> creet + very wary or the wolves will be after her +
> she'll be ruined. . . . It has just come over me that
> Edith belongs with Joan of Arc, according to Shaw's
> analysis of Joan in his preface to the play, as I remem-
> ber it, the formula fits Edith, too. This explains why
> certain people dislike her so violently, why she is be-
> loved by some + hated by others.[1]

George Bernard Shaw's lengthy preface to his 1923 play
Saint Joan does have several lines that might apply to Edith:
"As her actual condition was pure upstart, there were only
two opinions about her. One was that she was miraculous:
the other that she was unbearable." Or: "When she was
thwarted by men whom she thought fools, she made no
secret of her opinion of them or her impatience with their
folly; and she was naïve enough to expect them to be obliged
to her for setting them right and keeping them out of mis-
chief."

While staying at her brother's apartment in New York,

Hathaway crossed paths with Edith: "Edith Farnsworth came yesterday, feeling rather desperate, hating New York and hating all people. Yet she has so much vitality + courage she isn't crushed, only passionately rebellious. I liked her very much. She had very good looking clothes."[2]

When she presented herself at Georgia Lingafelt's dinner party in 1945, Edith had been a doctor for five years. She worked on the staff at Passavant Memorial Hospital, which had a new building and had become a teaching hospital for Northwestern's medical school. Passavant had strong connections to Chicago's Gold Coast. Colonel Robert McCormick, the newspaper baron from whom Edith had purchased her nine acres in Plano, gave $2 million for the new building. The Wards, as in catalog merchants Montgomery Ward, were also huge benefactors, along with collateral Swifts, Armours, and Rockefellers.

In a letter supporting her application to Passavant, Northwestern's A. C. Ivy testified that "Miss Edith Farnsworth is a young woman of excellent character and habits. She is neat in personal appearance and expresses a pleasing personality. I am sure that she will be liked by patients and the attending staff."[3]

Passavant was an old-fashioned charity hospital, founded by a Methodist minister and sustained by deep-pocketed donors. In Edith's first years of practice, male doctors were scarce, having been absorbed by World War II. She saw private patients and tentatively ventured into kidney research, in the field that would come to be known as nephrology.

Edith's friends described her as "correct," quite finicky,

and, as a maturing woman in her thirties and forties, conservative on questions of etiquette and behavior. She was hyperintelligent and spoke in a breathy voice, the product of decades of chain-smoking.

"She had a very sharp tongue, and she was quick to be critical of almost anybody even if you were sitting there," remembered Ellyn Kivitts, one of several Plano residents whom Edith befriended after purchasing her Fox River acreage. Kivitts recalls Farnsworth telling gritty stories of her medical training, which amounted to a crash course on How the Other Half Lives. "When she practiced medicine in Chicago, she would make house calls, and tell us about the awful hovels that she would go into," Kivitts recollected for an oral history. "This woman called her into her home where she was going to have a baby, and of course it was very nasty in there. They somehow got a lot of newspaper and put it on the floor and delivered the baby. Edith was appalled by the condition of this awful place."[4]

Writing about her doctoring, Edith sounded a bit old-fashioned, calling attention to her status as a new, but not particularly young, doctor. In one memoir entry, she writes that "the laying on of hands" sometimes helped patients. Like her twenty-first-century counterparts, she regretted that physicians and patients spent so little time together.

Edith had a cranky streak, evinced throughout her adult life. "She was very bright, and had a difficult personality," according to her Chicago friend Parkie Emmons, who bought property near Edith's in Plano. "But like so many difficult people, she also had a very appealing side. She had an attitude that most doctors have, that when they give an order they expect people to get up and do it."[5]

Finding herself in the office with her patient Miss Wetherly, a librarian from northern Michigan complaining about her "drives," Farnsworth could barely contain her scorn. Miss Wetherly had happened across an article in a popular psychology magazine, and then consulted a psychiatrist who "explained how not getting married at the right time made [Wetherly] hostile towards life, so both hostilities and sexual drives were repressed."

Farnsworth's reply, recorded in her journal: "The common human day is full of signs of impatience and bad temper," for example a baby's tantrum, or a missed putt in golf. "Would it be sensible of us to magnify these little outbursts and restate them in the pompous terms of theoretical psychology, let alone psychiatry?"

"But how about my drives?" Wetherly asked. "And my repressions?"

There are more familiar terms for these feelings, Farnsworth responded, like "impulses" and "upbringing." These "old names are like domestic animals—the cats which are used to your hearth and the dogs whose ways you know—leave the safaris to other people who are trained for the jungle." Her journal entry continued:

Miss Wetherly regarded me dully. "I don't know what you mean, doctor."

"I mean that you have been talked into an interpretation of your life and self which has shocked and frightened you, a crude and violent interpretation which is completely unsuitable to you, but because it was offered by a person with authority you feel that you must accept and believe it."

Her duties kept Edith extremely busy. Not only did she have hospital obligations and outside clinical commitments, she also held an appointment as an assistant professor at Northwestern Medical School. In the mid-1940s, right around the time she first met Mies, she started working in her own lab, researching applications of synthetic hormones in improving kidney function for diabetic patients.

The three roles took a heavy toll. "The strain of those early years was great not only because of the weight of the responsibility, but because of the wild-cat calls for a physician which come into any hospital," she wrote.

These included corpses washed up on the beach, as well as all of the usual incidents to be expected in the life of a great city and were apt to come from the wrong side of the tracks or from transients in hotels of various levels. Many of these were neither pleasant nor safe.

On Sunday afternoons I used to stretch out on the sofa and listen to the New York Philharmonic on the radio. Often I dropped off to sleep during the program, and wakened to the gripping timbre of [Catholic radio evangelist] Msgr. Sheen, as he worked his vineyard. As spring came on one year, I came to the conclusion that something would have to be done about those tired, dull Sundays.

Like well-to-do Americans before and after her, Edith was thinking of a country retreat. A small cottage next to a river, perhaps; a convenient hour's drive from the center of the city.

DR. EDITH FARNSWORTH

CHAPTER 3

"LET THE OUTSIDE IN."

Aerter the dinner party at georgia Lingafelt's, Edith Farnsworth hurried home to figure out just who Mies van der Rohe was. Leafing through some art books, she noticed that Mies was "an architect who seemed to have a singular predilection for luxury materials." And, furthermore, "an architect whose austerity had kept him from popularity and whose manner was determined by his insight."

He had definitely made an impression, and their meeting was most fortuitous. Edith and a friend had gone property hunting southwest of the city some months before and happened upon a flower-strewn meadow sloping down to the Fox River. A young girl riding along on a pony told the women that the land belonged to the sprawling 1,300-acre Tribune

Farm, an experimental property in Plano, managed by Colonel Robert McCormick, the wealthy publisher of the *Chicago Tribune*.

Plano was about an hour's drive from the city. Landed gentry other than the McCormicks owned property there, including theater operators A. J. Balaban and Sam Katz; the heirs to the Horlicks malted-milk fortune; and the Simmonses of the fast-growing mattress empire. After some dickering, Colonel McCormick sold Edith a nine-acre parcel of land, including the scenic meadow, for a few hundred dollars.

As soon as the weather warmed up, Farnsworth started driving Mies out to the Fox River site in her Chevrolet coupe, always in the company of her white cocker spaniel:

> We set out for a day in the country, to inspect the property with a view to the ideal weekend house. . . . I stopped at 200 East Pearson to call for Mies, and he came out wearing an enormous black overcoat of some kind of soft, fine wool which reached well down toward his ankles. Installed beside me in the little Chevrolet, he put up only feeble resistance to the advances of my white cocker who sprawled across his knees for the duration of the trip. Finally we reached the dooryard of the farmhouse and I could open the car doors. The emergence of Mies and the cocker was spectacular, as it turned out that the latter had yielded most of his white coat in a soft frosting over the black wool of that splendid overcoat, and we had nothing on board with which to remove.

From then on, Edith reported that the two of them "made frequent Sunday excursions out to Plano. As the warm weather came on we had to cut pathways through the weeds and meadow grass down to the shore. From the bank we studied various sites for the house and drove a few tentative stakes."

Edith's acreage was magnificent. The plot emerged from a forest that abutted a road to the north, then sloped gently down to a broad meadow spread along the banks of the river. The site afforded almost total privacy. The river road lay well to the north, and the deciduous forest screened Edith's property from travelers. The nearest bridge was half a mile to the west. The opposite river bank was undeveloped, and in the unlikely event that campers or canoers came floating by, there was the possibility of nesting a house behind a gigantic black sugar maple, one of several trees scattered near the riverbank.

Farnsworth isn't always a reliable narrator, but she was telling the truth when she recalled how much Mies loved the site:

> We walked down the slope, through the frozen meadow grass and dormant brush, and I worried for fear a European might be unable to see the beauty of the mid-west countryside at so unfavorable a season; but midway down, Mies stopped and looked all around him. "It is beautiful!" he said, and I didn't doubt the spontaneity of his exclamation.

The forest, the natural meadow, and the quiet flow of the river enchanted Mies.

"We talked about possible materials for the house, about brick and stone," Mies later commented. "As I remember Dr. Farnsworth did not like brick, and as it was raining she suggested we visit a nearby quarry."[1] Brick was one of Mies's favorite building materials, but he must have intuited that it was ill-suited for the bucolic meadow spreading out in front of him. During a subsequent visit, when Farnsworth asked him what kind of materials he planned to use for the house, he didn't answer her directly. "I wouldn't think of the problem quite like that," he replied.

I wouldn't think, "We'll build a brick house or a reinforced concrete house." If we were building in the city or in the suburbs, on the other hand, I would make it opaque from outside and bring in the light through a garden courtyard in the middle. I would think that here where everything is beautiful, and privacy is no issue, it would be a pity to erect an opaque wall between the outside and the inside. So I think we should build the house of steel and glass; in that way, we'll let the outside in.

A question presents itself: If Mies had an idea for the Farnsworth House, was it wholly original to the place and the moment, or did it spring from a design or idea that he had had before? Cautiously, Miesians mention a single sketch elevation, *Glass house on a hillside,* as a possible antecedent for the Farnsworth House design. The sketch dates back to 1934, and is thought to be an idea for a summerhouse—Mies's own, theoretically—in Merano, a town in the Italian South

Tyrol, where he and Reich had vacationed. The 1934 glass house assumed a rugged hillside and addressed the landscape with a cantilever, rather than the five-foot piers that Mies eventually chose for the Plano meadow.

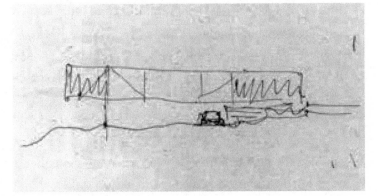

GLASS HOUSE ON A HILLSIDE, 1934

Closer in time, Mies had generated hundreds of provocative sketches for the Resor House in Wyoming, for the rich couple that first invited him to the United States. The Resors owned some beautiful open country next to a wild river, and, instead of putting their house on one of the banks, they and their first architect, Philip Goodwin, had decided to plant the house astride the river. In his follow-up designs, Mies proposed an elongated open-plan home that shared many design elements with the Farnsworth House: It was sited above ground level, and the exterior walls facing up- and down-river were glass. In the end, the river proved too wild to tame. A flood washed out one of the home's concrete piers, and the Resors lost their enthusiasm for the project. But Mies definitely intended to "let the outside in," to subordinate his architecture to the magnificence of the Big Sky site.

CHOOSING THE SITE FOR a house or building can be the most important and creative decision an architect makes. The Roman architect/engineer Vitruvius obsessed about the correct sites for cities, temples, and residences in *De Architectura*, published around 30 B.C. He was the Goldilocks of architectural theorists, prescribing (1) Don't build on high promontories—too windy! (2) Don't build in lowlands—marsh gases! But (3) Build somewhere in between, and arrange your corridors along breeze lines to sweep foul odors and pestilence from your doorstep. Vitruvius was also the first writer to recommend building on an east–west axis, to take advantage of the southerly course of the sun.

Great houses rise on great sites. Frank Lloyd Wright's decision to build Edgar Kaufmann's Pennsylvania summer home, Fallingwater, *atop* the scenic waterfall that ran through the department store magnate's property made architectural history. "E.J., I want you to live with the waterfall, not just look at it," Wright told his client.

Often site choices are more subtle, although just as important. Wright built a suburban home for his clients Isadore and Lucille Zimmerman along a diagonal on a square lot in Manchester, New Hampshire, in part to use the site's longer hypotenuse for a façade, and in part to make the house stand out from its boring suburban grid. The long diagonal had the added benefit of facing southwest, rather than squatting in the shadowed, north-facing array of the other homes on the street. Mies's insistence on setting his famous Seagram Building back a hundred feet from the Park Avenue sidewalk, leaving millions of dollars of prime Manhattan real estate for a tasteful plaza, likewise made history.

As they began inserting stakes in the riverside property, Mies and Edith made a fateful decision. They chose to put the house on the meadowed floodplain, about seventy-five feet from the river. Edith thought the house might sit better higher up the slope, but Mies prevailed. Mies later insisted that he had conducted some due diligence, consulting local landowners about the possibility of flooding, and he obviously thought he could create a house that would rise above the occasional inundation. Myron Goldsmith, a young associate who would supervise construction of the Farnsworth House, later commented that Mies was anxious to site the house catty-corner to a resplendent, golden maple tree, which placed the structure near the river—and five feet off the ground. "Of course, then it led to the terrace, the stair and all that," Goldsmith said. "So maybe you could have cut the cost a third by moving it up [the hill.]"[2]

Mies had a second reason for placing the house close to the river. He not only had the huge maple tree looming over what would become the living area, he also had a line of trees to the south and west, screening the house from the Fox River. Privacy didn't factor into his decision, but what we would now call passive solar design did. "We placed the house very carefully underneath the trees to cover it as much as possible against the sun," he later explained. "I observed the angle of the shadow at many hours, and we moved the house so close to the trees that we kept the sun as much as possible out in the summer and we would like to have the sun in the winter."[3]

One day Karl Freund, a local cabinetmaker who was to become one of the main contractors for the house, was walking the site with Mies and Edith. "We were standing on the flood plain," Freund recalled, and "Mies asked me where I'd build the house. I said 'Not here.'" He continued:

> We had just walked from the woods. Turning in their direction, I said, "There." And Mies said, "No, here, by the beautiful tree!" He was pointing to the two hundred year old black sugar maple tree.
> "I wouldn't build here. You'll get flooded."
> Mies replied, "That is precisely what we want to show . . . that we can combat that. It's easy. You have a canoe there, and if it floods, you take the canoe to the house. It isn't much. It's an adventure, but that belongs to life."[4]

THE YEARS OF 1946 and 1947 were the *Wunderjahre* of the Mies-Edith relationship. They spent many weekends in Plano making plans for the house, and plenty of time in the office, reviewing drawings or just joshing around with the younger architects. Farnsworth, an avidly interested client, reveled in the company of Mies's junior confederates and often whiled away Saturday afternoons visiting the South

Wabash Avenue office, or on giddy picnics by the Fox River. "She treated us, the office staff, like a bunch of kings until the end," said Edward Duckett, one of Mies's young architects.

> She was so sweet and nice and always championed us. We could do no wrong it seemed. All we had to do was say, "Hey, let's go out to the site this weekend," and she would drop everything. She would prepare hamburgers and have wine for us. . . .
>
> She used to come to the office just about every other Thursday night, as I remember. I was doing some graphic chart work for her that related to the research she was doing so she would look at that as well as the drawings.[5]

PICNIC IN PLANO; EDITH FARNSWORTH WITH TWO OF MIES'S "BOYS": EDWARD DUCKETT AND JOSEPH FUJIKAWA

Occasionally, high jinks ensued. Duckett remembered Edith getting "peeved" when the "boys"—accomplished adult architects every one—started horsing around on her half-built marble terrace:

> Mies and Edith were on the upper deck and Myron and I were just standing around. There were a lot of big stones on the site, and I went over, just having fun, got some of the stones and placed them on the corner of the [terrace]. Myron had to outdo me, so he went over and put some stones on top of my stones, and then I put some more on top of his. We were just fooling around and didn't mean any harm. Mies laughed because he thought it was funny. But she did not! After it dawned on us that she was getting sore we got busy in a hurry and got those stones off there.[6]

Mies was someone who put the *ur* in urbanite. He had, after all, emigrated from one of Europe's great cultural and industrial centers to Chicago, then reveling in its muscular expansionism as America's fast-growing "second city." (Mark Twain once wrote a lengthy feature for the *Chicago Tribune* about Berlin, "The Chicago of Europe.") Yet the Plano site exposed a sentimental appreciation of nature rarely mentioned by friends and colleagues. "One time we were out at the Farnsworth House," Duckett recalled,

> and Mies and several of us decided to walk down to the river's edge. So we were cutting a path through the weeds. I was leading and Mies was right behind me.

Right in front of me I saw a young possum. If you take a stick and put it under a young possum's tail, it will curl its tail around the stick and you can hold it upside down.

So I reached down, picked up a branch, stuck it under this little possum's tail and it caught onto it and I turned around and showed it to Mies. Now this animal is thought by many to be one of the world's ugliest, but I remember Mies looked at it and said, "Isn't nature wonderful!" So he studied that possum for some time and commented on how unusual it was. How beautiful its fur was, the texture of it, and so on.

"Mies was exceedingly excited about the house," Myron Goldsmith remembered. Goldsmith, still in his twenties, probably spent as much time with the client as Mies did, allowing that Mies was seeing Edith socially after hours. Long after relations between the principals soured, Goldsmith, who later became an internationally renowned architect, had some fond memories of Edith:

First of all, she was a brilliant writer, she had a wonderful command of the language. She knew exactly what she was getting and wanted what she was getting.

[Edith] would come into the office almost every Saturday afternoon. Mies had a model of the house on his desk and they would talk. If there were anything new and interesting on the house, he would talk about it with her.

In later interviews, Goldsmith emphasized that Mies treated the Farnsworth commission as a special project. "I think he had great fun with this," Goldsmith told an Art Institute of Chicago interviewer many years later:

GOLDSMITH: I think Dr. Farnsworth said, "Mies, build it as if you were building your own house." The understanding was that she would let him use it sometimes. I think that was the spirit of the whole thing.

QUESTION: Do you think he had such a personal interest in this because he was interested in the client in a personal way?

GOLDSMITH: It probably had something certainly to do with it, and that she had said, "Build it as if you were building it for yourself." I don't know what was said and what was understood, certainly I had understood that he would be using it. It also was a thing in which he was interested because he had full control of it. It wasn't like an apartment building where you don't really have control of every detail. He had control of every detail here. It was understood that it would be built as beautifully as it could be done.

MIES AND EDITH WERE spending a great deal of time together, their relationship abetted by Lora Marx's temporary disappearance from Mies's life. For the past several years, Marx and Mies had enjoyed an easy romance based on shared interests—she was an artist who spoke fluent German and moved easily in Mies's social and professional milieus—and their respective independence. Marx's former husband, the architect and art collector Samuel Marx, provided her with enough money to live comfortably and dabble at her profession. A brief *Chicago Tribune* item about their 1936 divorce noted that Samuel left her "half the $15,000 a year income from her husband's interest in Oklahoma oil wells."

Marx met Mies shortly after he arrived in Chicago, and said she experienced "love at first sight" upon encountering the well-traveled refugee from Nazi Germany. Mies exuded a charisma that affected both men and women. "Mies cast an aura over everything," according to his colleague Alfred Caldwell. "He was absolutely infallible."[7]

Marx and Mies were lovers and at times very much in love, but each valued their solitude. They lived in separate apartments and had no plans to marry. Mies had been married, had never divorced, and once was enough. "I don't belong to the people who cannot live alone," he once told Marx.

Marx and Mies shared another pastime: drinking. Fueled by alcohol, the pair had been known to paint the town red. Literally. On a famous toot, Mies and Lora once slathered lipstick over the face of a marble nymph in the lobby of Chicago's historic Blackstone Hotel. Another wild revel lasted all night inside the ruins of Edith Rockefeller McCormick's Villa Turicum estate in Lake Forest, where a friend was the caretaker.[8]

In 1947, the drinking broke them up. Marx decided to join

Alcoholics Anonymous on the advice of her physician. Marx and Mies shared the same doctor, Bertha Isaacs, but she made no headway trying to steer the architect into twelve-step land. He consumed several braces of martinis in an average day, sometimes three at lunch and five or more in the evening and nighttime. "I have to wait until the music dies out" is how he explained his marathon solo drinking sessions to Marx.[9]

With Marx out of the picture, Edith assumed the role of favorite in Mies's life. She provided medical advice when asked, especially to Mies, who was entering a period of relative infirmity that would last the rest of his life. He suffered from painful ankylosing arthritis of the right hip, and Farnsworth shepherded him through one of his hospitalizations.

Mies and Edith inhabited a world of unusual intellectual and spiritual intensity. He insisted that she read the Italian-born German theologian Romano Guardini, who published an important book, *Vom Geist der Liturgie* (*The Spirit of the Liturgy*), during World War I. Guardini's informed skepticism about the emptiness of the vestigial Roman liturgy in the twentieth century influenced two cardinals who would later become popes—Ratzinger (Benedict XVI) and Bergoglio (Francis)—although what Edith was supposed to make of the text isn't clear.

"I read Guardini," she noted, "as he urged, and tried to lend myself to the concept of 'liturgy' as an element in the 'hierarchy of values,' or a mystic dimension of religion, or a sitting-up exercise in the hygiene of the soul—as almost anything which might enrich my own awareness, presumably by showing me how Mies had been enriched."

He likewise introduced her to the theoretical writings of

Le Corbusier, with whom he had worked on the experimental workers' housing complex in Stuttgart. "I dutifully contemplated Corbu's modules," Farnsworth recalled later, "although I was never able to see any organic connection between the proportions of the human body and those of the [Villa] Savoye or any other house, or what such a connection could have meant if it had existed."

For her part, she insisted that Mies read *What Is Life?*, a popular science book of the time by the eminent physicist Erwin Schrödinger. Subtitled *The Physical Aspect of the Living Cell*, Schrödinger's short tome is quite dense, and full of state-of-the-art medical vocabulary belonging to the immediate pre-DNA era.

Farnsworth reported that Mies admired "a kind of heroic abstemiousness in Schrödinger's reduction of life to observable crystals, organic or inorganic."

At his apartment one evening, she found him "pacing his living room, limping, clearly agitated."

FARNSWORTH: Don't you approve of the
Schrödinger book, Mies? You seem so upset.

MIES: It is unspiritual. What about man and his
hopes for immortality? Does Schrödinger think I can
sit staring at the snowflakes on the window or the salt
crystals on the dinner table and be satisfied? I want to
know what I have to expect after death.

Farnsworth later wrote: "I was struck with the force of Mies's preoccupation with death, and it lent a mystic context even to the project of the house by the river, and an undefinable dimension to the personality of Mies."

Lora Marx reported that Mies remained enthralled and bewildered by the Schrödinger book until the end of his life. While certain that her partner of many years was a committed atheist (as was Farnsworth, who called the Bible "a beautiful myth"), she saw him as a spiritual seeker not satisfied with purely scientific explanations for human existence. "He was baffled by the final chapter of that book," she told biographer Franz Schulze. Schrödinger's conclusion is markedly unredemptive, accepting the construct of identity and consciousness, and dismissing spirituality and the putative soul as "gross superstitions." One wonders what kind of spiritual awakening Mies was expecting from a particle physicist, and a German particle physicist at that.

Marx is one of several observers who thought that Mies and Edith had a brief dalliance during her absence. "There was a short 'little thing' between them but no real affair— strictly professional," she told Schulze. Philip Johnson, who knew both parties, didn't mind gossiping about their relationship, with his characteristic choler: "God, who could sleep with that woman? None of us could figure it out. Life is strange."[10]

Edith's sister, Marion Carpenter, likewise testified that Edith "was mesmerized by [Mies] and she probably had an affair with him." Mies found little favor in Edith's family. "I found him indigestible," Carpenter continued. "My husband called him a big German lump. He didn't talk or respond. Nothing but silence. They told us he didn't talk unless he was pumped full of liquor. Evidently we didn't pump him enough."

Edith's nephew, Fairbank Carpenter, recalled an awkward luncheon when Edith dragged Mies to the Carpenters' new home on the North Shore. "Mies sat across from the rest of us and he didn't utter a word," Fairbank remembered. "He was just an object."

The Mies-Edith love affair had definitively ended by 1948, when a teetotaling Marx felt confident enough to resume relations with the martini-swilling Mies. More to the point, two of Mies's daughters arrived in Chicago from Germany, unbidden, to live with their father. Mies's apartment had only one guest bedroom, so one of the girls slept on his couch. "Our presence annoyed him," Georgia wrote, confirming other accounts.

He felt restricted in his freedom, in his bachelor existence. No woman, let alone two women, had ever lived with him. But it did not occur to him to rent us a room someplace. Maybe he shunned the expense. Sometimes I would have liked to just take off, but I didn't have the money to do that because as so-called exchange students we were not allowed to earn any money. In the harsh Chicago winter I often did not have enough money to take the bus four times a day from house to house. When we asked our father for money, he pulled five dollars from his pocket or he borrowed money from his housekeeper Caroline.

We often sat until 4 in the morning, talking, and I'd fall asleep right on that sofa. My father told me about his amorous encounters and was curious to hear about mine. The topic intrigued him yet made him jealous at the same time, which I did not realize at the time.[11]

Mies's late-night drinking dictated his daily schedule. "My father's day began around noon," Georgia wrote.

> Most afternoons he spent a few hours in his studio where he worked with a number of young architects. At 6 pm sharp, he came home to watch gangster films on TV that played in Chicago of the 20s. He often invited guests for dinner, and those evenings were always very interesting and relaxing for [my sister Waltraut] and me. My father was a charming and animated entertainer of his guests, never superficial or trivial or uninteresting.[12]

Peter Blake, who knew Mies in Chicago, also commented on what he called Mies's sui generis lifestyle. Blake described Mies's apartment as essentially unfurnished: "Its only décor is Mies's magnificent collection of Klees, carefully hung on white and otherwise empty walls, and just as carefully lit." (Mies also hung some Kurt Schwitters collages, and, in his bedroom, a magnificent Max Beckmann nude, *Alfie with Mask.*)

In his book *The Master Builders,* Blake dilates on Mies's "rather peculiar schedule":

> As he rarely talks until after dinner . . . he does not go to bed until the early hours of the morning,

and does not rise until fairly late the next day. No one who values Mies's friendship would telephone him before 11 a.m., at which time he may, under extreme duress, produce a few pleasant and thoughtful grunts.

In the office, Blake writes,

Mies may communicate with others by an occasional smile between puffs of his ever-present cigar. There are not likely to be many spoken words, and the atmosphere tends to be that of an operating room while a great surgeon is preparing to perform a revolutionary operation for the first time.[13]

Edward Duckett had similar recollections: "Mies used to have people come in and they would just sit there. We would watch them from our drafting boards and they would just sit there and look at each other."[14]

"And smoke their pipes," his colleague Joseph Fujikawa added. When it came time to build the Seagram Building in 1958, the clients rented a suite for Mies at the Barclay Hotel, and couldn't help noticing that he never seemed to do much. He was often holed up in his room, smoking a cigar. Philip Johnson, Mies's collaborator on the Seagram, inquired, "What do you do all the time?"

Mies's reply: "Ve think."[15]

In a cloud of cigar smoke and in a shallow lake of martinis, the beautiful buildings got built.

LIKE DR. FARNSWORTH, MIES was busy. While juggling many professional assignments and personal relationships, he still saw a great deal of Farnsworth. In her memoir, she describes a peremptory summons for dinner at Mies's apartment, sans daughters. Farnsworth recalls arriving at the apartment with no places set at the dining table. Instead, Mies's maid had left them two food trays in the kitchen, with a lamb chop on each plate. They ate dinner sitting on the armrests of Mies's sofa and plush armchair.

"Nothing could be heard but the occasional fumble of silverware on china or teak, and the soft sounds of food consumption, not to say digestion," Farnsworth wrote. After eating, they returned the trays to the kitchen and sat facing each other in the living room.

> [Mies] sat there with half-closed eyes, his face as impassive as a landscape—and talked about his past life, from his childhood in Aachen to the present. So I pictured Mies as a small boy attending the local trade school and earning a few pennies in his spare time by picking up nails where building was in progress.
>
> "The best part of the day" [Mies recalled] "came when the work was finished and we boys went to the factory and stood at the gates, waiting for the weavers' daughters to come out," he remarked with a reminiscent smile.
>
> "Waiting for what, Mies?"

"The weavers' daughters," he replied, unperturbed. "To try to get a kiss from them. They were
beautiful!"

But the monolithic Mies was not much given to
nostalgic recollections of his childhood, nor was there
anything about him to suggest that he had ever been
"brought up" or modified by anyone.

One reference made by Mies to his parents that slid
open like a little trap door and revealed a dark space;
then the aperture closed without a sound and for years
he forgot that it was there.

It happened late one evening: the cigar was burning down toward the wet, macerated end and the glass
on the end of the table had been refilled many times.

"Did your parents continue to live in Aachen after
you left home, Mies?"

"My parents? They didn't know much about me
after I went to work in Behrens's office. Once I started
to go back to see them in Aachen but I met some
friends on the train and we were drinking and I forgot
to get off at the station."

"So you got off at the next stop and went back?"

"The next stop? No, I never went back."

"Never at all? You never saw them again?"

"Why should I?"

MIES AND EDITH TRAVELED together to see the Museum of
Modern Art's retrospective show *The Architecture of Mies
van der Rohe*. The show was an act of prestidigitation by

Philip Johnson, the onetime director of (and in 1947 consultant to) MoMA's Department of Architecture. Johnson had been promoting Mies since their first meeting in Berlin, in 1929. He commissioned Mies and Reich to design his Manhattan apartment, and frequently visited Mies's office in Chicago. The young Johnson was a besotted fan. An enthusiastic road tripper, he hopped in his car and viewed Mies's Tugendhat House before Mies bestirred himself to see the finished masterpiece in Brno. "Of all the great modern architects," Johnson wrote in a monograph to accompany the MoMA show, "Mies van der Rohe is the least known."

Although Mies had been in the United States for almost a decade, he remained somewhat obscure in his adopted homeland. He had created a master plan and designed several academic buildings for the Illinois Institute of Technology—the Armour Institute became IIT in 1940—where he was director of the architecture department. He had also designed a twenty-two-story tower, the Promontory Apartments in Chicago's Hyde Park, which would become a commercial success but was hardly a masterpiece. The relative paucity of completed work in the United States mattered not a whit. Johnson conjured a superb show, designed by Mies, that showcased his most dramatic German work, as well as examples of Mies's Barcelona and Tugendhat furniture, which were already part of MoMA's permanent collection. Johnson added a model of one of his very favorite Mies designs—the Farnsworth House.

Johnson wrote a rhapsodic monograph to accompany the show. (Mies inscribed Johnson's personal copy: "To Philip: It would not be without you; It could not be without me.")

He compared Mies's spare, black steel structures at IIT—
much of them as yet unbuilt, and some destined never to be
built—to Gothic cathedrals:

> He has conceived the design in terms of steel chan-
> nels and angles, I-beams and H-columns, just as a me-
> dieval design is conceived in terms of stone vaults and
> buttresses. . . . Whereas the medieval architect relied
> on the collaboration of the sculptor and painter for his
> ultimate effect, Mies, so to speak, has had to perform
> the functions of all three professions.

The show was a hit. The *New York Times* review lauded
Johnson's monograph, and praised Mies for being not *too*

MIES AT THE 1947 MOMA SHOW, WITH A RESOR HOUSE
SKETCH IN THE BACKGROUND

modern. "Mies van der Rohe never goes off the deep end merely to create something startling or sensational," the paper reported. "Everything he does is soundly reasoned." On the threshold of his own legendary career, architect and designer Charles Eames praised Mies's hall design in *Arts and Architecture* magazine: "Certainly it is the experience of walking through that space and seeing others move through it that is the high point of the exhibition."[16]

After visiting the MoMA show, Mies remained in the city, and Edith returned to Chicago. She noted to herself that the Farnsworth House model "was the pivotal point of the exhibit, and I was happy as I boarded the train back to Chicago, reflecting that our project might well become the prototype of new and important elements of American architecture."

Mies spent some time in New York escorting the talented, beautiful, and wealthy sculptress Mary Callery, an on-again, off-again paramour for whom he designed an artist's studio on Long Island. Johnson had introduced the couple, yet another of his interventions into Mies's life. Twice married, Callery cherished her independence almost as much as Mies did, and she could match him drink for drink. Mies's daughter Georgia reported that "one Sunday, I had to return from Mary Callery's country house on Long Island by bus, because both of them were too drunk to drive."[17] Mies didn't drive, which explains why Farnsworth was always at the wheel during their visits to the Fox River house site.

Mies's associate Duckett remembered accompanying Mies to New York to help install the MoMA show, while Callery "mother-henned us":

One night after we had been working on the exhibition, we were sitting in her kitchen having a few drinks and feeling no pain, and she said something, and Mies said, "Oh, you're a woman, stay in the kitchen!" or something like that, and she ate him alive. So he may have been the worst male chauvinist in the world, ever known. I don't know, but it definitely had been the wrong thing to say to her.[18]

In a posthumously published interview with Robert A. M. Stern, Johnson offered up some gamy comments about Callery's and Farnsworth's relations with Mies. Stern asked if Callery was a longtime girlfriend of Mies.

"No, Farnsworth was first," Johnson replied. "Then Mary wasn't around a very long time. She was too temperamental and he wasn't really able to screw much. He was too big and heavy. So it wasn't a satisfactory love affair."

Johnson was wrong. Callery and Mies continued to see each other off and on for the rest of their lives. Although Callery and Marx were willing to indulge Mies's precious "freedom" and share him with other women, Farnsworth was not. From 1948 on, she was Mies's client, but not a girlfriend, mistress, or lover.

BACK IN CHICAGO, FARNSWORTH placed herself at the center of a famous tiff that effectively ended Mies's relations with Frank Lloyd Wright. Mies was one of the few European architects whom Wright could abide, although he at various times accused almost all of the continental luminaries—

Mies, Le Corbusier, and Gropius—of stealing his ideas. In his book *Fallingwater Rising,* author Franklin Toker reports that Wright antedated some of his early twentieth-century drawings "to remind the world that Wright was the source for German modernism." Toker further notes that "whenever Wright swatted flies at Taliesin he would gleefully announce the window-kill as 'Got Gropius . . . got Mies . . . got Le Corbusier.'"

Yet for some reason Wright liked Mies, repeatedly reinviting him to his Wisconsin headquarters. The feeling was mutual. On the occasion of a 1940 MoMA show, Mies wrote an adulatory "Tribute to Frank Lloyd Wright" that never made it into the official catalog, although a typescript ended up in Wright's files. In the essay, Mies wrote about discovering Wright's work at a famous Berlin exhibition in 1910:

> The work of this great master revealed an architectural world of unexpected force and clarity of language, and also a disconcerting richness of form. Here finally was a master-builder drawing upon the veritable fountainhead of architecture, who with true originality lifted his architectural creations into the light.[19]

Wright sashayed through the MoMA retrospective, and was overheard calling the show "much ado about next to nothing." This was a carefully aimed arrow, because Mies promoted his belief that architects need to do *beinahe nichts,* "next to nothing," to make great art.

Learning through the grapevine that he may have offended Mies, Wright fired off a non-apology apology.

Somebody has told me you were hurt by remarks of mine when I came to see your New York show. . . . But did I tell you how fine I thought your handling of materials was?

You know you have frequently said you believe in "doing next to nothing" all down the line. Well, when I saw the enormous blowups the phrase "Much ado about 'next to nothing'" came spontaneously from me.

Then I said the Barcelona Pavilion was your best contribution to the original "Negation" and you seemed to be still back there where I was then.

This is probably what hurt (coming from me) and I wish I had taken you aside to say it to you privately because it does seem to me that the whole thing called "Modern Architecture" has bogged down with the architects right there on that line. I don't want to classify you with them—but the show struck me sharply as reactionary in that sense. . . .

But this note is to say that I wouldn't want to hurt your feelings—even with the truth. You are the best of them all as an artist and a man.

Wright then recalled that he had invited Mies to Taliesin several times since 1937, and he urged another visit, "unless the break is irreparable."

Farnsworth claimed that she helped Mies compose his famous *réplique* ("We drafted a dignified complaint having a dim bearing upon negation") that they sent off to Taliesin:

My dear Frank,

Thank you so much for your letter.

It was an exaggeration if you heard that my feelings were hurt by your remarks at my New York show. If I had heard the crack "Much ado about next-to-nothing" I would have laughed with you. About "Negation"— I feel that you use this word for qualities that I find positive and essential.

Mies allowed that yes, the two men should meet again at Taliesin to discuss the subject further. They never communicated again.

THE 1947 MOMA SHOW produced another curious artifact: an article by Edith Farnsworth about Mies's architecture. Its genesis became clear several years later, when Mies and Edith were airing their dirty laundry in public. *ArtNews* magazine had commissioned a former student and colleague of Mies to write an overview of the van der Rohe oeuvre, timed to coincide with the opening of the MoMA show. Speyer proved unequal to the task, and Edith stepped into the breach.

"There had to be an article written," Myron Goldsmith recalled, "and Mies gave it to somebody. It might have been written by Speyer or somebody like that. [Mies] didn't like it, so she said, 'I'll rewrite it.' She did, and showed very great understanding of what it was all about."

The result, not surprisingly, is a fulsome, erudite love letter to "possibly the greatest architect of his generation. . . . Ludwig Mies van der Rohe is one of the founders of contemporary architecture," the article began, and gathered enthusiasm from there:

> Mies van der Rohe is almost unknown to the architectural public at large because of his extreme modesty and reluctance to seek or accept publicity. . . . Mies van der Rohe's accomplishment of the last thirty years shows unwavering consistency. There is no compromise. It is an orderly record of innovating and refining.

When Mies was telling stories about his childhood in Aachen, Edith was paying close attention. "In all of his subsequent planning," she wrote,

> one can see what he learned from the old city; from its spatial quality—the fluctuating contrast between narrow streets and wide squares—and from the meaning of the compact, walled town mass in relation to the long, rolling fields of the lowlands.
>
> But it was probably in the Chapel of Charlemagne that he learned his best lesson. His mother took the boy to this chapel each morning for devotion. There he was fascinated by the wonderful hall, and he searched the walls, counting stones and tracing joints during the visits. In time he understood the mysterious beauty to be the result of the stone construction, realizing that the architecture was a direct expression

of the structure. It is among his most vivid recollections.

The article heaps praise on the open plans of the Barcelona Pavilion and the Tugendhat House, and mentions three of Mies's works on the drawing boards: the IIT Administration Building, the Drive-In Restaurant for Indianapolis, and the Theater of 1947, the latter two of which were never built. There is no mention of the Farnsworth House, even though the model would be displayed at the MoMA show.

MIES'S PROPOSED DRIVE-IN RESTAURANT
FOR INDIANAPOLIS

The *ArtNews* conclusion calls attention to its actual author:

He has often been called a genius, but the compliment worries him. He mistrusts the individualistic traits which are inherent in genius. His philosophy of life and of architecture revolves around the idea of "order," and he believes that too great individualism produces irresponsibility, a form of self indulgence which destroys order. Those of us who know him intimately, know him to be a great man, a great teacher, and a great architect.[20]

DESPITE THE NUMEROUS TRIPS to the house site in Plano, construction of Edith Farnsworth's dream house took more than two years to begin. Mies was by nature dilatory, and after creating a beautiful watercolor sketch of the home, and a couple of plywood models, he more or less ignored the project for almost two years. He and Farnsworth realized that their initial idea of building a cottage for $10,000 was unrealistic. Back in Chicago after the MoMA show, Farnsworth popped into Mies's apartment for one of her regular visits. "I wrote down on the edge of the drawing table before him the sum $40,000 and listed the assets it represented," she wrote in her memoir.

Mies put on his glasses, and said, "Let me check your addition," and I ribbed him a little at the oddity of his checking my addition.

"Now can we have the house?" I asked, half believing that the question was rhetorical in view of the extreme simplicity of the design.

"I should think so," Mies replied. "We haven't made any estimates yet, but it must be a cheap house— it's almost nothing."

"Are you going to be happy building a small house

out of conventional building materials, without any onyx?" I asked.[21]

Edith was thinking of the onyx walls she had seen in photographs of the Barcelona Pavilion and of the Tugendhat House. A few years later, under oath during their epic lawsuit, Edith said Mies "thought if there was a criticism of the Tugendhat House, it was because it showed a certain youthful exuberance in the use of fancy material and he would build this house for me and would be glad to use common building materials."

It is notable that Mies called a $40,000 house "cheap." That is the equivalent of more than $450,000 today, and expenses would continue to mount.

Mies's reply: "I will build this house for you as I would build it for myself!"

CHAPTER 4

"THE MOST IMPORTANT HOUSE IN THE WORLD"

HAVING SHOWN MIES THE COLOR OF HER MONEY, Farnsworth was eager to goad the architect forward. Alfred Caldwell, a student and collaborator of Mies's who taught at IIT, recalled a telephone call from Edith: "Caldwell, how can I get Mies to do my house? Every year it's postponed, he says he's too busy. That man, I can't get him to do anything, I love the house, I want it. He keeps putting it off. Will you talk to him about it?"

Caldwell bearded Mies, who responded, "Ja, we have a lot of work and I can't get my mind on it because I've got so much work. There is nobody in my office who can draw that plan, nobody can do the actual drawing. If I had somebody to do it, I would do it."

Caldwell, an architect specializing in landscape

design, agreed to start working on the plans. He described the process in an oral history interview many years later:

> I spent two or three weeks and Mies was busy on other things. I drew as much as I could. With something so personal for Mies one can only go so far. The big trouble with Mies was to find out what he wanted. Everybody wanted to give him what he wanted, but he wouldn't tell you what he wanted.

> INTERVIEWER BETTY BLUM: Did he know at the time?

> CALDWELL: Not only about this, but with anything, with anything. He was an extremely interesting and elusive person. Elusive is a very good word for Mies. Anybody who knew him well—you go ask [his associate George] Danforth, he will tell you that.
>
> Finally, when it really came down to the crux of something, then Mies gave the order. But he fought it. He didn't want to.

Although construction wouldn't begin until May 1949, Mies and his client began to make some basic choices. Preliminary sketches depict some ideas considered and abandoned. For instance, Mies entertained the idea of running steps to the terrace both from the river side of the house and from the meadow. The single staircase and the house itself eventually faced south, toward the river. He likewise thought of screening off the kitchen behind glass partitions, then jettisoned that idea.

The site was locked in. Even though locals continued to mention that they had seen Edith's land underwater, no one in Mies's office could find hard evidence of a recurring problem. There are archived letters to the Army Corps of Engineers, and letters to Kendall County flood-control officials, but the exchanges all succumb to bureaucratic lethargy and doublespeak. No, we don't know, maybe, try someone else. Goldsmith later said that a neighbor to the west once had river water in his swimming pool, "so we measured that." Likewise, "there was a man who owned a pop stand and a picnic parking and boat renting establishment south of the bridge who had been there for very many years and we inquired of him"[1]

Contractor Karl Freund, who claimed to have warned about the site before it was chosen, later testified that high water carried away his lumber forms during construction, and submerged a pile of steel framing and a generator in winter.[2] But by then, the die had been cast.

The decision to elevate the floor above the floodplain added considerable expense to the home. Problems that would easily resolve themselves in a normal design, for example, sending the plumbing and drainage directly into the ground, became engineering challenges for the Fox River house. For aesthetic reasons, all utility functions were gathered into a four-foot-diameter cylindrical tube, or "stack," that descended to the ground below the kitchen, partially masked by the magnificent two-tiered staircase. The densely packed stack, which brought electrical power, heating oil, and water into the house and also expelled all waste, would later present its own headaches for Edith, long into the future.

The client made some key decisions. Farnsworth chose not to lay a driveway from the county highway on the northern border of her property directly to her house. Various contractors lobbied for a road, which would have made it easier to deliver materials, and to build an electric line to the house, but she vetoed both. The electric line was buried, avoiding the prospect of unsightly poles, but, again, raising the cost. There is still no such road on the property. One approaches the house obliquely, through a patch of woods to the east of the building, on a riverside path.

Edith asked for bigger closets for guests to hang their clothes, and for larger mirrors in the bathrooms. She also wanted a fireplace, and "Mies acquiesced," Goldsmith later said. "It didn't work. I think a fireplace was a mistake. It was hardly ever used, and to have it burning on the travertine floor—when it wasn't burning, it was a mess. But Mies seemed to accept it. He didn't have any theological problems with it."[3]

Mies and Edith collaborated on many decisions, for instance, limiting the amount of stainless steel used on the kitchen countertops, for cost reasons. "We asked somebody who designs kitchens for restaurants for his advice," Mies later explained, "and then we sent out his specifications for bids, and then it was too expensive, so we decided to make the front of the kitchen just in white enamel."[4] Mies rejected a contemporary electric range because he didn't like the dashboard design that rose above the counter surface. Instead, he and Farnsworth settled for two smaller stoves.

Mies chose the steel elements, the concrete, and the glass. The Pittsburgh Plate Glass Company delivered the huge glass panes to the work site and cut them to size in situ. The quarter-inch-thick plate glass, normally used for storefronts, was made by rolling molten glass into uniform sheets and polishing them until smooth. The largest panes, on the north (road-facing) and south (river-facing) exteriors, were nine feet tall and eleven feet wide, mounted between white steel mullions.

Chicago's Wendnagel Steel Company furnished the columns and steel girders, which they measured, assembled, bolted, and disassembled before sending the materials on to Fox River. Wendnagel had worked with Mies before, and were familiar with his demand for strict, one-sixteenth-of-an-inch tolerances. In the middle of construction, Goldsmith jerry-rigged a six-foot-long mercury level to make sure that the lines and corners trued up all along the seventy-seven-foot-long house frame.

Much second-guessing would attend Mies's decision not to use double-paned, insulated glass, or thermopane, for the house, which could be exposed to extreme hot or cold in the Illinois flatlands. Mies had little use for thermopane, which cost several times as much as single-layer glass and was not available in the huge expanses called for in the Farnsworth House. Mies "had a high disregard for insulating glass," his associate Duckett later said. "He thought it was criminal to propose insulating glass in a large quantity because at that time you could only get a five-year guarantee whereas the glass itself has an inherent guarantee." Unlike some other design elements, this was never subject to debate.

The travertine marble flooring *was* debated. Mies loved unpolished travertine, the soft, porous stone that lent his Barcelona Pavilion a muted elegance. He had laid travertine in his Berlin apartment, and just as he was finishing up the Farnsworth House, he started work on one of his skyscraper masterpieces, the twin buildings at 860/880 Lake Shore Drive, both set upon an open plain of travertine. The same marble reappeared in the interior of his famous Seagram Building, on New York's Park Avenue—even in the executive washrooms.

On-site, Mies, the stonemason's son, explained the difference between Colorado travertine and Roman travertine: "I explained that the Colorado travertine was a little cheaper than the Roman travertine, but that it was too unquiet, because it was not smooth enough in the color."[5] "Travertine is a very fine stone," he was more than happy to explain. "They call it sometimes marble but it is a sweet water deposit in fact."

He was later questioned about his favorite stone:

Q: Can you describe what it looks like?

MIES: It is a grayish yellow stone with holes in it, quite a lot of holes in it coming from the air into the position.

Q: Where does travertine come from?

MIES: Oh, it is in many countries. In this country is Colorado, travertine from Colorado. Then in Europe

you have travertine in Germany and in Belgium
and you have travertine in France and Italy.

Q: Is there any in Vermont?

MIES: No, it isn't especially—in Vermont is not an
original travertine. That is this stone quarries there
[*sic*]—who get travertine from Italy and cut it in
slabs.[6]

Mies adored travertine.

Travertine was expensive. After the fact, Mies realized
that half of the cost of his famous Barcelona Pavilion was for
marble—travertine, and the famous *onyx doré* slabs.

Of course there were many other options for flooring—
limestone, bluestone, precast concrete, tiles, and so on. Mies
indicated his preference for travertine, and reported that the
stone could be sourced from a quarry in Carthage, Missouri,
not so far away in the grand scheme of things. (Mies had
previously contacted his brother Ewald, who ran the family
business in Germany. Ewald explained that even with a substantial discount, European marble would cost too much.)[*]

"With some apprehension I agreed to travertine for [the
floor]," Farnsworth reported, possibly unaware that she had
just added several thousand dollars to the cost of her house.

---

[*]   Mies's biographers Franz Schulze and Edward Windhorst write
that Ewald liked to take clients to cemeteries to examine different
kinds of stone. Mies's colleague Gene Summers took such a tour, noting that "not only can you see [many] types, but you can also see how
they age."

The total cost of the travertine was between $12,000 and $13,000. Mies and Goldsmith decided that the exposed stone floor would require inlaid radiant heating, which itself would require more insulation in the subfloor. The additional insulation cost $850.[7] Because the radiant system heated the house slowly, Mies and his associates realized the home wouldn't warm up quickly enough if Edith arrived on a winter weekend. (A thermostat maintained a fifty-five-degree temperature when she was absent.) So they installed a second furnace to blow hot air into the house, placing the furnace and fan in the utility stack.

Mies later recalled that "[Dr. Farnsworth] was a little afraid about the holes in the Roman travertine," a prescient concern, as ice can expand inside the marble pores and cause damage. For the outside terrace, Mies designed a sophisticated drainage system, not unlike a shower pan, and he even tilted the terrace at a slight angle toward the river. Nonetheless, some of the travertine has suffered damage over the years.[8]

INEVITABLY, MIES DESIGNED AN open-plan house.

There is some irony here, because Mies himself didn't choose to live in an open plan. His two-bedroom apartment on Pearson Street had a reception hall, a butler's pantry, and a maid's room. But his generation of European modernist architects were famous for building interiors short on walls and long on a "natural" flow of living spaces, with the living room melding into a sitting area, and so on. The Barcelona Pavilion was a completely open plan. All the living spaces of the elegant Tugendhat House flowed into one another, too, though the clients insisted on closed-door bedrooms for themselves and their children.

Unlike Herr and Frau Tugendhat, Edith Farnsworth would not be able to close her bedroom door. Her bed was placed against the east side of the house's only fixed partition, the "core" island that comprised the fireplace, kitchen, and two bathrooms. Her pillow faced the dawn over the Fox River. A large, teak-clad wardrobe screened the Spartan sleeping quarters from the living and dining areas.

"Another contested point was the 'open plan' of the interior," Edith wrote,

> according to which a guest would have a bathroom but no bedroom. He, or she, could sleep on a sofa or I would spread a mattress on the travertine floor. We would co-habit a sort of three-dimensional sketch, I in my "sleeping space" and he in his—unless sheer discomfort and depression should drive us together.

According to Edith, Mies's original plan lacked windows that could open and close. "I told Mies that I couldn't spend a night without an open window and would never accept a house without at least one window," she wrote.

> I felt almost as strongly about a second door.
> "I think I should have two ways of getting in or out," I complained. "In case of fire, or other emergencies. I'm not too happy about the 'glass box' motif and I rebel at a glass trap."

Mies added two in-swinging hopper windows at the east end of the house, which themselves caused further problems. "In the end I got two large windows and no 'back door' nor partitions," Farnsworth said. A second door would require a second set of steps, and she agreed with Mies that that "was bound to look like an automobile showroom."

Farnsworth had noticed the chromium-plated steel columns in photos of the Barcelona Pavilion and the Tugendhats' Brno house, and made clear that she found them garish. Because Mies carried the entire weight of her house on the eight steel exterior columns, no chrome invaded the Fox River design. Edith had many ideas for the wardrobe exterior, but Mies insisted on teak, and on expensive primavera wood for the larger kitchen/bathroom/fireplace "core."

Mies had wanted only one bathroom, with a shower, but bowed to Farnsworth's request for two. (Mies later commented, ungenerously, that the purpose of the second bathroom was to "keep visitors from seeing Edith's nightgown on the back of the bathroom door.") She made sure one of those had a tub, and a porcelain tub at that—not the metal one called for in the original design. Like many a couple before and after, they visited a Crane showroom together, to choose lighting fixtures for the bathrooms. It was at Crane that they decided to install an electric fan in the bathroom, to help it heat up more quickly.[9]

There is no doubt that Edith Farnsworth could be troublesome, for example, fretting where and how to install her record player. "She had an idea from one of the leading orchestra musicians in Chicago how [her Victrola and records] should be arranged," Mies said, "and then she talked it over with somebody else and she heard that somebody in California had a good knowledge about how to place the loud speaker and then she was referred from this man to somebody else in Chicago, so we had to change it several times."[10]

Architect and client disagreed over curtains, in some detail. Farnsworth wanted to add some color inside the house, but Mies understood the house to be transparent. The beautiful, changing palettes of the Fox River littoral and the surrounding forest would provide the wallpaper. Mies had strong views on this subject:

> Nature should also have a life of its own. We should avoid disturbing it with the excessive color of our houses and our interior furnishings. Indeed, we should strive to bring Nature, houses and people together into a higher unity. When one looks at Nature thru the glass walls of the Farnsworth House, it takes on a deeper significance than when one stands outside. More of Nature is thus expressed—it becomes part of a greater whole.[11]

A few years after the house was finished, he offered his opinion that "the Farnsworth House has never been truly understood. I myself have been in this house from morning until evening. Until then I had not known how colorful Nature can be. One must be careful to use neutral tones in interior spaces, for outside one has all sorts of colors. These colors are continually changing completely, and I would like to say that it is simply glorious."[12]

Mies wanted curtains made of raw shantung silk, which has a light fawn shade. He knew a lot about silk, having designed an exposition space for the German silk industry in 1927, and he hung heavy shantung silk curtains—dyed blue—in his Berlin apartment. "She claimed [the shantung] would fall to pieces from the sun," Goldsmith later recalled. "He claimed that he had some in his apartment in Germany, and when they had to be replaced, they made dresses for their daughters out of it."[13] Mies thought Edith didn't like the shantung "because it is used in cheap clothes now and she wanted another material."

The pair spent a whole day at the site discussing curtains and hanging different fabrics. "I tried to explain to her why I wanted that shantung silk," Mies later testified.

It was a natural shantung silk and I wanted to have those natural colors, the travertine and the wood and the natural colors for the curtains and I explained why I have to have this particular color, this natural color because of the character of the glass house, that the color from the outside—from the nature should not be destroyed by the strong colors she wanted, and she looked at it and we hung large pieces from the ceiling down—looked at it from inside the house and from outside and tried to visualize when it was dark what the light inside would do to the appearance outside.[14]

It didn't help matters that Edith solicited curtain advice from another, younger, Chicago architect, Harry Weese. "I discussed it with Harry Weese and he thought [the curtains] should be brown," she told Goldsmith. Supposedly brown would blend better with the autumn colors infusing the glass house. Inevitably, Weese's opinion got back to an "absolutely fuming" Mies. "I don't know whether I reported this to Mies or how he knew," Goldsmith recalled. "He said, 'If I would have known that she would be so difficult I would never have touched the house,' something like that."[15]

Gene Summers, who, like so many of Mies's young associates, would go on to become a successful architect, likewise noted that the back-and-forth over the curtains was the first dark cloud to float over the otherwise undisturbed horizon of architect-client relations:

> She wanted yellow curtains, and Mies wanted beige. When I say beige, it's actually natural silk, which is beige. It's a gorgeous color. Mies wanted that, and his idea was perfectly obvious and objective to us in the office, because these beautiful trees around were golden, natural golden and red in the fall. Why put a yellow or put any kind of a strong color there that would be in competition with these beautiful natural colors? The floor was travertine, and it worked together and it made sense.

A few years later, queried about the curtain discussion, Edith rejected the notion that the subject was "discussed": "*Discussion* should be qualified. It was not that Mr. van der Rohe wanted any opinion from me on the curtains. So that really there was no discussion there. . . . He wanted a certain kind of curtain, and the question was whether I would agree to it."[16]*

AS ANYONE WHO HAS ever tried to build a house understands, there are several forces at play here. Mies had a lifelong commitment to perfection, in materials and craftsmanship, dating back to his youth in Aachen. "Because God can see it" was generally Mies's credo, making only occasional exceptions for clients who insisted on economical materials to suit an unforgiving bottom line. But his greatest works—Barcelona, Tugendhat, Farnsworth, and New York's Seagram Building— rose largely free from budgetary constraints. Edith Farnsworth proved to be both Mies's client and a patron. That she thought of herself as Mies's friend and soul mate first, client second, and patron not at all, was becoming a source of friction.

Great architects often have problematic relations with their clients. "I'm never concerned with my clients, only with their architectural requirements" is a quote ascribed to Howard Roark, the egomaniacal protagonist of Ayn Rand's novel *The Fountainhead*. Roark is supposed to be Frank Lloyd Wright, who in truth had more complicated feelings

---

* Curtains were a subject that Mies took very seriously. Van der Rohe was a "big pain in the ass," reported the poet Isabella Gardner, who was married to Mies's business partner Robert H. McCormick and lived in one of the Lake Shore Drive apartments. "Mies had determined that everybody who lived in that building had to have the same curtains. It was one of the first glass buildings ever and no one had any experience with this. So people moved in and they began putting up their curtains, and he would say NO."

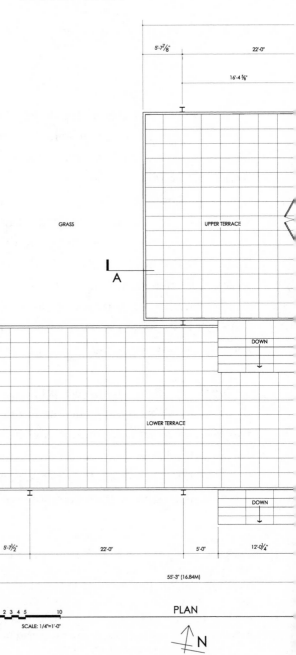

PLAN

SCALE: 1/4"=1'-0"

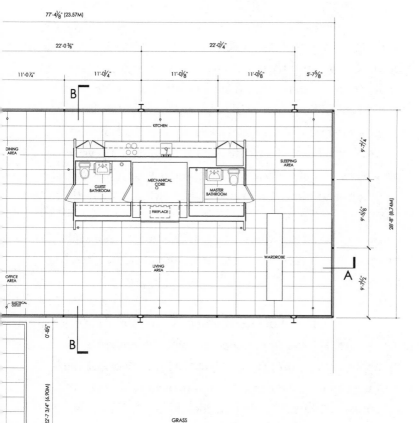

77'-4⅛" (23.57M)

22'-0⅜" 22'-0¼"

11'-0¼" 11'-0¼" 11'-0⅛" 11'-0⅛" 5'-7⅝"

B

DINING
AREA

KITCHEN

SLEEPING
AREA

GUEST
BATHROOM

MECHANICAL
CORE

MASTER
BATHROOM

FIREPLACE

9'-7¼"

9'-5⅝"

28'-8" (8.74M)

WARDROBE

LIVING
AREA

OFFICE
AREA

A

9'-7½"

ELECTRICAL
OUTLET

0'-8½"

B

22'-7 3/4" (6.90M)

0'-8½"

GRASS

-7½"

2   3

SCALE: 1:48

THE FLOOR PLAN: THE RECTANGLE AT LOWER LEFT
IS THE TRAVERTINE TERRACE AND STEPS FACING
SOUTH, TO THE FOX RIVER. THE UPPER RECTANGLE
IS THE LIVING QUARTERS. THE "CORE," WITH THE
SOUTH-FACING FIREPLACE AND THE KITCHEN
ORIENTED NORTH TO THE MEADOW, IS OUTLINED
IN DARK BLACK. INSIDE THE HOME, EDITH'S BED
("SLEEPING AREA"), UPPER RIGHT, IS FACING EAST.
A LONG WARDROBE SEPARATES THE SLEEPING AREA
FROM THE LIVING ROOM. THERE IS A SMALL DINING
TABLE (UPPER LEFT) AND A WRITING DESK (LOWER
LEFT).

about the men and women who paid his bills. Wright loved to design every aspect of a house, including furnishings and gewgaws. He even tried his hand at dress design, suggesting appropriate clothing to accompany his architectural work. Wright called built-in furniture "client-proof." But Wright's chief draftsman John Howe said his boss "had the highest regard for each of his clients simply because they were *his* clients; he found virtues in them which were indiscernible to others and almost refused to acknowledge their short-comings."[17]

Mies adhered to the less-client-interaction-is-more school of thought. "Never talk to a client about architecture," he once said.

> Talk to him about his children. That is simply good politics. He will not understand what you have to say about architecture most of the time. . . . Most of the time a client never knows what he wants. He may, of course, have some very curious ideas, and I do not mean to say that they are silly ideas. But being un-trained in architecture, they just cannot know what is possible and what is not possible.[18]

In an interview, Mies revealed mixed feelings about one of his most famous clients, the Brno businessman Fritz Tu-gendhat, whom he viewed as a conservative fuddy-duddy: "He was a very careful man. He did not believe in one doctor only—he had three." Mies realized that Mr. Tugendhat was probably expecting a solid, bourgeois home of the kind that

Mies built for clients before World War I, apparently un-aware that his more artistic-minded wife was looking for-ward to owning a modernist landmark. "I remember it was Christmas Eve when he saw the design," Mies recalled. "He nearly died." His wife, Grete, eventually convinced him to proceed.

Grete was the proverbial "high spirited personality"[19] whose artistic passion drove the project, and she reported no problems interacting with Mies. She objected to the "open plan" bathrooms on the second floor, and asked that they open not into the family bedrooms, but into a hallway. She also asked Mies to move his projected freestanding columns into the wall on the second floor, to open up the space, and to add shades onto the broad window expanses, to prevent overheating in the summer. "Mies accepted all these requests without objection," she reported.[20]

Her husband acquiesced to everything except the fur-niture. Mies cannily arranged to have the furniture deliv-ered just before lunch. Mr. Tugendhat flew into a rage, as predicted, but then calmed down after a toothsome Czech repast. Architects often win these battles, and Mies pre-vailed here. The twenty-four "Brno chairs" that Mies and Lilly Reich arranged around the Tugendhats' dining room table indeed became internationally famous. The house also featured two freshly designed "Tugendhat chaises," and two Barcelona chairs upholstered in emerald-green leather. Against the glass wall, Mies hung his favorite shan-tung curtains, in black and in the silk's natural color, fawn-beige.[21]

Mies's conclusion: "I think we should treat our clients as children."[22]*

THE FARNSWORTH WAS MIES'S first American house. His second, designed more or less simultaneously for Robert H. McCormick, a relative of Colonel Robert R. McCormick who sold Edith her Fox River acreage, was a pale imitation of the Farnsworth. It is obvious in retrospect that Farnsworth would be a bespoke creation.

"This was not a normal house, nor were we normal architects," Goldsmith recalled.[23]

> [Mies] told us how he wanted the windows detailed. He personally went to the plywood warehouse to pick the panels for the primavera panels. When the steel was almost erected he came out and squinted along the beams. I think once he said, "Goldsmith, this corner is low, fix it."

Attorney Dick Young remembered a confrontation between Mies and a local contractor who had arrived to grade the site. "Mies was so fastidious that he wanted a grade to within a tenth of an inch, and this guy just told him to go to hell," Young recalled. " 'Little lumps of dirt are bigger

---

* There is an exception to every rule. When Samuel Bronfman expressed an opinion about the cladding for his Seagram Building, Mies was all ears. "Just in the talk we had, he said, 'I like bronze and marble.' I said, 'That's good enough for me!' "

than that,'" the contractor said. Mies hired someone else for the job.

Nothing like the Farnsworth House had been built before, and all elements, except for the rolled steel columns and floor channels, and the concrete flooring slabs, would be handcrafted by one of Mies's associates or by a special workshop. There is a memo in MoMA's Mies van der Rohe archives titled "Miscellaneous Steel #1," stating, "Very precise workmanship will be required in the execution of this contract. The standard of excellence will be the metal sash on the Alumni Memorial Hall of Illinois Institute of Technology, 32nd and State Streets, Chicago Illinois."

The finished white-painted steel is beautiful, and was the result of painstaking work. Mies initially sandblasted the rolled steel columns to smooth them down. "When the steel comes from the mill," Mies explained, "it has often a very fine metal skin, and when that is not carefully removed, then it has rough texture and will rust much earlier."[24]

After sandblasting, Mies ordered the columns to be sprayed with a rustproofing zinc coating and "finally," Peter Blake wrote, "the white paint was applied with such care that the finished surfaces look almost baked on."[25] Mies insisted on four coats of paint.

Then Mies had the welding plugs ground off of the metal surface, so the columns seem to cling to the horizontal steel beams magnetically.

Once the office swung into action, the commitment to the Farnsworth project was all-absorbing. "[Ed] Duckett, Bruno Conterato, and I worked full-time on it for weeks," Goldsmith later said. "This was almost the entire office force. We made full-size models of the window frames and Mies personally decided even the smallest details. . . . There is no other building in the American work that Mies followed so closely. He examined every visible detail."[26]

A STEEL SUPPORT BEAM RISING FROM THE GROUND SEEMS MAGNETICALLY ATTACHED TO A FLOOR CHANNEL, WITH ALL TRACES OF WELDING REMOVED.

The intellectually curious Farnsworth was nothing if not an engaged client. "She was there when we were pouring the foundations," Goldsmith recalled, "and putting in the foundations, and the tanks and the underground cables and so forth. I remember pointing out and explaining everything to her that was going into the ground, showing her the oil tank, the septic system, explaining the underground pipes coming from the well and the oil tank."[27]

The aluminum curtain rods were hand-fashioned in the downtown office, increasingly frequented by Farnsworth in her off-duty hours. The office produced several wooden versions of the stainless-steel andirons for the fireplace, and erected a wooden model of the famous two-tiered staircase at the site, to see its proportions in situ.

Gene Summers recalled crafting the wooden study models for the house's aluminum mullions:

SUMMERS: I never will forget I built those mullions. [They were] actually for the terrace of the Farnsworth House, which was an enclosed screen. We had our office in Ohio Street then. I built those mullions on a wood saw in the office full size. They were nine and a half feet high, or nine foot four inches high. There were two of them. I put them on my shoulders, took them to the railroad station and took them to Plano and walked from the train station to the house and installed them so that Mies could see them the following weekend, full scale.

INTERVIEWER PAULINE SALIGA: That was above and beyond the call of duty.

SUMMERS: It's all part of it, it was great fun. I felt a little silly going through the Loop with these two big pieces of wood over my shoulders.

Custom building would prove to be expensive.

Mies tasked the young Goldsmith, who was emerging as primus inter pares among the Farnsworth crew, to model the house in three different sizes, at three different costs: 84′ × 30′ × 10′ at $69,250; 77′ × 28′ × 9′ at $59,980; and 77′ × 28′ × 10′ for $60,980. They chose 77′ × 28′ × 9.5′, with Mies hoping to keep the costs around $60,000. Goldsmith later calculated that siting the house in the lower floodplain increased the overall cost by one-third, requiring the house to be lifted off the ground and adding the elegant staircase and terrace as design elements.[28]

Money concerns would return to haunt Mies and Edith again and again. For context, the median U.S. home price in 1950 was $7,354, roughly one and a half times the average household income. Edith was, by any standard, a well-to-do woman who "didn't have to worry about where the next dollar was coming from," according to her attorney and contemporary Dick Young.[29] Great architects were building great houses at the American midcentury, but they weren't costing this much. Between 1952 and 1955, Richard Neutra built his famous residence for Occidental College art professor Constance Perkins in Pasadena for $17,000. A 1948 *Time* magazine feature on modern architecture, featuring Neutra on the cover, listed several chic homes that would cost a fraction of the eventual Farnsworth bill: a $30,000 Walter Gropius house in Massachusetts; a $45,000 Ralph Twitchell home in Sarasota, and so on.

On the one hand, costs were piling up. On the other hand, the word *fun* crops up again and again when the principals remembered the summer of 1949 when Farnsworth House construction began.

"[Mies] absolutely enjoyed it, was fascinated by it, followed everything," Goldsmith recalled. "He loved to go out there."

At Mies's office, Farnsworth later wrote, spirits were high: "In the big drafting room, the boys sat at their tables, transfigured. 'This is the most important house in the world,' they crowed."

CHAPTER 5

"COMPARED TO THE
FARNSWORTH HOUSE,
IT'S JUST A TOY."

A FUNNY THING HAPPENED ON THE WAY TO building Mies's glass house. Philip Johnson built it first.

Johnson had played a huge role in promoting Mies's distinctive style and his European accomplishments to the American audience. An eager acolyte with a sharp tongue and generally impeccable (if snobbish) taste, Johnson boosted Mies and his other favorite European architects such as Oud and Le Corbusier, in the groundbreaking 1932 MoMA *International Style* show, and again in the 1947 exhibition devoted solely to Mies's work.

Philip Johnson was a complicated fellow. In the first half of his long career as an architect—he died at age ninety-eight in 2005—he was derided as "Mies van der Johnson," so often did he swipe from the master's canon. "I have always been delighted to be called Mies van der Johnson," he replied much later in life. "It has always seemed proper in the history of architecture for a young man to understand, even to imitate, the great genius of an older generation."[1]

For his part, Mies didn't mind being borrowed from. "Sometimes people say, 'How do you feel if somebody copies you?'" he commented in a 1960 interview. "I say that is not a problem for me. I think that is the reason we are working, that we find something everybody can use. We hope only that he uses it right."

In the final decades of his life, Johnson renounced and even vilified Mies. But in 1939, when Johnson, at age thirty-three, finally decided to attend architecture school, Mies loomed so large in his life that Johnson felt intimidated. Instead of attending the Armour Institute (later IIT), where Mies chaired the architecture department, Johnson registered at Harvard's Graduate School of Design (GSD), then led by Mies's Bauhaus rival, Walter Gropius.

"I was very frightened of Mies directly," Johnson told interviewer Peter Eisenman. "I wasn't sure how I could make out with all those drawings of bricks, and so on." Johnson said he would feel more comfortable at "Mother Harvard," and "What was this 'Armour Institute,' for God's sakes?"

In a 1968 interview with his grandson, the architect Dirk Lohan, Mies drolly confirmed Johnson's reasons for studying architecture in Cambridge. "Well, you see, Harvard is a special school, you know, only the better people go there," Mies observed. "Now they went on strike too [in 1968], the better people. [Johnson] had already been at Harvard earlier as a poor student. And Gropius was not so bad that you'd be expected to turn your back on your alma mater."[2]

Surprising no one, the dauphin Johnson built an elegant Miesian "courthouse" for his graduation project at the GSD.

He was rich enough to buy a house lot in the center of Cambridge, and he was rich enough to finance construction of 9 Ash Street, an elegant bachelor pad surrounded by a nine-foot-high wall. Johnson lived at Ash Street for a few months

in 1942, before he was called away to the army. Among the attendees at his legendary parties were Gropius, the future Yale architecture chairman George Howe, and a young MIT architecture student, I. M. Pei.

It did not go unnoticed that Ash Street was pretty much a direct copy of Mies's plans for the Hubbe House, an unbuilt project to be sited on an island in the Elbe River near Magdeburg, Germany. It was not even Johnson's first copy: "My first design [at the GSD] was the usual little seaside house," he told Robert A. M. Stern years later. "It looked just like the Barcelona Pavilion. So it looked as if I was accomplished; I wasn't. They didn't know Mies at Harvard, you see." Johnson's classmate Ulrich Franzen said that 9 Ash Street "was the

THANK YOU, MR. VAN DER ROHE: 9 ASH STREET

first Miesian house that any of us had ever seen."[3] Johnson's first biographer, Franz Schulze, sardonically noted that "Philip had built the first Miesian court house anywhere."[4]

Once out of Harvard, Mies recalled, Johnson was a frequent visitor to his Chicago office: "[Johnson] always came here, snooped through all the details and copied them. The mistakes that he makes in the details happen because he did not work to obtain them, but was just snooping around."

Johnson's visits became the stuff of legend. "He would get his little cards out, and say 'What's new, boys?'" Mies's associate Joseph Fujikawa remembered.[5]

> He was in and out of Mies's office ever since we were in the Champlain Building. He'd come walking in Monday morning. "Well, what's new, boys?" Then he'd go around where each of us was working and ask questions, "What are you doing?" I guess he picked up quite a bit of information which he then ran back to New York and used.

Fujikawa's colleague Edward Duckett added: "I don't think [Johnson] ever had an original idea in his life."

Johnson was, of course, familiar with the Farnsworth House design. Not only did Mies have a model on display in his office from 1946 onward, but one of the Farnsworth House models was featured in the 1947 MoMA show.

There is scant evidence that the two architects conferred about Johnson's house, which he planned to build atop a low hill overlooking a pond on an eleven-acre property he had just purchased in New Canaan, Connecticut, about forty-five miles from Manhattan. At a 1961 symposium, Johnson said he once "pointed out to [Mies] that [a glass house] was impossible because you had to have rooms, and that meant solid walls up against the glass, which ruined the whole point; Mies said, 'I think it can be done.'"[6]

In a quixotic *Architecture Review* article published in 1950, just after the completion of his New Canaan house, Johnson wrote:

> The idea of a glass house comes from Mies van der Rohe. Mies had mentioned to me as early as 1945 how easy it would be to build a house entirely of large sheets of glass. I was skeptical at the time, and it was not until I had seen the sketches of the Farnsworth House that I started the three-year work of designing my glass house. My debt is therefore clear, in spite of the obvious difference in composition and relation to the ground.

The open-plan interior, Johnson admitted, was cribbed from Mies, too:

> The whole arrangement inside the house, the planning of the house, was done from a simple, Mies-ian arrangement of planes and blocks. That is, the closet into the bedroom makes one plane, the kitchen makes another, both of them anchored by the circular bathroom.[7]

And so was the idea of placing Elie Nadelman's five-foot-high papier-mâché sculpture group *Two Circus Women* at the edge of the open sleeping area. "The sculpture provides the type of foil which this kind of building needs," Johnson wrote, adding "(Mies again established the precedent in the Barcelona Pavilion.)" In Barcelona, Mies had placed Georg Kolbe's nude *Dawn* in an elegant, marble-framed water basin.

Mies was later asked under oath if he thought Johnson had "pirated" his Farnsworth House design, and he waxed indifferent.

Q: The Glass House is pretty much a copy of your plan, isn't it, of your model?

A: I would not say that it is pretty much a copy because it is quite a different house.

Q: Did he copy it with your permission or without your permission?

A: [Mies demurs.] The conception is different. It rests on the ground. It has no porch, it has no terrace. He has a different window division. He has four doors in the house, steel doors.

Q: What other differences are there?

A: He has a brick cylinder as a bathroom, and the fireplace. He has a freestanding counter kitchen.

I think if somebody would look at it he would think it would be an absolutely different house. The details may be similar somewhat.[8]

In the *Review* article and many times afterward, Johnson claimed several other, non-Miesian inspirations for the Glass House: "Malevich, the Parthenon, the English garden, the whole Romantic Movement, the asymmetry of the 19th century . . . The footpath pattern between the two houses I copied from the spider-web-like forms of Le Corbusier."[9] He compared the approach to the Glass House with the processive revelation of the Parthenon as one climbs the Acropolis, and pointedly excluded his cylindrical, brick service core, where he stashed a bathroom, from Mies's influence. He claimed, shockingly, that the brick cylinder sprang "from a burnt wooden village I saw once where nothing was left but foundations and chimneys of brick." Given that Johnson almost certainly saw this tableau when he accompanied Hitler's Wehrmacht as a pro-fascist, fellow-traveling journalistic observer during the 1939 invasion of Poland, his citation was curious and grotesque.[10]

Some of Johnson's woolgathering is nonsense. *Épater les architectes* was one of his favorite parlor games. Well into his eighties, the spotlight-loving Johnson ("Attention *à tout prix* . . . we choose any direction as long as it is different enough to get attention in the architectural magazines")[11] addressed the idea that building a glass house was "a form of exhibitionism": "A great number of [people] have said that. In fact, they went so far as publishing in a magazine, 'People that love in glass houses should ball in the basement.' But I don't have a basement, so I don't ball in the basement."[12]

It would have made for less interesting copy for him to explain that he had built a separate house altogether, the neighboring Brick House, with a garishly canopied guest bedroom suitable for any pleasures. In a *Commentary* review, the art critic Hilton Kramer noted that the Glass House

> proved to be so egregiously uninhabitable even for an aesthete like Johnson that he at once undertook to build an alternative, *anti*-Miesian retreat on the same property that would afford him the privacy and amenity which the doctrinaire transparency of the Glass House precluded.
>
> In this regard, I recall a lecture Johnson delivered at Harvard in the spring of 1951 (when I was a student there). Asked by a member of the audience if the Glass House was not fundamentally incompatible with the needs of family life, Johnson declared with his customary hauteur that the family should be abolished.

The primary difference between the Farnsworth House and the Glass House derives from the sites. Mies examined Edith Farnsworth's riverside acreage and decided to build in the floodplain. Hoping to avoid high water, he elevated his glass house five feet three inches above the ground. Johnson had no such problems. The gently flattened hilltop offered a natural pediment for his house, and he set it atop a stage of bricks, invoking the design language of Greek temples and of monumental nineteenth-century architects like Karl Friedrich Schinkel, who also designed stage sets for Berlin opera houses. Schinkel was one of Mies's architectural heroes.

Mies and Johnson treated their equally attractive sites quite differently. Mies and Farnsworth let the house inhabit the wild acreage. Aside from mowing the hillside field that rolled upward to a road parallel to the river, they landscaped only minimally. Cars approached on a dirt road coming down the hill from the east; Edith never wanted a paved road on the property, and never built one. Johnson's Glass House, by contrast, was the centerpiece in a fully programmed landscape, connected to the Brick House by manicured gravel paths that soon led to a small swimming pool and perfectly trimmed expanses of bordered lawn. "It's very expensive wallpaper, of course—landscaping," the urbanely urban Johnson remarked. "Because if a tree falls and ruins your landscape it's an expensive little piece of wallpaper to fix."[13]

THE GLASS HOUSE, WITH PATHWAYS LEADING TO THE BRICK HOUSE AND OTHER BUILDINGS ON THE PROPERTY. THE BAR/KITCHEN FACES US ON THE LEFT; THE CYLINDRICAL BRICK HEARTH/ BATHROOM CORE IS TO THE CENTER-RIGHT.

Mies let nature be, with occasional untoward consequences. That is a chance Johnson never took. Nature can be
unfriendly, as Mies and Edith would discover soon enough.

Johnson's house departed from the Farnsworth House
prototype in other fundamental ways as well. Johnson en-
cased his transparent box in black girders; Mies chose white.
("White is always powerful and positive," said Le Corbusier.) Mies's eight elegantly engineered columns cantilevered
about a third of the Farnsworth House's floor plan out over
the site. Johnson placed his eight columns conventionally,
four of them in the Glass House corners, where they would
be in any ordinary building.

The two houses had different dimensions. In fact, the
Glass House's 55´ × 33´ rectangle was closer to the original
proportions of the Farnsworth House—and to the 3:5
"golden rectangle" ratio—which were downsized for budget reasons. Johnson's house has four doors, each in the center of a glass plane. Farnsworth has only one. In both houses,
furniture divided the open space into living rooms, dining
room, and sleeping area. The two architects had different vi-
sions of their service cores, that is, where to place the kitchen
and bathroom. Mies located these services in a rectangular
structure floating asymmetrically at the back of the Farnsworth House. Johnson, who had zero interest in cooking,
installed a notional kitchen in a line of cabinetry that more or
less defined a "dining area." The Glass House's single bathroom was tucked into Johnson's cylindrical core of glazed
brick, which also housed the fireplace.

The different approaches to service functions subtended
a gaping distinction between the two structures: Johnson had

no intention of living in his glass house, while Edith Farnsworth did. Johnson later explained that the house he'd wanted to build on his scenic knoll simply wouldn't fit, so he erected the glass "pavilion" atop the hill and the separate Brick House eighty feet away. Designed simultaneously with the Glass House, the Brick House came together a few months before the Glass House, in 1949. "It contains the guest rooms and bathrooms and the necessaries and the heating," Johnson explained. "So, in that way, we make an anchor for the Glass House."[14]

In practice, Johnson and a companion would generally overnight in the sumptuous Brick House, in a Topkapi-style double bed. The very first night Johnson spent in his newly constructed, uncurtained glass house, his own reflection frightened him. (Edith Farnsworth, with her hard-won shantung curtains, never complained of being frightened in her Fox River home. Johnson telephoned his architectural partner, Landis Gores, who rescued him. Soon thereafter, Johnson retained lighting designer Richard Kelly, who had worked at the Yale theater department, to install a remarkable state-of-the-art illumination system. Kelly attached floodlights to the eaves, "illuminat[ing] the lawn around the house, giving the illusion, from within, that the floor is suspended above the ground." Spotlights installed at the bases of tree trunks uplit the immediate landscape, and Kelly dug a trench around the Glass House perimeter and trained floodlights up and onto the ceiling of Johnson's dwelling.

Architect Phyllis Lambert, who later retained both Johnson and Kelly to design the Four Seasons Restaurant inside Manhattan's Seagram Building, wrote that "the lighting scheme Kelly and Johnson created for the Glass House evoked Schinkel's aesthetic vision of a stage 'essentially atmospheric in nature, employing lighting and painterly *Stimmung* [mood] as the main devices for the creation of theatrical effects."[15]

Johnson appreciated theatrical effects as well as any architect, and it was hardly surprising that he alerted *The New York Times* to the crowds of gawkers "blocking traffic on Ponus Ridge in this conservative old community of early colonial homes," meaning New Canaan, during the Glass House construction. In December 1948, the newspaper reported on "hundreds of residents turning out in holiday mood to inspect Philip C. Johnson's all-glass house. While workmen put the finishing touches on the 'private' residence and the adjoining guest house, startled, uninvited visitors tramp about to view the results with mingled expressions of awe, wonder and indignation."

The Glass House was completed in 1949. Johnson told Mies that the house cost $60,000 to build, and that number cast a long shadow across the Fox River project. An undated memo in the Farnsworth construction file notes that "Mies had been a guest at the home of P. Johnson and had discussed the heating of the home with Mr. Johnson. That house was heated by radiant coils in floor and ceiling. . . . Philip's house proved slow to heat and was sluggish to variations in heat loss. This convinced Mies that air heat or at least partial air heat was a necessity."

In late 1949, Goldsmith dashed off a quick note to Johnson inquiring about door handles for Plano:

Dear Philip:

We are going to need a pair of lever-handles for the Farnsworth house door.

Mies said that you had good ones on your house.

Would you please tell us where they can be obtained.

Johnson's prompt response:

Tell Mies I stole them from him!

The lever handles that Mies saw at my house were based on a design of his that I used on my first apartment here in 1930. They are currently available at Ostrander and Eshleman Inc.[16]

Johnson had a Prospero-like gift for conjuring up fawning press coverage. *House and Garden* called the Glass House "a truly original [!] building of timeless elegance and classic simplicity, as well as a conclusive demonstration of the fact that modern building techniques have come of age." *Life* magazine gushed:

Philip C. Johnson . . . likes to build extremely modern houses and try them out on himself.

His latest experiment, amid the hilly scenery of New Canaan, Conn., is the current conversation piece of American architecture. . . . After living transparently for nine months, Johnson regards his experiment as a success. For friends who joke about the perils of stone-throwing, he has an answer: "People don't throw stones at shop windows, why should they throw them at mine?"

In the fullness of time many critics forgave Johnson his magpie-like borrowing and accepted the Glass House as fundamentally "different in character" from the Farnsworth House. Peter Blake elaborated in his book *The Master Builders*:

> Johnson's home is symmetrical in its elevations; the Farnsworth house has a porch and a lower deck at one end and is quite dynamically asymmetrical. Johnson's house sits on the ground like a delightful little classical temple; the Farnsworth House is virtually airborne. . . . Finally, the Johnson house has a strong post-and-beam look, a feeling of compression in the columns; whereas the Farnsworth house has a sense of tension, of steel being stretched out to its ultimate potentials. The white steel columns of the Farnsworth house are so precisely welded to the horizontal steel fascias of floor and roof planes that the steel "sings" like a tuning fork when it is lightly tapped.[17]

Both Blake and another later MoMA curator, Terence Riley, think the Glass House is essentially European ("a tiny, classical palazzo" —Blake) while the Farnsworth feels more American ("dynamic, cantilevered, almost in motion" —Blake again). "Philip understands Mies almost better than Mies does in a certain sense," Riley argues.

Philip always understood Mies through the lens of Schinkel, and in Berlin the countryside was where the king lived. Berlin relied on the countryside for its art and its cultural history. Philip was very aware of a countryside full of allusions, and his house is like a European villa, vertical and aristocratic, something that Schinkel might have constructed in Potsdam. The Farnsworth House is very American compared to that.[18]

It would not have surprised Johnson to read some extremely harsh critiques of his New Canaan project. "In spite of its moniker," architect James Biber wrote in a collection of Glass House essays, "the Glass House is, when compared with Farnsworth House, a brick."

It sits, earthbound, heavy, black, ironically solid, and dependent on an array of other elements and an expansive site to make it a livable place. The Farnsworth House is sui generis, an entire world in one building. It is like smoke,—magic, elusive, both solid and vapor, and always in flux.[19]

In this same collection, Phyllis Lambert wrote of the Glass House that "architecturally, compared to the Farnsworth House, it's just a toy."[20]

Architect David Holowka reviewed Johnson's preliminary drawings for the Glass House and concluded that "After 25 tries, Johnson's tortured resignation that the Farnsworth

House was not to be improved upon is on full view in penul-
timate scheme 26's nearly actionable plagiarism of its plan."[21]
Edith Farnsworth herself used the "p" word when asked to
testify about her house in 1951: "There was a great deal of
talk about plagiarism on the part of Philip Johnson when his
house was completed."[22]

There is another way of looking at the Glass House: as a
heartfelt homage to Mies, in whose footsteps Johnson had
faithfully trod since 1930. If it was a theft, it was certainly
acknowledged, with honesty and even affection. For instance, Johnson chose to decorate the Glass House's minimalist living area with copies of the same furniture, in the
same arrangement, that Mies and Lilly Reich had chosen to
decorate Johnson's one-bedroom Manhattan apartment in
1930: two Barcelona chairs and a Barcelona couch and otto-
man, arrayed around Mies's famous glinting steel-and-glass
X table, also designed for the Barcelona Pavilion.

On the north side of the house, at the edge of the putative
"sleeping area," Johnson placed the bespoke leather-topped
desk that Mies designed for him in 1930. This was not a copy,
but the actual desk that Mies shipped to Johnson for their
first project together. It remains in New Canaan to this day.

CHAPTER 6

"YOU GO BACK TO YOUR NEPHRITIS WHERE YOU BELONG."

WITH CONSTRUCTION HUMMING ALONG in mid-1949, Edith allowed herself a moment of ebullience in her diary: "That summer was marvelous because it fulfilled my ideal that persons trained in different fields of the arts or the sciences should seek to understand the principles common to all fields of advancement." Few appreciated it at the time, but Mies's career in America was turning a corner. A partnership with Chicago developer Herbert Greenwald was landing him work that would soon make him more famous in the United States than he ever was in Germany. Simultaneously, Farnsworth's career was gathering momentum.

The years of her acquaintance and relationship with Mies were also the time that Farnsworth's name began to appear in leading research journals, such as *The Journal of Laboratory and Clinical Medicine, The American Journal of Medicine,* and the *Proceedings of the Society for Experimental Biology and Medicine.* Edith was working both as a clinician and as a researcher/assistant professor in kidney diseases at Northwestern University Medical School, in the field that would soon be called nephrology. Initially, she published basic studies of kidney function. She then focused on the potential of the synthetic hormone ACTH (adrenocorticotropic hormone) for treating a common form of kidney disease known as nephrotic syndrome, one form of which was previously called Bright's disease. In the early 1950s, Chicago's Armour and Company was the rare supplier of ACTH, a "fluffy, magic compound"[1] derived from the pituitary glands of hogs. This work was key to the later, very effective use of certain steroid medications, e.g., prednisone, for this disorder.

Edith's fans have sometimes insisted that her work deserved a Nobel Prize, which sounds like hyperbole. Yet in 1950, two American researchers from the Mayo Clinic, Edward Kendall and Philip S. Hench, shared a Nobel Prize for Physiology or Medicine with Swiss chemist Tadeus Reichstein "for their discoveries relating to the hormones of the adrenal cortex, their structure and biological effects."

"The Nobel Prize was for both lab work on the adrenal hormones (not just ACTH, the regulator of adrenal hormones, so to speak) and for therapeutic uses," according to Dr. Steven Peitzman, a Drexel University professor of medicine and historian of nephrology. "The dominant use was for rheumatoid arthritis, for which it made a remarkable difference for some patients." Edith's experiments with ACTH and Bright's disease represented a closely related, narrower field of endeavor.

Edith was running her own small, well-equipped lab of five researchers, funded both by the research division of the U.S. Public Health Service, a precursor to the National Institutes of Health, and by a charitable research fund from Cook County Hospital. She also received private donations from well-to-do friends and social acquaintances. Dr. Homer Smith cited her work in his famous "kidney bible," *The Kidney: Structure and Function in Health and Disease*, the postwar cornerstone of the burgeoning field of dialysis and renal medicine.

"It was unusual for a woman to be leading a lab and publishing as first author in scientific journals," Peitzman says. "Often key women were relegated to the background. She was doing what we call solid, 'normal science.' Adding little bricks to the building up of knowledge about kidney function. She was very productive, and this was critical work."

In October 1949, Farnsworth traveled to Atlantic City for a conference on her specialty, the use of ACTH in curing kidney diseases. The conference achieved notoriety for pitting the Old Guard of kidney research against a new generation of Young Turks, including Farnsworth. Edith felt that she had to attend:

> I had come under criticism in the research world as a poor "laboratory man" and was thus bound to alter such an impression in order to save my reputation.
>
> That was the way it was for me when, a novice, a

midwesterner, and a woman, I packed my toothbrush and my little box of slides and started for Atlantic City to give a paper. . . . My contribution to this lordly-sounding conference was a painstakingly abstruse paper on the behavior of the renal tubules under stimulation by ACTH. I had masses of irreproachable data which I arranged in well-advised but impenetrable ratios.

She described approaching the dais in a huge auditorium in front of a large crowd, "the audience extended before me, acres of dark faces with pipes gripped in their teeth, for the

most parts scouts for the research establishment." She delivered the final paper of the symposium. "My knees were shaking violently as I put the manuscript and notes on the lectern." When the conference moderator tried to hand her the pointer and pinpoint flashlight, "I wasn't in condition to manipulate either one."

Her account of the conference ends there.

In her autobiographical journal, Edith resumed the story of her life with Mies:

By the summer of 1950 the Fox River house had a roof, and the slabs of travertine waited in rows outside the brooding house. Students of all callings arrived in busloads to mill around open-mouthed and to drop a line into the river in the hope of carp. Architects came from various European countries and we brought one or two of them out from town with us about every weekend. Most of them were fulsome in their words of praise and wonderment at the miracle which was taking form in that rural spot; one or two of the German ones exclaimed, "Master!" and crawled across the terrace to [Mies's] feet where he sat on a low aluminum deck chair, impassively awaiting the throaty plaudits of the visitors, "Grossartig!" [Masterpiece!], "Unglaublich!" [Unbelievable!].

EDITH IN THE MEADOW, WITH POODLE. THE BARE TREES LINE THE BANK OF THE FOX RIVER.

In this same vein, Farnsworth described "the travertine drama."

Mies was fanatical about stone, and, as noted, in love with travertine. He spent two full days "in bitterly cold weather" examining the 2´ × 2´9˝ slabs as they arrived in Plano. "When the travertine came he was on the site and looked at every piece," Myron Goldsmith recalled. "If they were different quality than what was first quality, what was second quality went into the corners and into unimportant places, and what was to be discarded."[2] Mies's categories were "Accepts, Rejects, and Dubious."

The Mies archive at the Museum of Modern Art has a huffy letter from the Acme Marble Company to its supplier, the Carthage Marble Corporation of Carthage, Missouri. The letter explains that in one session, Mies rejected nineteen delivered slabs and labeled fifty-seven "as being sub-standard and subject to rejection upon later re-appraisal." Mies agreed to pay for the 85 percent of the shipment that he deemed acceptable. Acme's letter quoted Mies to the effect that marble represented one-quarter of the overall cost of the house and needed to be perfect. Carthage contested Mies's dour assessment of their work and insisted that all of the marble had been inspected before delivery.

Looking back, Farnsworth took a jaded view of what she had come to view as quality-control theatrics:

> The blue canvas deck chair became the pivotal point in the travertine drama which drove the first nails of incredulity into my hitherto well-guarded tolerance. The slabs had been selected before they left

the yards of the marble firm and delivered at the farm-house. Mies assigned them to one of three categories; first quality, second quality, or reject. This seemed appropriate and I took it for evidence of the architect's meticulous concern for the best use of his building materials.

On second viewing, as it were, Farnsworth felt that what she first experienced as connoisseurship had become farce:

> When, however, the travertine ceremony was once again enacted, this time with Mies in the blue deck chair while a crew of men filed by, each man carrying a slab of stone like a precious painting before the eyes of a divine appraiser, I turned a corner in my regard for Mies. The absurdity became dramatic when it was discovered that there had been a misunderstanding about which pile belonged to which category and that there was no agreement between First Viewing and Second Viewing.

In the end, Mies rejected forty-six slabs, and used about six hundred.

By 1949, Mies and Edith were no longer intimate friends; they had reverted to the roles of architect and client. Lora Marx had reentered Mies's life and would remain at his side until his death. Mies was still occasionally seeing the elegant Mary Callery, who visited Chicago now and then, according to his daughter Georgia. An incident at the building site reinforced Edith's no-longer-specially-favored status: Mies

MIES ENJOYING A CIGAR AT THE WORK SITE

saw Farnsworth standing on the terrace below the patio. "Turn around, I want to look at you," he said. Farnsworth shifted to face him, only to learn that "he was just considering the scale and not her beauty," Goldsmith reported. "Mies was always thinking architecture."[3]

Relationships drown in puddles, not lakes, and suddenly small construction problems were acquiring outsized importance. For instance, Edith's cherished fireplace.

Fireplace design was not one of Mies's fortes. He initially intended to use travertine for the bottom of the firebox. "One Sunday when I was there in Plano," Farnsworth remembered, "we put a piece of travertine on the ground and lighted a fire to see if that would break." When the fire was extinguished and the marble cooled, it did break. She suggested using stainless steel for the firebox, and they did.

Around the same time, she phoned Mies to complain that his office's custom-designed stainless-steel andirons "are beautiful but they are much too far apart." Mies had expended considerable energy on the andirons, commissioning several different wooden models of the log holders.

"I will teach you to make a fire with them that way," Mies said in a telephone conversation, Edith recalled.

"It wouldn't be one fire, it would be two fires," Edith said. "The andirons are useless."

"Use bigger logs," Mies advised, before hanging up.

Other features integral to the design were triggering doubts in the client's mind. "I found that the utilities had been jammed together so ruthlessly [in the house's tight, cylindrical service stack] that only the most emaciated of heating and plumbing men could service the equipment," Edith wrote.

As for the chimneys and dampers for the oil furnaces, they could only be reached by the plumber's oldest boy, a thin wiry child who could be poked back among the pipes and was just old enough to carry out orders.

After one such session, the plumber dusted off his child and stood him on his feet. "You haven't chosen a name for the house yet, have you? My suggestion would be: 'My Miesconception.'"

IN HER MEMOIR, WHICH SHE almost certainly hoped to publish as a book, Farnsworth related several social encounters that began to erode her faith in Mies. One evening in Chicago, she wrote, she found herself at a party in the studio of her friend Hugo Weber, an émigré Swiss painter/sculptor/aesthete/boulevardier who shared her interest in European poetry. She attended with Mies, who was in a gloomy mood, partly because he had been drinking, and partly because several of the guests taught with Weber at the Institute of Design, the "American Bauhaus" founded by László Moholy-Nagy. Moholy-Nagy was the artist and photographer who helped design and teach the famous "preliminary course" (*Vorkurs*) at the German Bauhaus.

Mies disliked Moholy-Nagy, whom he viewed as an undisciplined dilettante, and he disdained the perennially cash-short American Bauhaus, whose trustees were angling for a merger with IIT. Furthermore, Mies thought Moholy-Nagy and Gropius, who had both been more assertively anti-Nazi than he, had stolen the name *Bauhaus,* which rightfully belonged to him, as its final director. (After Moholy-Nagy's untimely death at age fifty-one, his widow, Sybil, proclaimed to the rooftops that Mies had been an ardent Nazi. She evinced no sentimental fondness for Gropius, either, calling New York's Pan Am Building, erected above Grand Central Station, "Hitler's Revenge.")[4]

The arty folk got plastered with cheap wine, Farnsworth wrote, while Mies sat "in gelid silence." When she passed into an adjoining room, she reported that "a stranger grabbed my elbow."

"How did you ever happen to involve yourself with Mies?" the man asked. "You surely know that this is nothing but a very queer man with a queer name—"

"I was shocked and hurt on Mies's behalf," Edith wrote, "but before I had recovered enough to think of a reply he had moved past me and disappeared among the other guests."

Some time later, Edith confessed to Weber that his friend, who turned out to be an art historian and a former habitué of Jean Arp's studio, also frequented by Mies, had planted some seeds of doubt:

> I'm so accustomed to the premise that Mies is great that I was really shaken by the curt finality of those words. Of course I have been aware of his brutality for quite a while now, but I never seriously questioned his place and value in architecture. And yet I wonder if what I'm saying now is strictly true. Perhaps, in addition to a real and growing dislike for his arrogance and his monumental selfishness, I have been having some shadowy doubts concerning the sanctity of the rectangle. I mean as an absolute and not only one but the only one—

"Hugo, did you ever hear anybody else express a similar viewpoint about Mies?" Farnsworth asked.

"A queer man with a queer name?" Weber replied. "Not precisely. But it wouldn't surprise me to hear that he has adverse critics in Europe. Anybody who achieves prominence has adverse, even hostile, critics, and I don't quite see why you should feel so upset about it. De-bunking has been a popular exercise for quite a time now."

"But your friend's message goes a good bit further than that."

"True. But don't forget that Germany of the Inflazions-zeit must have been pretty nasty. . . . At any rate, so far as Mies and his rectangle are concerned, they have to be taken or left—the Emperor wears the most superb cloak in the world or else he is naked. And it seems that neither the Trustees of IIT nor the architects of Chicago thought he was naked."

Farnsworth also described her conversations with British architect Fello Atkinson, whom she invited to the Fox River house on a snowy evening. "The first snow had fallen during the night," she wrote, "when I stopped for him at the Chicago Avenue YMCA and when we reached the river bank the rustlings and cracklings of autumn were muted by a light covering of crystalline white."

Atkinson gathered some wood for a fire, and in conversation, clearly had misgivings about the house, specifically the yet-to-be-chosen furnishings. He warned her against "overstuffed furniture," but ventured that reed or wicker would be just as ineffectual; Edith would feel as though she was "camping on travertine." Furnishings will be a challenge, he said:

> I suspect that the difficulties have to do with an abstract quality which is perhaps the dominant one. It will be interesting to see what means you will find to live happily in your weekend house. For it would be dreadful if you were not to be happy here.

Edith invited Mies to her apartment for a nightcap to meet Atkinson, after the pair drove back to Chicago. The rendezvous fell flat. "Conversation moved heavily in spite of anything I could think of to get it off the ground," Farnsworth reported, "and by eleven Atkinson took his leave and offered to drop Mies at home on his way back to the Lawson Y."

The next day, Atkinson barged in on Edith, explaining that he was returning to London and wanted to offer some comments about her new house:

The thing I have on my mind is this; the history of architecture is badly served with quarrels between architects and their clients. . . . These stories do no credit to architects and have done a great deal of damage to architecture. The situation seems even worse in recent years because we architects have broadened our pretensions and come to feel that we should not only design and execute the house itself, but furnish it as well.

Edith was doubtless aware that architects bent on decorating and furnishing the houses they designed was hardly a new phenomenon. But Atkinson wanted to make a broader point.

And here we come back to your problems and your situation with respect to Mies, which is the reason for my visit this evening. It should be possible for you to go ahead together until the project is complete, but I'm afraid you're not going to be able to. I kept thinking of it last night as you and he were sitting here on the sofa. He is a very stubborn man and you are far removed from the masochistic German women he's accustomed to dealing with—I'm terribly afraid that it's going to turn out to be impossible for you to keep on with him.

"That is certainly possible," Edith replied. "I am sure that he would like to put several examples of the Barcelona chair, done in pink suede, beside that enormous glass coffee table, although the subject of furniture has never come up between us." She continued:

> I think the Barcelona chair is very handsome but it is fearfully heavy and utterly unsuitable for a small country house—the place would look like a Helena Rubinstein salon. There is already the local rumor that it's a tuberculosis sanitarium. The fact is that Mies has no taste and if you stop to think about it, that is not surprising. I would hate to be forced to break with him, but I would never consent to his ideas on furnishing. One's house is almost as personal as one's skin. I don't see how he could seriously think that I would go with him beyond the erection of the house itself.

"Mies has no taste" is an example of a comment that Farnsworth would never have made when they were close friends, and was a judgment she almost certainly didn't believe. It was true that she and Mies had different tastes. Mies collected Klee and Kandinsky, Schwitters and Beckmann, while Edith invested in Asian art. But in the first years of their partnership, she had nothing but admiration for his work.

Her guest Atkinson offered his opinion: "I'm afraid that this story is going to end badly."

"I suppose you have good reasons for your predictions, Fello, and I listen with a very heavy heart," Edith replied.

It may well be that I have been mistaken in my impressions of Mies. Perhaps, as a man, he is not the clairvoyant primitive that I thought he was, but simply a colder and more cruel individual than anybody I have ever known. Perhaps it was never a friend and a collaborator, so to speak, that he wanted but a dupe and a victim. There are also the possibilities of a ruinous financial mess, in case our gloomy prognostications should really turn out to be well-founded.

YET AGAIN, CONCERNS ABOUT costs were coming to the fore. The possibility of a "ruinous financial mess" seemed quite real. By 1950, Mies's office was aware that building the house for between $50,000 and $60,000 was becoming unlikely, not only because of decisions about premium materials, but also because the onset of the Korean War had jacked up prices of such basic materials as concrete and steel. Billable hours, which were not exactly the coin of the realm in Mies's chaotically organized office, eventually rose to 5,884. This was more than double the number of hours that Mies's firm would bill for the twin apartment towers scheduled for construction at 860/880 Lake Shore Drive.[5]

The "boys" were hiding certain problems from the client. Mies and Goldsmith had hoped to hire Mies's IIT colleague,

William Goodman, to sort through the challenging heating and plumbing constraints at the Fox River House. But Goodman wasn't available, and his replacement, Norman Beutter, "had very much underestimated how much work was involved and wanted $700 more," according to Goldsmith. "Also he had made an error on the electric supply to the house which we caught before work commenced. For some reason, I began to have misgivings about Beutter's work."

Ultimately they decided to hire Goodman to check and redo Beutter's work. The running total for heating and plumbing was $4,115 at the beginning of 1950, and $5,680 by midyear.[6] It would eventually come to $7,000.[7]

The office knew that costs were rising above $60,000, and that they had allowed a misunderstanding to linger in Edith's mind. When she and Mies started casually discussing the cost of the house in 1946 and 1947, they hovered around the number $40,000. Even though Mies informed her that Philip Johnson spent $60,000 for his house, it's not clear that the new total had registered with Edith. When construction began in 1949, a file memo reported that the building permit valued the project at $60,000. "There is not the slightest doubt that when we started building [summer 1949], we all believed that the house would cost $60,000," according to the anonymous memo writer. "The $40,000 figure Dr. Farnsworth speaks about was a 1946 figure."

The $20,000 difference in 1949 would be worth just over $200,000 today. Even for someone with money, these were not trivial sums.

On June 13, 1950, Goldsmith wrote a file memo entitled

"Increase in Cost and Informing Dr. Farnsworth," reporting, "I made a new estimate . . . $67,899. When I told Mies, he was very surprised. . . . Mies had great difficulty in telling Dr. Farnsworth but when he did, I think we were very surprised that she took it calmly."

Farnsworth and Goldsmith had complicated relations of their own. He was the "customer's man," appearing at the site more often than anyone, including Mies himself. Goldsmith also acted as a general contractor for the project, because Mies never found a local builder to take on the finely crafted Farnsworth House. Goldsmith admired Farnsworth, but he occasionally rubbed her the wrong way. At the work site, she thought she heard him making questionable choices, using crushed rock instead of local gravel for a concrete mix, or overpaying for a steel delivery.[8] In her memoir, Farnsworth recalled complaining to Mies that "the young man who had been delegated as supervisor"—Goldsmith—was interrupting the construction workers with "stupid questions":

> On this point I expostulated to Mies: "The workmen are complaining and I get the impression that he is really raising our building costs through his inexperience."
>
> Mies hesitated for a moment. "You go back to your nephritis where you belong and leave me to build your house without interference."

"It was a tough moment," Farnsworth recalled, "and Mies and I were not far from a rift. But a house cannot very well be abandoned half finished. So we softened our voices and parted friends."

But not for long.

On August 1, 1950, Mies's office told Edith they had spent $69,868.80 on the mostly completed house. One week later, she sent Mies a letter "stating that no further amount should be committed over this figure and to cancel the screens" for the porch. By this time, she had sent him checks totaling about $69,000 for construction expenses, and nothing for architects' fees. In all their hours spent together, the subject had never come up. One day, with the house nearly complete, Edith mentioned to Goldsmith that "Mies and I have never discussed a fee for this house." Goldsmith was understandably surprised:

> Apparently she had trouble bringing it up and he never brought it up. She said, "I wonder if I should offer, he's going to be able to use it, we will work out an arrangement when he can use it when I'm not using it. I also want to give him something, perhaps a painting." I'm sure she had been thinking of a major painting. I did not mention this to Mies but I thought, my God, this thing has been going on for years and they have never discussed it.

Farnsworth would eventually send in two checks, one for $1,000, and another for $2,500, more like tips than fee payments, which would have amounted to 10 percent or more of construction costs.

In September, Edith typed out this chilly missive to Mies:

Dear Mies:

*I received your statement for the chairs, stool and table.
I am delighted that you were able to manufacture these
pieces, but, as I originally stated, I wanted them in the
dull finished steel. If it was not possible to make them
with the stain finish, I think you should have advised me
that such was the case. . . . In any case I prefer to
purchase the frames alone in order to choose the material
for the cushions. Likewise I wish to select the material for
the table top. . . .*

> *Cordially yours,*
> */s/ Edith*
> *Edith B. Farnsworth,*
> *M.D.*

Mies had assumed that Farnsworth, like the Tugendhats,
would want modernist, "Barcelona" furniture inside her
house, but she clearly had other plans.

In February 1951, another memo on costs appears in
Mies's files, written by Goldsmith: "We sent a statement
showing that the final cost of the house was $74,167.95. I told
Mies about this figure and we were both wondering how Dr.
Farnsworth would take it because the $4000 minus the cost of
her screens *represented a complete surprise to us as well as to
her.* [Emphasis added.] Mies told me to call her."

Edith later recounted this phone call, under oath:

GOLDSMITH: Are you sitting comfortably, so that
you could sustain a shock?

FARNSWORTH: Yes, go ahead.

GOLDSMITH: Well, it seems as if there had been a little mistake about the total cost of the house.

FARNSWORTH: I presume that is in the negative sense. It would hardly be in the advantageous sense. . . . What is the extent of the mistake?

The discrepancy, Goldsmith told her, amounted to over $4,000.

"I could hardly imagine how this might have occurred," Edith testified, "and I believe he said something about the electrical bill."

Goldsmith remembered that Edith "was very cold and wanted to know why Mies had not informed her himself."

The next month, Edith again sat down at her typewriter.

MARCH 1, 1951

Dear Mies:

The serious confusion into which the Fox River Project has projected me serves to convince me that it is unsafe for me to close the account without the advice of a specialist competent to protect my interests. For this reason, I am turning the matter over to Randolph Bohrer . . . [and request] "an affidavit giving details of work, labor and material furnished." . . .

It is, of course, understood that no further

*commitments of operations on the Fox River House have
my authorization.*

> *Yours truly,*
> */s/ Edith B.*
> *Farnsworth*
> *Edith B. Farnsworth,*
> *M.D.*

Bohrer was a lawyer whom Edith had met at the hospital.
The marriage of art and intimacy was over. The parties now
contemplated divorce.

CHAPTER 7

"A VIRGILIAN DREAM"

W HAT HAD MIES WROUGHT? THE INITIAL reviews of the Farnsworth House were rapturous. *Architectural Forum*, the leading journal of the day, featured the house on its cover and re-produced the site plan, as well as several interior photos in a fulsome appreciation. "This is the first house built by Ludwig Mies van der Rohe since he came to America in 1938," the magazine announced.

To some it may look like "nothing much"— just a glass-sided box framed in heavy, white steel; but to many partisans of great architec-ture it is the most important house completed in the U.S. since Frank Lloyd Wright built his desert home in Arizona [Taliesin West] a dozen years ago. For the Farnsworth House near Chicago has no equal in perfection of workmanship, in precision of detail, in pure simplicity of concept.

There were elements of finery that excited this specialty magazine:

> The plaster ceiling has the smoothness of a high-grade factory finish. The primavera panels of the service core were matched with infinite patience. And the steel frame was welded to such precise dimensions and so tautly that the column flanges seem almost in tension. When you strike them with the palm of your hand, they sing like a tuning fork.

The unbylined appreciation (by Peter Blake) called Mies a "subtractor," but "what remains after Mies's subtraction is a concentration of pure beauty, a distillation of pure spirit." The Farnsworth House, Blake concluded, exuded "a subtle influence, the influence of a great artist, of a great work of art, of a great discipline, of a great belief that man in architecture should be free."

The London-based *Architectural Design* magazine also slapped a photo of the Farnsworth House on its cover, even though reviewer Mark Hartland Thomas admitted that he was judging the house based only on pictures. "It is such a powerful work of art that even the photographs make a profound impression," Thomas wrote. "One feels that one has already been there." He continued:

What about the human values? Is not this too cold and hard—an impersonal *thing* too complete in its own perfection to admit human life? On the contrary, it has been the deliberate aim of the architect to keep the building quiet and simple in character as an unobtrusive background to the people and the life they will lead in it. There is an important lesson for us here.

The important lesson, according to Thomas, was that "all the chattels that surround our lives . . . proclaim themselves too loudly. The ordinary things that we use should be unobtrusive, giving way to the few things that should be seen, but above all to people themselves."

Architects, generally, have loved the Farnsworth House. There are numerous tiny epiphanies that can be appreciated

TRAVERTINE STAIRS LEADING TO THE (NOW) UNSCREENED PATIO

by specialist and layperson alike. For instance, the magical marble stairs that float off the riparian meadow, first to a broad terrace and then to the west-facing open patio of the house itself. Each travertine riser is separately cantilevered by a steel frame hidden underneath the stairs. The stairs are firm underfoot, but sustained by forces barely visible below.

The lighter-than-air feeling extends to the house itself, a surprisingly large structure of glass expanse, marble-and-concrete flooring, and steel roofing that at first glimpse seems to float over the Fox River meadow. Sandblasting the massive H-beams, which are normally used to buttress foundations, and painting them white lightened their effect on the eye. Natural iron color or black—the color Philip Johnson chose for his earthbound Glass House—would have sunk the house down into the earth below. "If it were black, you wouldn't have the same image of geometry in this forest," the Swiss architect Pierre de Meuron commented after a 2014 visit. "If you make it white, you [bring] it much more to the foreground."[1]

White is the color of the Greek temple, and the stairs-terrace-stairs sequence reinforces what architects call the procession, meaning the curated approach to a house or building. The most famous procession in architecture is the path to the Parthenon in Athens, where the visitor passes through a gateway partway up the Acropolis, signifying the transition between profane and sacred ground. The as-yet-unseen temple is the dwelling place of Athena, the patron goddess of Athens.

Frank Lloyd Wright was famous for making visitors enter his homes through cramped hallways that opened up into glorious, welcoming, high-ceilinged hearth rooms at the physical and psychic center of the house. Naturally he created a dramatic procession for the visitor to his studio/home in Taliesin, Wisconsin, as Witold Rybczynski has explained:

> In a choreographed sequence, the visitor drives up a winding road that circles the house, passes under a porte cochere, makes a sharp turn, and arrives in a courtyard between the building and the crown of the hill. . . . Before entering the house, the visitor passes under a shaded loggia that—finally—offers a panoramic glimpse of the Jones Valley below.[2]

So Mies built only one set of stairs, forcing visitors to approach Farnsworth's house from the south, or river side. As you walk up the stairs, especially in sunlight, you see only dizzying white, a fleeting hallucination of heaven if there is such a thing. "Mies wanted steel to look as refined as Greek marble," according to architecture critic Blair Kamin, and Mies succeeded. For some visitors, the Farnsworth House is indeed holy ground.

Mies's decision to grind off the exposed weld plugs holding the horizontal channel beams to the eight support columns further liberates the building. The beams look as though they were glued together, or attached magnetically. There is no visual cue to explain how the floor and ceiling, each of which weighs several tons, hover effortlessly above the landscape.

Philip Johnson saw the house just after completion and fired off a letter to Mies:

There is no way I can tell you how much I admire the architecture. Your brilliant solutions of the problems that have been plaguing all of us for years are breathtaking.

The steel connections are so inevitable, so clean, so beautifully executed, that I believe no one will ever improve on them. Their problems are solved once and for all. Their execution is also a wonder to me. I am amazed that you found workmen to execute them so well. I cannot be specific, because each one is as good as the next. It exhausts me to even imagine what work you have been through.[3]

The interior, one large room measuring fifty-five by twenty-eight feet, was a near-perfect articulation of architecture's open plan. There is a single entrance door, made of glass, and two millwork doors for the small bathrooms, one with a bath and the other with a shower. There are no walls. A rectangular service core placed at the back of the house separates the front living area from the narrower rear-facing kitchen and bathrooms. Even without walls, the furniture— a dining set and some Barcelona chairs, per Mies's original vision—defines the entry space as a parlor, a receiving area, and a dining room. Moving farther into the house, a soft-leather Barcelona chaise longue and the stainless-steel fireplace invite guests to sit, or suggest relaxation or reading to the single occupant. This is, after all, a second home in a secluded meadow, an hour's drive from the city.

A movable wardrobe, originally clad in teak panels, defined a sleeping area in the eastern quadrant of the house.

The wardrobe provided badly needed storage, and what passed for privacy in the transparent house. Farnsworth, who was nearly six feet tall, groused about its initial height, which didn't fully conceal her from guests in other parts of the house.

If the house had an Achilles' heel, it was the cylindrical utility "stack," a barrel-wide channel of pipes and ducts that brought gas, water, and electricity into the house, expelled sewage into the ground, and sent combustion by-products to the roofline, to be vented by a low chimney. As would become clear shortly after Edith moved in, certain elementary measures of mechanical engineering had either been overlooked or underemphasized. The house needed two separate boilers, for the forced-air heating and hot water systems, and a total of three fans to properly distribute warm air in the winter. Condensation—and worse—collected on the plate glass walls because no warm air flowed upward or downward along their planes in winter.

There was no air-conditioning—still a rarity in the late 1940s—and Mies never seriously studied the need for proper summer ventilation. He had designed mosquito screens to enclose the west-facing patio, but Edith refused to pay for them. "It is undeniable that the Farnsworth House suffers from serious and elementary design faults," the architect Maritz Vandenberg concluded in an elegant appreciation of the structure:

> It was perfectly predictable that a badly-ventilated glass box, without sun-shading except for some nearby trees, would become oven-like in the hot Illinois sum-

mers, and that single-thickness glass in steel frames, devoid of cautionary measures such as convection heaters to sweep the glass with a warm air current, would stream with condensation in an Illinois winter. Mies's disregard of such elementary truths illustrates his greatest weakness as an architect—namely, an obsession with perfect form so single-minded that awkward problems were loftily disregarded.[4]

WHEN DISCUSSING PROJECTS, ARCHITECTS ask, What is the program? Meaning, what will this structure be used for, where is it located, and how will that affect the design? Programs can be simple: an elementary school in Southern California needs classrooms, but not an enclosed hallway. The Mediterranean climate allows students and teachers to circulate through the building under covered breezeways.

After he left Mies and joined the architecture firm Skidmore, Owings and Merrill, Myron Goldsmith designed a repair hangar for United Airlines' base at San Francisco airport. The hangar, of course, had a tightly defined program. It was designed to fit four DC-8 airplanes, so its purpose dictated its dimensions. The DC-8 had a 142-foot wingspan, and the tail rose 42 feet off the ground. So Goldsmith erected a vast (tasteful) barn with reinforced concrete piers to hold welded steel girders that cantilevered 142 feet in two directions.

The program for the Farnsworth House was to create a retreat, a summer house, a second home for a city dweller. In another time it might have been called a villa, a place in which Pliny the Younger, who owned two sumptuous summer homes, remarked that "there is no need for a toga." Le Corbusier said of his villa clients, "Their domestic life will be inserted into a Virgilian dream."[5] But when Corbu built his famous Villa Savoye outside of Paris, he remembered to include three carports for the Savoyes' automobiles. Neither Mies nor his client Farnsworth considered building a road to her house, much less a garage. Likewise, Le Corbusier created an elegant, landscaped approach to his masterpiece. Mies left the landscaping to nature on his meadowed, riverside site.

Perhaps Mies never intended to build a house for Edith Farnsworth. Instead he was indulging in an architectural exercise of consuming interest to himself. While still in Germany, Mies professed great interest in an obscurantist tract by Siegfried Ebeling, *Der Raum als Membran* (*Space as Membrane*). Ebeling described the space of a house as equivalent to a "skin" or a "membrane between men and exterior space." Mies inserted an exclamation mark in the margin of his copy of *Membran*, alongside this particularly opaque passage that explained architecture as an attempt to "equalize the three-dimensional, physical, determined space of a three-dimensional, biologically determined membrane between our bodies, as plasmatic, labile substances, and the latently given yet biostructurally apprehensible emanation of the spheres."

Exclamation mark indeed.

The young Mies of the Weimar avant-garde would certainly have come in contact with the somewhat dotty speculations of the poet, art historian, and science fiction writer Paul Scheerbart, author of "Flora Mohr: A Glass Flower

Novella" and the better-known *Glasarchitektur* (*Glass Architecture*). Scheerbart provoked gnomic speculation in his Expressionist friends, for example, "The Gothic cathedral is the prelude to glass architecture," a quote attributed to Bruno Taut, an architect and theoretician who co-edited the progressive journal *G: Materials for Elemental Form-Creation* with Mies. Taut, who contributed a building to Mies's 1927 Weissenhof Estate project, had earlier built a famous mortar-shell-shaped Glass Pavilion, for which Scheerbart wrote a dedicatory couplet:

> Glass brings us the new age
> Brick culture does us only harm[6]

Scheerbart wanted to declare war on "closed spaces":

> If we wish to raise our culture to a higher plane, so must we willy-nilly change our architecture. And that will be possible only when we remove the sense of enclosure from the spaces where we live. And this we will achieve only by introducing Glass Architecture.[7]

The critic Walter Benjamin, a Mies contemporary, opined that "to live in a glass house is a revolutionary virtue par excellence. It is also an intoxication, a moral exhibitionism, that we badly need." Mies's reputation as one of Germany's most innovative architects of the early 1920s was based in part on two famous unbuilt skyscraper designs, both entirely clad in glass. In 1927, Mies and Lilly Reich designed a *Glasraum* for the Deutsche Werkbund exhibition, commissioned by the German glass industry. "It consisted [of] a large fluid space, organized in three areas by free-standing glass panes with different degrees of transparency, which [interacted] with the reflections from the shiny chromed steel furniture," according to architect Ramon Esteve.[8]

In an interview published a few years after completing Edith's assignment, Mies said, "I hope to make my buildings neutral frames in which man and artworks can carry on their own lives. . . . We should attempt to bring nature, houses and human beings together into a higher city. If you view nature through the glass walls of the Farnsworth House, it gains a more profound significance than if viewed from the outside. . . . It becomes part of a larger whole."[9]

It is important to remember what Mies had the freedom *not* to think about. Edith had no abutters, no nearby intersections, no hankering for a tennis court, a dock, or a swimming pool. She barely required a road, and, aside from mowing the field uphill from her house, she had no landscaping interests at all. Somehow he convinced her not to worry about rain gutters. He and Goldsmith designed a roof-draining system that channeled runoff water to the utility stack. Not an ideal solution, as it happened.

Edith was social, but she didn't ask the house to be. She could serve drinks to friends at midday on the patio, or inside, in front of the fireplace. If she had an overnight guest, it would be one person, at most, probably sleeping on the day bed in the "living area." Remember Mies's remark "I don't belong to the people who cannot live alone"? That was a trait he shared with Edith Farnsworth.

Mies's concessions to summerhouseness in this commission seem quite modest. There is virtually no storage space for, say, horseshoe sets, croquet mallets, or badminton equipment. Mies insisted on furnishing the house sparely, and exclusively with luxury furnishings: the aforementioned Barcelona chairs, an expensive (and beautiful) Brno chrome steel coffee table of his own design, and an elegant complementary dining room set of MR tubular chairs, another of his famous designs. There are no walls to hang art on, and attaching works to the primavera paneling of the kitchen-bathroom core, or to the teak-finished wardrobe, seems sacrilegious. When Farnsworth later installed wicker furniture, Chinese statuary, and family photos in the home, Mies—or at least the Miesians—scoffed.

The architectural historian Alice Friedman, author of a monograph on the Farnsworth House, believes that Farnsworth was more of a patron who midwifed brilliant ideas from Mies, rather than simply his client. "I think she was truly a patron; she was trying to introduce an extraordinary work of art," Friedman told me. "The fact that she had to inhabit the work of art, like any work of art, it teaches you something that you didn't expect when you got it."

As program, the Farnsworth House was "almost nothing . . . a quantity of air caught between a floor and a roof,"[10] according to Arthur Drexler, the Museum of Modern Art curator who acquired Mies's MoMA archive in the 1960s.*

---

* Just a few years later, when Mies, Philip Johnson, and Phyllis Lambert were collaborating on the Seagram Building in Manhattan, Johnson told Lambert that Mies was impatient "with anything that had to do with an elaborate program."

"This assessment was accurate," concluded Lambert, for whom

Although it is easy to see the Fox River building as a Platonic meditation on the essence of a house, Drexler linked Mies's philosophical aspirations to a great American tradition:

It is often said that Mies could have realized his ideas only in the United States, and that only Europe could have produced him. But Mies has seemed more American than the Americans: *the Puritan tradition and the transcendental philosophers of nineteenth century New England must seem sentimental beside Mies himself.* [Emphasis added.]

There was indeed a Transcendentalist-era American antecedent for a house of one room, planted in the middle of nature: Henry David Thoreau's famous cabin next to Walden Pond. "Walden's setting of the stage for a minimal, open, one-room house is uncanny," David Holowka wrote, in an appreciation of the Farnsworth and Philip Johnson glass houses:

Thoreau's grasp of man's unconscious attitudes toward shelter and of the inherent drawbacks of shelter and possessions goes far toward explaining the lasting appeal and influence of the two glass houses built nearly a century later. . . .

Mies was "a conceptualist concerned with architecture's epochal role, the idea of structure, and the proper use of materials, not with intricate programming."

The two glass houses' use of nature for privacy is prefigured in Thoreau's statement "that it costs me nothing for curtains, for I have no gazers to shut out but the sun and moon."

He almost seems to be idealizing his cabin into the future Farnsworth House when he writes, "This frame, so slightly clad, was a sort of crystallization around me, and reacted on the builder. It was suggestive somewhat as a picture in outlines. I did not need to go outdoors to take the air, for the atmosphere within had lost none of its freshness. . . . I found myself neighbor to the birds; not by having imprisoned one, but having caged myself near them."[11]

Thoreau, of course, was an original "less is more" devotee. When he set to cabin building, he made himself "consider first how slight a shelter is absolutely necessary," adding, "the walls must be stripped, and our lives must be stripped, and beautiful housekeeping and beautiful living be laid for a foundation."

"I sometimes dream of a . . . house," Thoreau wrote, "which shall consist of only one room . . . a house whose inside is as open and manifest as a bird's nest." It is no accident, as the Marxists like to say, that Mies kept a copy of *Walden, or Life in the Woods* in his library.[12]

Terence Riley, one of Drexler's successors at MoMA, detected a fundamental change in Mies's early American work. In Germany, Mies famously designed a "Concrete Country House" and a "Brick Country House," both of which sit quite heavily on the landscape. "I find it interesting that Mies comes to America, he doesn't even really speak English, but he finds a lot of German culture in Chicago, so he begins to think he could move here.

> So he winds things up in Germany, he's a bit of a cad with [Lilly] Reich, and he designs the Resor and Farnsworth houses. His first two projects in America don't even touch the ground. It's as if he left Germany and he was no longer rooted, I think there is something significant in this, the unrootedness of the Farnsworth House, this notion that the essential connection between the earth and the structure seems to have been broken.

The British architect/critic Reyner Banham likewise picked up on the theme of Farnsworth as the House-of-No-House: "The 'house' is little more than a service core set in infinite space, or alternatively, a detached porch looking out in all directions at the Great Out There," he wrote in a 1965 essay.[13]

In a co-authored meditation written after a 2014 visit to the Farnsworth House, the Swiss architects (and winners of architecture's most prestigious award, the Pritzker Prize) Jacques Herzog and Pierre de Meuron elaborated further on the possibility that Mies was designing an idea, and not a house. Noting that "the intensity and radicalism of his quest increased after he moved from Germany to the United States," they argue that Mies was exploring "the universal language of architecture":

He was driven by an idea and by the will to translate that idea into a reality: Farnsworth House—a project of that kind cannot be the outcome of a planning process and an exchange with a client. It is much *more the expression of a will* and a conviction that something great must be created and that this was the moment to do so: pure architecture, essentials, nothing superfluous, *no traces of authorship*, timelessness, eternity, beauty! [Emphasis added.][14]

Mies would have been flattered. To have his work described as the "will of an epoch," or of a specific moment, was his highest compliment, previously reserved for medieval cathedrals or the Pyramids.

Had Mr. van der Rohe built his dream house? "The house is more nearly a temple than a dwelling," his biographer Franz Schulze observed, "and it rewards aesthetic contemplation before it fulfills domestic necessity." In an essay published in Tokyo, architect Dirk Lohan, Mies's grandson, argued that the Fox River house "is closely related to the Japanese teahouse where life became a celebration of the spiritual." The house "owes its stature . . . to its spiritual rather than its functional values," Lohan wrote.

The concept, a country retreat from the big city, has been elevated to such a spiritual abstraction that it demands complete acceptance of its inner logic from the occupant. So unconventional is the house that every move and every activity in it assume an aesthetic quality which challenge behavior patterns formed in different surroundings.

In designing the Farnsworth House, Lohan argued, "Mies had his own ideal retreat in mind. If anyone could have lived in it, it would be the philosopher Mies van der Rohe himself."[15]

Mies was a man almost entirely without domestic necessity. "You must learn to live differently—you mustn't keep things," Mies told Lora Marx. In the years after his youthful marriage, Mies strove to lead an attachment-free life, and that applied to possessions as much as people. He enumerated to Marx his valued possessions: "Cigars, whisky, clothes." To his friend the architect Paul Schweikher, he added, "My Schwitters," referring to his beloved Kurt Schwitters collages that (sparely) decorated the walls of his Chicago apartment. Mies also owned a Picasso, some works by his friend Paul Klee, and almost a hundred etchings and lithographs by Edvard Munch. When asked why he owned no works of geometric abstraction that would appear to echo his architectural style, he answered, "You don't have to have everything."[16]

Mies had never inhabited a living space like the form-free open-plan dwellings he designed for Edith and for the Tugendhat family in Brno. His personal habits were "monastic," Schulze reported. "His apartment was furnished simply, neither richly nor scrupulously; what he did for the Tugendhats was hardly necessary for himself."[17] The three-bedroom, two-thousand-square-foot Berlin apartment that he inhabited with his family, which later became his office, was likewise quite normal. "The domestic Mies was very, very different from the public Mies," Schulze has said. "I mean, his apartment did not look like the Farnsworth House. The building he lived in did not look like the Barcelona Pavilion. I think he didn't care that much about his immediate domestic surroundings. Mies, it seems to me, lived to a large extent in his head."

In his essay collection *Looking Around,* Witold Rybczynski dwelt on the subject of "houses by famous architects":

There is no sense of time in these perfect houses, springing fully formed from the minds of their creators. There is no room for the peculiar but endearing idiosyncrasies that are revealed when houses are lived in and lovingly molded to fit the lives of their owners.[18]

ALL CREATIVE WORKS REPLICATE precedents. If so, what does the Farnsworth House look like, imitate, or draw from? What contemporary or classical sources had influenced Mies?

That is a hard question to answer and may explain why the Farnsworth will never drop out of the Architecture 101 slide deck. Except for his hasty esquisse of a putative "architect's house" in the Italian Alps or his sketches for the unbuilt Resor House in Wyoming, Mies's earlier domestic work contained few hints of the radical minimalism of the Farnsworth project. His previously best-known home, the 1910 Riehl House in Potsdam, was a relatively conventional stucco-and-brick creation. There is one Farnsworth-esque

design in the Mies archive, his unbuilt riverside house for a
wealthy client named Margarete Hubbe, who had inherited a
two-acre parcel of land on an island in the Elbe River in
Magdeburg, Germany.

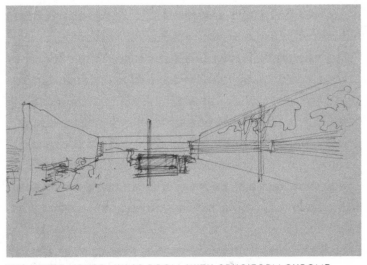

THE HUBBE HOUSE LIVING ROOM, WITH CRUCIFORM CHROME
COLUMNS, GLASS WINDOWS, AND A FREESTANDING MARBLE
PARTITION ON THE LEFT

Although the Hubbe House exposed mainly glass fronts
to the river view, it also had two bedrooms with walls and
doors, a much more conventionally organized kitchen, and
even modest servants' quarters. The stated program might
well have suited Dr. Farnsworth:

Though [Hubbe] was going to be living in the
house alone, she wanted to be able to maintain a casual
social life and hospitality. The inner arrangement of

the house is designed for this purpose as well, once again offering the necessary privacy in conjunction with the fullest freedom of open spaces.[19]

At the very same time that Mies was designing Farnsworth, architect John Entenza was launching the famous Case Study House project in California. In his Los Angeles–based *Arts and Architecture* magazine, Entenza published memorable plans of glassy, light-on-the-eyes California homes by such architects as Richard Neutra, Craig Ellwood, Eero Saarinen, and Charles and Ray Eames. Many of the Case Study Houses were built, and several—certainly Pierre Koenig's dramatic Stahl House, cantilevered above the Los Angeles skyline—remain in the architectural canon.

There is no evidence that Mies was influenced by the designs that Entenza was publishing, although it is likely that the director of an architecture school would have been aware

"MIES MANQUÉ?" PIERRE KOENIG'S STAHL HOUSE, IN LOS ANGELES

of trends around the country, such as the so-called Bay Region style, a moniker that critic Lewis Mumford attached to a genre of attractive suburban ranch houses springing up around San Francisco.

It is much more likely that the younger West Coast practitioners were influenced by Mies's Barcelona and Tugendhat drawings, or by the widely reproduced Farnsworth model displayed at the Museum of Modern Art show in 1947. Witold Rybczynski has gently chided the Case Study movement as Mies manqué. He called the Entenza-promoted designs "a sterile exercise in reductionism: Mies, but without the substantial and somber solidity of the German master."[20]

There was one architect who was most certainly influenced by the Farnsworth House: Mies van der Rohe. Biographers Franz Schulze and Edward Windhorst explain how S. R. Crown Hall, Mies's famous home for IIT's architecture and design departments, owes a great deal to the Farnsworth concept. Like Farnsworth, "Crown Hall's clear-span structure is a spiritual ideal made real. It has no programmatic justification, but as a representation of the potential of Miesian steel-and-glass architecture, it approaches an idealized perfection."

Again like the Farnsworth, the Crown is a glazed—glassed—structure, with an innovative design for massive glass plates, anchored by steel stops to the off-the-shelf rolled-steel beams. "The technology is essentially that of the Farnsworth House, completed five years before," the authors write.[21] The famous Crown Hall stairs are recognizably copied from the Fox River blueprints. "The porch and stairs are pure aesthetic gesture," the authors write,

THE ALL-GLASS CROWN HALL, WITH THE FARNSWORTH STAIRCASE

"modeled on those of the Farnsworth House."[22] Un-air-conditioned, it resembled the Farnsworth in another way, too: "Climate control was problematic."

Katharine Kuh, for whom Mies designed a small art gallery, likewise noticed the Farnsworth principles applied to Crown Hall, on her first visit: "I was struck by the uncanny marriage of interior and exterior space. Inside the predominantly glass structure, one does not merely look out; one feels that the outside actually floats in."[23]

The Farnsworth design also had a direct impact on the twin skyscrapers Mies was designing on an enviable Chicago site facing Lake Michigan, at 860/880 Lake Shore Drive. "If you extrude Farnsworth up thirty stories you get 860," says his biographer Edward Windhorst, who lived in the 880 tower for thirty years. Terence Riley agrees: "Mies made the bridge in an amazing way, he's taken a Lake Shore Drive apartment, pulled it out and put it on stilts." A visitor rhapsodizing about a stay in a Lake Shore Drive apartment might have been describing a night on the Fox River: "It was a glorious starry night. I couldn't sleep, for I had the feeling the stars would fall on my head. I was between heaven and earth."[24]

The floor-to-ceiling glass was the same, the flowing open plan was the same, the presence of "architecturally exposed" steel wide-flanged H-beams on the exterior all echoed the Farnsworth. Initially, the exterior glass walls had narrow, unscreened, floor-level hopper windows for ventilation. Fairbank Carpenter remembers his aunt Edith Farnsworth remarking how "it was a miracle that pets and small children didn't come cascading out of the upper floors."

Even the St. Charles kitchen cabinetry was the same. The famous beige curtains reappeared at 860/880. While Mies didn't mind what curtain designs faced into the apartment, he insisted on uniform, outward-facing Farnsworth-colored blinds.

In 1957, the 860/880 Lake Shore Drive owners' association published a "Glass House brochure," hailing the livability of the twin skyscrapers: "In all of Chicago, there is not a more desirable location for gracious modern living than The Glass House." A purported tenant's testimonial rhapsodized:

> We take PRIDE in our Glass House, not because it is world famous and created by Mies van der Rohe, but because it is truly beautiful in design, proportion and

materials. . . . Never before have we lived in a place that gave us constant JOY in nature—the ever-changing beauty of the lake, sky, sun, moon and circling birds.[25]

The legendary towers shared some of the same problems with the Farnsworth. "The glass was at the heart of the problems [at Lake Shore Drive]," Schulze and Windhorst write, "whether it was the blistering heat or the bucket brigades conducted by unhappy owners during rainstorms." Instead of air-conditioning, the Lake Shore Drive buildings used the small hopper windows at floor level, much like the Farnsworth House. "The heat was somewhat tamed," the biographers write, "but the windows were beyond improvement until modern sealants and the permanent freezing of the once-operable upper lights made reasonable peace with the water. Indeed, widespread systematic leaks in the exterior wall . . . must be judged an embarrassment."

Both Schulze and German art historian Wolf Tegethoff, the author of a survey of Mies's country designs, have suggested that the Farnsworth experience soured Mies on residential home building.[26] In fact, Mies built only one more home, the McCormick House in the Chicago suburb of Elmhurst. It presses, flat and ungainly, against the ground in a way unlike either the Farnsworth or Tugendhat house. The house's current owner, the Elmhurst Art Museum, says McCormick emulates "the ground-hugging horizontality of Frank Lloyd Wright's designs"—a far cry from the magical lightness of the home next to the Fox River.

The Elmhurst house has plenty of outward-facing glass.

Indeed, the broad windows that use white steel girders for vertical mullions are copies of the (black-mullioned) Lake Shore Drive windows, which themselves were derived from the Farnsworth House plans. But the McCormick House, which architect Avram Lothan calls "an International Style version of a ranch house,"[27] has many more sops to convention: brick side walls, a carport, flexible wall partitions dividing living and sleeping spaces from the dining room and kitchen, and bedrooms with actual doors. McCormick had a wife and children, with normal expectations of a life in the suburbs. (Well, not completely normal. McCormick commuted to work in his Rolls-Royce.)

It should come as no surprise that the magpie-like Philip Johnson was designing a glass house at the very same moment for his friend and business manager Robert Wiley in New Canaan, Connecticut. Johnson understood that the Wiley family wouldn't want to live in a transparent fishbowl like his nearby Glass House, so he built the house on two levels—a stone and concrete ground floor with bedrooms, bathrooms, and a sitting room, underneath the now-familiar glass box: a second floor with a living room, dining room, and kitchen. Johnson called the Wiley house

one more attempt to reconcile the (perhaps) irreconcilable. Modern architectural purity and the requirements of living American families. Why can't people learn to live in the . . . pure glass prisms of Mies van der Rohe? No, they need a place for Junior to practice the piano while Mother plays bridge with her neighbors.[28]

Mies and McCormick were likewise hoping to domesticate the glass house design, in their case for suburban tract homes. However, the absence of a basement and air-conditioning meant the McCormick design couldn't compete with the garden-variety ranch houses springing up around every major American city.

Great architects have always dreamed of making homes for the middle class, most notably Frank Lloyd Wright's Usonian adventure, when he tried to build easily constructed versions of his Prairie Style houses for the masses. The smallish Usonian homes were generally elegant, but many ran well over the intended $15,000 or $20,000 budget. Mies, too, entertained Usonian dreams. A couple of years after completing the Farnsworth House, he and Goldsmith embarked on a formal study of mass-producing the Farnsworth in a fully glassed residential project called the 50 × 50 House. The 2,500-square-foot open-plan home was intended for family use, and, theoretically, might have been a less expensive version of the Farnsworth suitable for construction on housing tracts. It shared some design features with Edith's Plano home, for instance, an asymmetrically placed kitchen/bathroom/services "core" and a broad patio that replicated the suspended travertine terrace in Plano, although this terrace was earthbound. In a 1986 oral interview, Goldsmith explained that Mies had fallen in love with the idea of capacious, open-plan dwelling spaces, and thought American families might come to share his vision:

Mies was very interested in architecture just as background for people, to try to reduce the architecture as much as possible to nothing. . . . One sees the glimmer of this in some of the lofts that are being done now, unified, very high spaces, solving the elements like sleeping and everything at an absolute minimum. This was the idea of the Fifty by Fifty House, of how far you could go in one unified space and how you could live with it.[29]

The 50 × 50 also came to be known as the "core" house, because Mies & Co. marketed the earthbound glass house idea in different square configurations, for example, 40 × 40, 60 × 60, and so on. In August 1952, *Chicago Tribune* writer Anne Douglas ginned up what looked like a full-page advertisement for the glass house idea, headlined "Dinner in Yesterday's Bedroom—It's Possible in This Flexible Plan." The article, which showcased both a house model and a blueprint, treated the open-plan design as a curiosity. Douglas explained that the "immovables," such as the kitchen and bathrooms, were concentrated in one area, a "core"—exactly as at the Farnsworth House. "The family can arrange the rest of the house as it wishes," she wrote. "Storage partitions would serve as dividers. The partitions, stopping short of the ceiling, would not interfere with ventilation but would provide privacy. Interior curtains could be used for further separation if desired. Because the partitions would be movable, the room layout could be rearranged at will."

"A dozen people have come to us in the last few years and asked for a modern house in the range of $30,000 or $40,000," Mies told the paper. "Since there seems to be a real need for such homes, we have attempted to solve the problem by de-

THE NEVER-CONSTRUCTED 50 × 50 HOUSE

veloping a steel skeleton and a core that could be used for all houses. The interior is left open for flexibility. It would be suitable for a family with no children, one child, or several children."

Despite Mies's assertion of a "real need for these homes," no version of the 50 × 50 House ever found a buyer. Edith Farnsworth was the only owner of the unusual home design that bore her name.

CHAPTER 8

"THE FEAR OF MIES' IMPLACABLE INTENTIONS"

E DITH DECIDED TO SPEND NEW YEAR'S EVE OF 1950 in her new house. It was habitable, but not finished. Since her refusal to pay Mies any more money the previous August, there had been minimal communication between architect and client. Nonetheless, some of Mies's subordinates kept in touch with Edith, and offered her occasional help with the house. William Dunlap, who later became a partner at Skidmore, Owings and Merrill, did the finish work on the six-foot-tall primavera-faced wardrobe closet that acted as a wall between the home's living and sleeping spaces. Goldsmith remained available for the occasional chore. Mies-Edith relations were none of their business, and when they could be of service, they often were.

"On New Year's Eve I brought out a couple of

foam rubber mattresses and a number of other indispensable articles and prepared to inhabit the glass house for the first time," Edith wrote.

> With the light of a bare 60-watt bulb on an extension cord, I made up the foam rubber mattress on the floor, turned up the air furnaces, and got something to eat. Spots and strokes of white paint remained here and there on the expanses of the glass walls and the sills were covered with ice. The silent meadows outside white with old and hardened snow reflected the bleak bulb within, as if the glass house itself were an unshaded bulb of uncalculated watts lighting the winter plains.

Then, as if in an Alfred Hitchcock movie, "the telephone rang, shattering the solitary scene."

"Are you there alone in those cold meadows?" a voice asked. "I'm your neighbor from over the approach to the bridge. Won't you come and celebrate New Year's Eve with us? I'll send one of the boys to bring you over—I can't bear to think of you there all alone!"

"The voice was Leola's," Edith wrote in her journal, "the wife of Gar, the tavern keeper."

> It would have been easier to face the situation for which I was prepared: the new house, the seamy flood—meadows and the young moon over the black river. But I could hardly decline so warm an invitation; so it was not long before two dark forms

could be made out walking down from the farm-
house.

"We didn't know whether we could get down here
in a car. Do you mind walking up?"

"Not a bit. You can make it in a car but it's a little
hard to turn around. You did well not to try it."

Leola's cottage house still wore its Christmas trim
and all the lights were on when we knocked and entered. Leola herself was an immensely obese woman
who played the organ and adored music. Gar had to
work that evening, I was told, but there were five or
six couples gathered around a long table, and I took
one of several empty chairs. I remember nothing attractive about that evening except the haunting mel-
ancholy in the eyes of that tremendous woman who
was married to Gar and loved music.

Edith chose not to mention it, but she was learning a lesson about privacy along the Fox River: There was none.
Even though her house was screened by trees on three sides,
outsiders seemed fully aware of her comings and goings.
This is also the first mention of Edith's Plano neighbors,
many of whom became close friends of hers. The game war-
den across the street, Toomey Burson, and the Kivitts family
and their children would be part of Edith's social set for the
fifteen-plus years that she rusticated in Plano. "The local
people definitely socialized," Kelly Simms remembers of her
aunt, their friends the Bursons, and Edith. "But Edith wasn't
super social, they were a fairly small set."

When Edith arrived at the neighboring cottage, Leola

broached a difficult subject. "I could have cried when I saw you was going to build down by the shore," she said.

"You don't know how quick the river can rise. Often I can't sleep at night for fear it's going to drown us all. Once it came up and flooded your barn so that the farmers could catch fish with a pitchfork."

"Really, Leola? What year was that?"

"Oh, it was a good many years ago, but still you never can tell when it'll rise again and we'll all be drowned."

Finally the New Year came in, burdened with its future floods. I went home to my electric bulb escorted by one of the couples at the long table who lived just down the road.

It was an uneasy night, partly from the novel exposure provided by the uncurtained glass walls and partly from the fear of Mies' implacable intentions. Expenses in connection with the house had risen far beyond what I had expected or could well afford and the glacial bleakness of that winter night showed very clearly how much more would have to be spent before the place could be made even remotely habitable.

Perhaps it was not precisely the following morning—it might have been a few weeks later—that I went back to town to begin the week's work, deprived of any further doubt that my economic security had been seriously jeopardized by my architect and that my trust in Mies had been misplaced.

———

DURING CONSTRUCTION, AND DURING the period of goodwill between Edith and Mies, architects and architectural students routinely visited the construction site, often at Mies's invitation. But even with Mies out of the picture, the Farnsworth House groupies, responding to the rapturous reviews in the professional journals, kept coming. "They thumbed their way tirelessly aboard my distress and my exposure behind glass walls, to whatever satisfactions they were seeking," Edith wrote.

> Shirts fluttered from behind trees, cameras clicked, and heads encircled my "sleeping space" as I woke up in the morning. . . .
> It was hard to bear the insolence, the boorishness, of the hundreds of persons who invaded the solitude of my shore and my home, and I never could see why it should have to be borne. It was maddening and heart-breaking to find the wild flowers and ground covers so laboriously brought in to hide the scars of building, battered and crushed by the boots beneath the noses pressed against the glass.

One of the annoying visitors was a young Ronald Krueck, who, like so many actors in this story, would later make a name as an architect. (His firm helped refurbish 860/880 Lake Shore Drive in 2008–9.) "I was walking down by the river, and I came up towards the house, coming to a wooded area, and this little dog starts barking, a dead giveaway," Krueck recalled.

> Edith comes out and tells us to go away. She was rather insistent. "Go away!" she said, "You don't know what it's like living in a house and having eyes staring back at you."
>
> I yelled back at her, and soon we were screaming at one another, from two hundred feet away. "You shouldn't build a house like this if that's your concern," I shouted. It was one of the few times I said what I thought.

Engineer Dick Young remembered browsing for Indian arrowheads along the river—the Fox is named after an Indian tribe—when Edith told him to get off her property. When he explained his hobby to her, she became interested, and the two of them became friends.[1]

Mies invited Katharine Kuh to visit the mostly completed house in the summer of 1950. "I'm afraid his motive for encouraging me to tag along was not entirely disinterested," Kuh later wrote, "for it seems that the lady had earlier unleashed a litany of complaints over the phone and he hoped that my presence would deter her from further charges."

"As our visit progressed, Dr. Farnsworth grew increasingly truculent," Kuh wrote.

> Yet her lengthening list of indictments [the fireplace; the too-low partitions] elicited little more than

amused indulgence from Mies, though he did assure her that, wherever possible, corrections would be made. . . .

When we left after an hour or two, I found myself feeling sorry for her. There she was, the duenna of an already famous landmark that only fractionally resembled the flexible hideaway she had earlier envisioned. She later told me that despite paying for the house, it was never hers. It always belonged to Mies, for it was his dream child.[2]

Another visitor was the great California-by-way-of-Vienna-Berlin-and-Taliesin modernist architect Richard Neutra, who looked in on Edith with his wife, Dione, in the springtime,

when the forsythias were blooming. These were among the first gardening experiments to be tried indoors and half-a-dozen tubs of forsythia bushes were in luxuriant bloom when the Neutras came up the path to the terrace and I saw them from the bare ground outside. The California architect had just recovered from a coronary occlusion and he moved slowly as he came up the travertine steps, giving me the impression of a frail man. His wife was charming and we fell to talking about the broken friendship between Mies and myself. "I have built a good many residences," said Mr. Neutra, "but I cannot remember an instance in which I have left a client in the position in which you find yourself. This is a very sad story, to which the house stands as a monument. I do hope that finally you will find some degree of happiness here."*

Paul Schweikher, who would later become chairman of Yale's department of architecture, described a similar encounter around this time, one that began with a visit from Mies and George Howe, another famous modernist, to Schweikher's home outside Chicago. Mies and Howe, Schweikher's predecessor at Yale, were hoping their host could help them find Bruce Goff's just-completed "pumpkin house," a spherical dwelling in nearby Aurora, designed for clients Albert and Ruth Ford. Before leaving, Schweikher recalled, "we'd all emptied a rather large pitcher of martinis, which Mies loved, and so did George and I. So, off we went—"

Mies took one look at Goff's much-publicized oddity (during construction, the owners posted a sign reading WE DON'T LIKE YOUR HOUSE EITHER) and lost interest. So the

---

* In 1968, Dirk Lohan recorded this exchange with his grandfather:

LOHAN: Some time ago I met Neutra in Los Angeles. He was strange; he told me for instance that it was he who persuaded Mrs. Farnsworth to build the house. But did he even know her?

MIES: I don't think so.

LOHAN: He acted as if he had made the house happen; as if everything you had accomplished really had started with him, that's the impression he gave.

MIES: Is he ill?

LOHAN: I think so, yes. Other people were mentioning it, too. Craig Ellwood and the others, saying that he was getting a little delusional.

three architects and Schweikher's wife embarked on a drunken, cross-state ramble to the Farnsworth House, to drop in on Edith, "whom we knew quite well."

The inebriated band realized that a coffee stop might be in order, and interrupted their trip in a town near Plano. Schweikher picked up the thread:

> Mies said, "I must stay here. I can't go with you because Edith and I are having difficulties."
>
> We left Mies at the place where he sat down to have a cup of coffee and Dorothy and I took George and went on to call on Edith, who was home. She showed us through her whole house. I was disappointed, I remember walking in and finding some store chairs instead of the Barcelona chairs, which I had hoped to see. I hadn't realized that they had become a part of the altercation and were omitted deliberately, I guess, by Edith.
>
> We spent some time talking not about Mies but admiring the house and telling Edith what a beautiful place it was and in other ways probably annoying her and boring her. We all began to feel a little annoyed and bored with one another and then we left.[3]

Philip Johnson looked in on Edith in June 1951, and reported to Mies by letter that "Edith was very charming to me and was vociferous in her praise of the house. She did not mention your name, but said nothing about having any trouble during the building. I think she will calm down quickly

EDITH AMID HER UN-MIESIAN FURNISHINGS

now and I only hope she does before too much furniture is installed."

There were, of course, problems with the new construction. Without air-conditioning, the house was ferociously hot in summer, the small hopper windows notwithstanding. The lights inside the house clouded with condensation in the winter, because they weren't warmed by the radiant heat rising from the floor. Combustion in the oil furnace had not been properly calculated. In winter, sometimes inky black traces—uncombusted oil residue—dripped like black tears down the glass walls. Rust appeared on the edges of the window frames.

Before the kitchen was fully functional, Farnsworth reported heating a can of soup on a hot plate in the bathroom during one of her visits. She decided to set a fire in the fireplace, and learned "a curious fact, namely that the house was so hermetically sealed that the attempt of a flame to go up the chimney caused a negative interior pressure." Venting all kinds of exhaust would soon prove to be a problem.

The mosquitoes were rapacious. "Another Fox River phenomenon that Mies underestimated was the mosquitoes," writer David Dunlap recalled in 1999.[4] "Even today, they are fierce enough to be a source of constant complaint in the guest register."

David's father was the above-mentioned William Dunlap, both a student and then a colleague of Mies's. His mother, Beth, was a patient of Edith's. In their midtwenties, "They socialized with [Edith] at parties and jazz clubs," David wrote.

> They visited the house in Plano during construction. And as it neared completion, they stayed overnight. They did not exactly sleep there, however, since they were kept awake all night while Dr. Farnsworth's poodles, in an amorous mood, chased around the central core as if they were on a travertine dog track.
>
> "Isn't that cute?" Dr. Farnsworth said, when my mother told her of the disturbance the next morning.
>
> While the two women talked, just before the architectural historian Henry-Russell Hitchcock arrived

for a visit, my father recorded the scene with his Kodak Vigilant 620 camera. He caught a moment of weekend-in-the-country informality wonderfully at odds with the house's formalism: my mother is in pajamas, Dr. Farnsworth in slacks; they lounge on the cantilevered front steps, with cups of coffee and poodles nearby.

EDITH, BETH DUNLAP, AND POODLES

A few months later, Edith asked Beth, "Do you think Bill would design the screens?" According to David:

> My father was then [1952] drafting part time at $1 an hour, supported by my mother's income as a fashion illustrator for *Women's Wear Daily*. Learning of

the prospect, he said, "I'm going to call Mies and tell him there's a way to finish the screens without going to someone else."

Unknown to Dr. Farnsworth, my father then shared his drawings with Mies, to be certain they met with the master's approval. At least once, Mies was reviewing blueprints in my parents' apartment just before the client arrived to do the same thing—requiring some logistical dexterity to prevent a collision between the two warring parties in the alleyway.

"After all," David wrote, "Mies designed a monument, but my father first made it possible to live in."

Edith's nephew, Fairbank Carpenter, recalled his aunt's accumulating frustration with the Fox River house. "I remember her becoming dissatisfied with the process," he said. "Her line was 'My house is a monument to Mies van der Rohe and I'm paying for it.' "[5]

In her memoir, Edith recalled her friends "who were outside the charmed circle" criticizing Mies's invisible insulation: "You'll lose heat through all sides of your glass box!" they insisted. "He could at least insulate the floors and ceilings." There was, of course, a layer of insulation in both the floor and the ceiling panels, which didn't stop Edith from complaining mightily about her heating bills, which were considerable. (She paid $668 from the fall of 1951 until the spring of 1952—more than $6,000 today.)[6] Dick Young remembered "her complaints about the outrageous expense of having to heat the whole Fox River valley."

Furnishing the finished home remained a bone of contention. Edith related that "one of the boys from Mies's office telephoned one day to tell me that the furniture for the house was to be delivered, namely, two Barcelona chairs, the glass coffee table and two of the chrome spring chairs."

This was the same ploy that had worked successfully on the merchant prince Fritz Tugendhat in 1937. It didn't work on Edith Farnsworth.

> I answered that I had not ordered them and did not intend to use them.
>
> "You're not going to use them!" he repeated, stunned. "You can't mean it. They were ordered for you."
>
> "Evidently. But not with my knowledge, let alone, my agreement."
>
> A pause followed before he said darkly, "You'll be sorry!"

CHAPTER 9

"YOU ARE A GODDAM LIAR."

OR MOST OF 1951, EDITH AND MIES REMAINED incommunicado and at loggerheads over money. Mies's firm calculated their total receivables on the house as $79,000, of which Edith had paid more than $73,000. She had said she wouldn't pay any more, and the issue of an architect's fee was hanging fire. Then two events occurred that would force this impasse to a resolution.

Yet again, Philip Johnson intervened in Mies's life. Mies had been complaining to Johnson that his office was in (its usual) financial disarray. Although Mies had a bookkeeper, he ran the practice more or less out of his hip pocket. He paid his junior staff laughably low wages for junior architects—between $1 and $1.50 an hour—but treated their association rather like Frank Lloyd Wright treated the Taliesin

Fellows, many of whom paid *him* for the privilege of working alongside the Master. Similarly, Mies's "boys" regarded their wage slavery as an invaluable apprenticeship. They generally enjoyed working with him, and many junior associates ended up as well-paid partners at the nation's blue-chip architectural firms.

That said, Mies ruled more as a philosopher-king than as a manager. "Extremely introverted" was how his associate Joseph Fujikawa remembered him; "I don't think Mies was a leader."

For a man who created buildings that spoke in the clearest possible tones, Mies was famously indecisive. "We would never have dreamt of saying, 'Mies we have so many hours to do this, and we've got to reach a conclusion,'" his associate Bruno Conterato recalled. "Mies was notorious for not making up his mind, and he had a host of ways to put off a decision."[1] Mies "had no interest in or even the slightest remote thought of efficiency of an office as far as getting a job done," Gene Summers said. "That just didn't enter his mind."[2]

He wasn't particularly savvy about money, either. Fujikawa remembers discussing with Mies "a potential client who seemed kind of dubious," and suggesting that the firm could ask for an up-front retainer as security for any work that might end up unpaid. "Mies chewed me out!" Fujikawa recalled. "He said, 'We don't do that here!'"[3]

At the end of the year, Mies hoovered up any excess cash in the firm's bank account and transferred it to his own. Each January brought its own financial challenges that eventually melted away as clients paid their bills and the revenue stream became a business-sustaining steady flow.

Mies knew this was no way to run a business, and he asked Philip Johnson for advice. Johnson sent him Bob Wiley, his friend and business manager, for whom Johnson had built the proto-Miesian house in New Canaan, Connecticut. Wiley spotted a $4,500 receivable on Mies's books—the balance due from construction costs on Edith's house. Let's collect that money, he suggested.

Around this same time, Edith met a fifty-nine-year-old man in the hospital whom she was treating for a kidney disorder. "As I entered the room, he stared at me from the bed," Edith reported.

Reversing the usual doctor-patient terms of trade, the man ventured: "You don't look very good yourself, this morning. Can't you sit down for a few minutes?"

Edith vented her troubles with Mies, with the house, and the looming battle over money. Wiley had approached her about collecting, and she had no idea what to do. Her diary picks up the story of the hospital room encounter:

> After hearing the principal reasons for my debilitated health, he sat up decisively. "Well! Now will you let me try to get you out of this mess?"
>
> There being no other value left to save except my economic solvency, I agreed and in the ensuing weeks I learned in considerable detail the facts of my situation.
>
> "Do you realize that he hasn't obtained waivers of lien from the firms who supplied labor or materials and that any or all of them could claim that they weren't paid and take you to court? And from the rec-

ords kept in that incredible office it's anybody's guess whether they were paid or not."

"Don't tell me any more awful things, Randy. I already have so much on my mind that I can't take any more. Put a period to the sentence—one that will stick—and then we'll see where we stand."

Edith's patient was attorney Randolph Bohrer, a business litigator who felt he owed Farnsworth a deep debt. "She had cured him of an auto-immune disease," lawyer William Murphy later explained. Murphy, a Harvard Law School classmate of Bohrer's son, Mason, became part of Mies's legal team. They were convinced that the Bohrers were representing Edith pro bono, because they thought she had saved the father's life. They may have been right. There are two letters in the Northwestern Medical School archives that testify to Bohrer's deep-pocketed affection for Dr. Farnsworth. The letters accompany checks of, respectively, $10,000 (over $100,000 today) and $5,000, donations for Edith's ACTH research. One letter reads:

> Though it is understood that the money is to be used for your ACTH research and experimentation program in the field of nephritis, it is intended primarily as a personal tribute to your relentless efforts in this field and your patience with, and compassion for and devotion to, your miracle seeking "guinea pigs."[4]

Bohrer asked that his donations remain anonymous. Wiley persuaded Mies to sit down with Bohrer to resolve the money dispute once and for all. Mies made what seemed like a generous offer. He asked for the $4,500 balance owed on building costs, and he would forgo his architect's fee, which could have amounted to $12,000. He never even mentioned a contractor's fee, which he could also have claimed. By mutual agreement, he and Edith had never retained a general contractor, who often pays himself a percentage of a project's building costs for his services. Paul Schweikher, who testified at the ensuing trial, called this "a German business arrangement in which Mies acted as the architect, the creator of the project, and the contractor who bought and paid for the labor."

Bohrer told Wiley that Edith was willing to settle for $1,500, a seemingly random number. At an impasse, Wiley put Mies in touch with one of Chicago's most powerful law firms, Sonnenschein, Berkson, Lautmann, Levinson and Morse. Senior partner David Levinson interviewed Mies and suggested that he sue Farnsworth. "I think this was one of the most unfortunate things that could have happened," Myron Goldsmith later remarked.[5]

Levinson and Mies filed suit. Bohrer and Edith counter-sued. *Ludwig Mies van der Rohe Plaintiff and Counter-Defendant vs. Edith B. Farnsworth, Defendant and Counter-Claimant* was under way.

BECAUSE THE ALLEGED EVENTS of nonpayment and architectural malpractice took place in Plano, the six-week-long courtroom drama played out in nearby Yorkville, the seat of Kendall County. The litigants agreed to dispense with a conventional trial in front of a judge or jury. Instead, they opted for a "special master in chancery" hearing, not uncommon in business litigation, in which a lawyer familiar with commercial law and contract disputes presides over a complex case. The litigants share the fee of the master, whose job is to create a Master's Report, with a suggested verdict, for a judge. The appointed master was Jerome Nelson, a future Kendall County state's attorney, who treated both sides with considerable indulgence.

The courthouse, now an office building that was added to the National Register of Historic Places in 1998, was a curious stage for an architectural dispute. Sixty-five years old, the grandiose Italianate courthouse, topped by a gold cupola, sat atop a small hill overlooking the Fox River upstream from Edith's house. Mies might have appreciated the graceful aesthetics of the facing twin circular staircases that rose to the second-floor courtroom from the first floor—itself already aboveground—though it must have been painful for him to negotiate the stairs, with his deteriorating hips.

Central Illinois was sweltering in late May and June of 1952, and nature failed to send the desired breezes down the river valley. On most days, the courtroom was a hotbox.

The Farnsworth case was in session from late May until July 3, and during much of that time, Mies chose to live in the posh Leland Hotel in nearby Aurora. A twenty-two-story landmark, the Leland was for many years the tallest building in Illinois outside of Chicago. Although the building was less than thirty years old when Mies stayed there, he was taken by surprise one evening when his bathroom ceiling crashed down on him while he was soaking in the bathtub.

Before the trial, Goldsmith reported, "Mies was very

worried, because her lawyer, who was a good friend of hers and a patient, was going to make Mies suffer, and got after his competence to design a house. So he was afraid he might lose his license. During this whole period, he hardly went to the office. He spent some nights in Aurora."[6]

Mies never missed a day of trial. "We met with him every day before the testimony," recalls William Murphy, a junior member of Mies's top-drawer legal team, led by Sonnenschein litigator John Faissler. Edith attended the proceedings only four times, when summoned. Murphy assumed her medical commitments took priority over the trial. "She was very busy with her professional practice, and she had a high degree of confidence in her counsel, so she really didn't follow it all that closely," Murphy later said.

In a 2004 oral interview, Murphy shared an amusing memory of the proceedings. He claimed that Goldsmith's main job in Yorkville was to keep Mies supplied with premium cigars: "He had this special coat, with lots of pockets, for all the cigars." Smoking was banned inside the courtroom, so Mies evolved a strategy of hiding his partially smoked cigars in mortar cracks in the courthouse's brick façade. Often he would return from court to find the cigar had disappeared. "Some of the oldsters had never seen cigars that good," Murphy says. "Mies would come out during the next recess, and a lot of the cigars would be gone."

Murphy's colorful story obscures the fact that Goldsmith, who knew more about the Farnsworth House than anyone, was probably the most important witness for both the plaintiffs and the defense. There is a November 1951 letter in Goldsmith's papers, urging him to return from his European sabbatical: "It is urgent that you return at the first possible opportunity," Mies's associate Ogden Hannaford wrote. Hannaford sent Goldsmith first-class airline tickets and a *Chicago Tribune* article announcing the litigation, "which, as you can readily understand, was very shocking to all of us when we saw it."

"Thinking that you might want to return to Europe," Hannaford continued, "I asked Mr. Wiley, Mies's business consultant, when he thought this affair might be concluded, and his reply was that the case would probably be settled by the end of this year."

The case wouldn't come to trial in 1951 and wouldn't be settled for many years to come.

Edith had sour memories of her time in court, although she did later recall "one light note":

> A whopping bumble bee which drifted into the court room from the lilacs outside and caused the attorneys on both sides of the table to erase their professional smiles and spring to their feet batting the air violently. The presiding judge displayed notable resourcefulness with respect to the bee and after chasing it around the room for a while, cornered it and put it outside with a heavy-duty broom, so that the legal squad could take their places again and mop their brows.

As the initiator of the lawsuit, Mies's team presented their case first, and Faissler acted as the master of ceremonies: "Your honor, this is a mechanic's lien foreclosure, involving the services and expenses incurred by Ludwig Mies Van der Rohe, who sits here . . ."

Edith's counterclaim alleged "that the plaintiff falsely and with intent to deceive held himself out as an unusually skilled, proficient and experienced architect." During the next few weeks, Bohrer and his associates would browbeat and humiliate Mies, accusing the former Bauhaus director of rank incompetence, as if he had been plying his trade at the level of a hapless intern from a community college. Mies withstood quite a bit of punishment and scorn, some of it capitalizing on his still-imperfect command of English.

(After Mies's death, Lora Marx shared some of her favorites Miesisms with Franz Schulze: Marx: "Is it raining?" Mies: "No, it's just mizzling." Or: "Tomorrow night at this time I will be in Mexico, drinking Kweela.")

Few subjects would be off-limits in the trial. Some interesting personal minutiae surfaced during the contentious pretrial depositions. For instance, it was revealed that Edith had treated Mies as a patient, had overseen one of his hospital stays, and had diagnosed his walking pains as "intense ankylosing arthritis of the right hip."

Bohrer asked Mies: "She was your physician, was she not?"

"Yes," he answered, "when I had something, you know, then I called her up, when I had a cold or something, I called her up, and asked what to do and she sent me some pills."

"We never discussed any kind of fee" for medical treatment, Farnsworth testified.[7] Friends don't charge friends for medical evaluations, nor, she testified many times, for building houses. "We started this as friends and there was no mention of fees. And my preoccupation was then to simply feel my way along and to treat him correctly."

The lawyers never probed too deeply into the intimacies of the Mies-Edith relationship. "We talked for years about God and the world" was Mies's brief comment. Asked what the pair talked about during their weekly car rides to the Fox River site, Farnsworth said, "Sometimes about philosophy, sometimes about teaching, sometimes about medicine, sometimes about the theory of architecture, sometimes about the past experiences of the architects, lots of subjects of conversation."[8]

Mies's lawyers devoted much trial time to establishing that the Fox River home was a bespoke creation, something that had never been built or even contemplated before, with attendant financial risks. "When we talked the first time about the house, at that dinner party," Mies said, "I told her I would not be interested in a normal house, but if it could be fine and interesting, then I would do it. . . . She knew that she would get a house that was not normal."[9]

In his deposition, Myron Goldsmith explained that several factors made this a special project: It's not normal to build a house exclusively from steel and glass; it's not normal to build a residence with just one open space; it's not normal to build a house that had to be elevated above a floodplain. "This was not a normal house," he testified, "nor were we normal architects."[10] Bohrer would press Mies on this point throughout the trial:

BOHRER: Was this an experimental house?

MIES: I would not say it was an experimental house. It is very difficult—to state the definition for this house. It was a new house. It was a house not built in the usual way and it was a house with new problems.

BOHRER: Isn't it a fact that you were interested in building this house because it was interesting?

MIES: Certainly, otherwise I would not do it. . . . If I build something I do it always in the same way, always with the same intention to develop something to—build something which is important in the architectural sense.[11]

Bohrer tried to lay the foundation for one of his arguments, that Mies had botched what should have been a relatively simple construction task.

BOHRER, SPEAKING OF THE HOUSE: It is a simple thing, isn't it?

MIES: Simple in an artistic way, yes. . . . It was a new concept of a house.

The depositions also provided a foreshadowing of the vitriolic exchanges between the two panels of lawyers. During Mies's deposition, Bohrer accused David Levinson, the supervising partner at the Sonnenschein firm, of coaching his witness.

BOHRER: I don't know what you coached the witness to say. I know what he would say if he weren't coached.

LEVINSON: You are a goddam liar. When you say
that I have coached this witness, you are a goddam
liar, and I don't want you to say that again.[12]

Edith appeared on the first day of the trial and quickly
adopted the persona of a Woman Who Doesn't Know
Much About This Kind of Thing. When questioned by
Faissler about construction details, she generally pleaded
ignorance.

Q: Now, there was some backfilling done, wasn't
    there, by a Mr. Zimmerman, or by Karl Freund?*

A: Backfilling?

Q: Backfilling.

A: I don't know what backfilling means.

Q: Well, pushing dirt around. . . . After that is done,
    then they push the dirt back.

A: Oh, I see what you mean.

* Freund, who was probably the third most important person on the
work site after Mies and Goldsmith, said in his eighties that he was
subpoenaed in the case but refused to testify. "If you want me to testify against Farnsworth or Mies, I won't. They are equally guilty of
making a thing without a solid contract. Building is a very delicate
thing, and if there's lovey-dovey stuff, it doesn't work." He claimed
that Farnsworth didn't understand the house and that "Mies should
have made clearer to her what she was getting into."

And:

Q: Well, there is a drain there, isn't there?

A: I don't really know anything about the drain.

Q: Do you have a bathtub?

A: Yes.

Q: Kitchen sink?

A: Yes.

Q: Water goes out through the bottom of them?

A: Yes. I don't really know anything about it. There are evidently drains.

And:

Q: There are flues going up from the core, are there not, for the furnace?

A: I don't really know anything about flues.

Of course Edith was a cultured and intelligent woman and no stranger to drollery. In one early exchange, Faissler tried to assert that she had considered other architects for the Fox River project:

Q: Did you ever tell anyone that you had thought of
Le Corbusier?

A: I have no such recollection.

Q: Or that you wanted Niemeyer?

A: Never heard of Niemeyer. I still have never heard
of Niemeyer.

Q: Well, you have now.

A: Yes. You have extended my education.[13]

In her first day of testimony, Edith laid down several
markers important to her case. She asserted that Mies had
kept her in the dark about essential construction details. Mies
was "not a person that one told to do things," she testified.
"May I explain the nature of the relationship? This was supposed to be a work of art; I was not supposed to know anything about it. I was supposed to keep out of art and stay in
medicine where I belonged, and I was not shown plans. . . .
Never did I examine any plans."[14]

This proved to be an inconvenient assertion for Edith,
when the plaintiffs produced a snapshot, taken by Duckett,
of Edith hovering over a drafting table next to Goldsmith.
She improbably explained that she and Goldsmith may have
been examining clinical graphs relating to a nephritis presen-
tation of hers, "because of the fact one of the boys in the
office had nephritis." In a normal courtroom peopled with

spectators, this assertion might have elicited a few chuckles. When Goldsmith took the stand, he offered a more truthful explanation: There was a General Electric kitchen catalog on the drafting table, he said. "We were talking [in late 1949] about the location and number of the fixtures in the kitchen, the accessories in the cabinet, knife holders and cup holders and etcetera."[15]

THE INCONVENIENT SNAPSHOT: FARNSWORTH AND GOLDSMITH REVIEWING DRAWINGS IN MIES'S OFFICE

Edith, of course, revisited the relentless ascent of construction costs, averring that "the cost was originally put as an eight, ten, or twelve thousand dollar modest country project." Then she told of visiting Mies's office with her "full inventory of personal property," her checking, savings accounts, and government bond holdings, which she said added up to $40,000. "He put on his glasses and said, 'Let me check your addition.'"

I said, "Now we can have the house?" and he said, 'Yes.'"[16]

In the end, she testified that she paid Mies $73,872.10.[17] This included $70,000 toward construction costs, and two random payments, more like gratuities, toward Mies's fees. She described one $1,000 check as "a voluntary contribution."

> I sent it with a note that would make it clear to the bookkeeper that I did not want it to go down the general rat hole. I had never been billed for a fee, but I thought a voluntary contribution would then be in order. It seemed to be wisest without discussion, because Mr. van der Rohe never rendered me a bill.

She later sent another $2,500 to "go toward a fee of which I suspect Mies stands in need."[18] She never mentioned the fact that, as she had confided to Goldsmith earlier, she thought she and Mies might share access to the property, or that she might buy him a valuable painting in lieu of a fee.

The following day, the sixty-six-year-old Mies took the stand and related his modest and astonishing biography: public school; the Aachen Cathedral school; trade school ("German, French, history, physics, chemistry, mathematics, and drafting"); apprentice bricklayer; apprentice carpenter; plasterer; draftsman in a stucco business; furniture design student, and, finally, in 1906, architect of record for his first house.[19]

Mies's imperfect grasp of English quickly manifested it-self on the witness stand:

FAISSLER: Well, after that time, say from 1914 on, what were your occupations?

MIES: Then I was in the war.

Q: And for how long?

A: No, with Germany.

Q: No, I say, for how long?[20]

Some of the great moments in the history of twentieth-century architecture flew by in the sleepy Yorkville court-room, as Faissler mentioned "doing something at an exhibition in Stuttgart" (this would be the Weissenhofsied-lung, the famous Stuttgart experimental housing project, overseen by Mies), then an allusion to Barcelona:

FAISSLER: Was that a World's Fair?

MIES: I designed and built the German pavilion.

And then:

FAISSLER: Now, calling your attention to Brno, Czechoslovakia, did you do any work there?

MIES: Yes. I built a very large residence.

Faissler spent the morning providing many examples of architect-client collaboration, including Mies and Edith's trip to the Crane company showroom to pick out bathroom fixtures. He then handed the witness over to Bohrer for cross-examination. During some introductory palaver, Bohrer homed in on Mies's name change:

BOHRER: Were you born with the name Ludwig Mies van der Rohe?

MIES: No. Ludwig Mies.

Q: Why did you add the name "Van der Rohe"?

A: For no particular reason.

Q: Wasn't it for the purpose of indicating some relationship to royalty?

A: No.[21]

Bohrer then perused Mies's résumé, highlighting some points that Faissler had left untouched. He emphasized that in the course of his education, Mies had never studied architecture, plumbing, or the fundamentals of electrical work. Bohrer interrogated Mies about the salaries of the welders, masons, plasterers, and plumbers who had helped build the

Farnsworth House, and about the price of cold-rolled steel. Mies had no idea what they were.

Bohrer hectored Mies about his decision not to use insulated double-paned glass for the house, which might have saved on heating bills. Mies replied that the estimated payback period of twenty years was too long, and that thermopane wasn't available in the sizes that he needed. Mies was quite firm on this point. He said they had used double-paned glass in Germany and "the seal was not tight . . . there was a dust film on the inside." Also, "it costs much more, and I think it has no more effect than if you pulled the curtains and closed the rooms."

Bohrer pushed back against the pushback. Upset by the avidity of Bohrer's interrogation, attorney Faissler intervened:

FAISSLER: I object to counsel shouting at this witness and badgering him. I want the record to show that he is standing within three feet of the witness, pointing his finger at him and yelling at him.

BOHRER: Good.[22]

"Why are you asking these questions?" Faissler interrupted.

Because, Bohrer replied, "We have pleaded that this man was negligent, that he perpetrated a fraud and did not know what he was doing, and was incompetent; that is what I have pleaded."[23]

This with Mies sitting in the witness chair in front of him.

Bohrer mocked and tormented Mies for no apparent reason. Absent an impressionable jury, it seems impossible that the sobersided Special Master Nelson would be swayed by his antics. For instance, Bohrer tried to portray Mies as indifferent to the possibility of flooding at the site:

Q: And if the water was high enough she could swim to the terrace, couldn't she?

A: It may be or maybe she could stay home for a day or two.

Q: And if she liked she could have a motorboat and launch at a dock in front of the house, couldn't she?[24]

Several hours into Mies's sixth day of testimony, Bohrer inquired:

Q: Are you tired and confused, Mr. van der Rohe?

A: I am confused about the question.

Q: Are you confused by the interruptions of counsel, or doesn't that confuse you?

A: No, the question. I would like to answer the question, but I tell you to repeat it all the time.

Q. Are you tired now?

A: Sure, I am tired.

Q: Were you tired this morning?

A: No, not particularly.

Q: Were you confused this morning?

A: I don't remember any more what happened this morning.[25]

During the six-week trial, both sides introduced leitmotifs that they replayed again and again. Bohrer delighted in mocking what he deemed to be modernist architecture's un-American pretensions, in this case, Mies's "open plan." He invited Mies to come over to a house model—there were two in the courtroom—and explain where people were supposed to sleep in the Farnsworth House.

Mies pointed to the bedroom on the eastern flank, separated from the living space by the hulking, teak-clad armoire. Thus someone could sleep over in the living area, he said, and someone else in front of the fireplace.

"What privacy would each person have?" Bohrer asked.

Well, Mies explained, it was a one-room house.

"Do you know whether or not people snore at night, Mr. Van der Rohe? I am really serious about that."

"That some people snore—I think I know that," Mies answered.

CHAPTER 10

"I THINK THE HOUSE
IS PERFECTLY
CONSTRUCTED,
IT IS PERFECTLY
EXECUTED."

LITIGATORS OFTEN USE THE TERM "BAD FACTS"
to describe details or occurrences that are
unhelpful to their case. The ultimate "bad fact"
rained down upon the Farnsworth House, and upon
Mies's defense, in mid-trial, on June 14, 1952.

Edith's version of events follows:

> One Saturday in early June I packed a few
> groceries in the usual thermos can and em-
> barked for the weekend in the country. Hu-
> go's little friend, the silver poodle, had had
> puppies and they too were packed in a little
> basket, but on the floor of the car, out of the
> sun. A violent thunderstorm overtook us on
> the way, and the river shore glimmered with

spectral drops as I crossed the travertine terrace carrying the three puppies and the rest of the paraphernalia. Shall I make a bed for Lucy out here where there is a bit of a breeze, or inside? I wondered as I fitted the key in the lock and opened the door.

Inside, however, I found the floor covered with water. The wood veneer of the core showed a high-water mark an inch or two above the floor, and the shantung folds which enclosed the entire house hung, stained and soaked, from their aluminum tracks overhead. Thunderstruck, I took off my shoes and waded around to check the possibility of a leak in the plumbing, but there was none, and it soon became clear that the water came from above, not below, and not from one point but from the entire periphery of the roof.

When the heating and plumbing man arrived, we set up the ladder and went up on to the roof which I examined then for the first time. It was a flat tarpaper and gravel covering with a slight pitch directed not toward peripheral gutters but to a pipe downspout leading down through the core to the ground below the house. Around the outer edge the tarpaper had been cut off where it reached the border or ornamental steel and in the absences of flashing, had responded to a half-year of weathering by bubbling and retracting. We found a defect broad enough to admit a finger, which extended all around the structure and had provided for the destruction of the hundreds of yards of shantung which curtained off the interior.

John Francis was the "heating and plumbing man." His wife, Jane, arrived at the Fox River house before he did, and testified in court about what she saw. "I could see puddles of water all over the place, just standing," she said.

> The drapes on the south side, which is the river side, were just wet from the ceiling down, dripping, and I walked on around the house. The shag rug in the front of the fireplace was soaked. Her bed, which is made up of mattresses at the side of the fireplace and the bottom mattress, was soaked clear through. I walked on around and there was water on the east side of the home and the drapes were wet from the floor up and the shag rug there was completely soaked, and puddles of water were all over.[1]

The nephritis researcher and the plumber's wife grabbed a pair of mops and went to work. They dragged the water-logged shag rug out to the meadow to wring it out.

John Francis showed up and ventured out onto the roof. "I noticed there was a crack between the roofing and the angle iron that forms the edge of the building," he told the court. Francis measured a three-eighths-inch-wide crack between the roof and the metal angle. Rain had come rushing in through an opening between the roofing and the top edge of the house.[2]

Edith had been taking a photography course with Harry Callahan at Moholy-Nagy's Institute of Design, so she hopped up on the roof with Francis.

A 1950S-ERA FLOOD

I spent a roll of film on flounces of tarpaper, on the border of ornamental steel which had supplanted the normal flashing, on the plumber's forefinger inserted in the crack, and the ruler which showed the breadth and depth of the defect.

All the negatives were masterly, and, helped by one of the teachers of photography from the Institute of Design, one evening was enough to provide me with a small album of photographs to present to the court at the next of its interminable sessions.

Bohrer showed the photos in court, Edith reported, "but it seemed nobody could believe his eyes, and a court session was called to meet on the roof. . . . All hands made it up the ladder and down again, I was told, including Mies, who had been present at all or most of the hearings." Faissler complained that "these are trick photographs" that exaggerated the water damage, and asked to have them expunged from the record.[3]

Inevitably, the finger-pointing began. "The roofing company accepted no responsibility for damages," Edith wrote, "since they had refused to guarantee a roof so constructed, and had acted under order of the architect."

Just a few days after the roof disaster, Bohrer summoned roofing contractor Harry Thiesen to the stand. Thiesen owned and managed a company that installed over a hundred roofs each year. He had loosely supervised some of the construction, and had revisited the site the day after the water incursion. He, too, testified that plastic roofing material seemed to have separated from the metal edge, possibly weakened by the heat of the sun. Then Bohrer embarked on one of his favorite themes:

Q: Did you ever see a roof constructed as the Farnsworth House is constructed?

A: No. . . . I have never constructed one like it.

Q: In what particular way is it different than the roofs you have heretofore constructed?

A: As a rule there is a metal flashing or metal edges used along the outside edge of a roof, when it ends off without a wall around it.

Thiesen brought samples of black gunk into the court-room that he said were hanging down on the inside of Edith's house when he arrived the day after the rain. The gunk was roof tar and an asbestos/asphalt-fiber weather stripping that had been laid above the plate glass. How it ended up oozing down Edith's windows was anyone's guess.

The roof disaster opened the door for Bohrer to argue that Mies was a European dandy who didn't have the first idea how to build a house. He found someone who agreed with him—contractor Carl Linder, whom Mies had consid-ered hiring to oversee the Farnsworth work. Linder testified that Goldsmith showed up at a work site in Aurora and "said he heard we were pretty good builders and thought he would come out and inspect our work. He mentioned he had an odd or unique type of structure he wanted to build and wanted to know if I was interested in it."[4]

In the summer of 1949, Linder visited Mies in his office. The two of them and Goldsmith examined the Fox River plans. The architects estimated the house could be built for $35,000 or $40,000. Even though the blueprints had yet to be finalized, "I said it couldn't be done for that," Linder recalled. "I called some of the construction screwy [and told Goldsmith I] didn't think much of the plate glass windows and the solid steel pilasters because they are great conductors of heat in the summertime and great conductors of cold in the wintertime."

Q: What did he say?

A: Didn't answer. . . . I told Mr. Goldsmith I did not like his type of construction, and he asked me why, and I told him there was too much glass and steel involved for a home.

Linder inspected the roof after the flood and noticed the crack around its entire perimeter. He testified that water poured into the house because it lacked proper flashing. Mies had relied on the mastic sealant above the glass to keep water out. Linder also said he saw "innumerable" water spots on the ceiling, each one about the size of a dime.[5]

Linder and Francis singled out other problems they noticed in the house, independent of the storm-induced cataract. "Farnsworth was having trouble with the heating system causing deposits of dirt and smoke on the [glass] walls," Francis told the court. He thought the chimneys should have risen higher off the roof for better drafting, but he said Goldsmith wanted them to lie low along the roofline.[6]

Linder said he visited the house just before the trial started and noticed that "the lower steel stops that retain the window glass were rusted in a lot of places." He also saw "water streaks" on the glass panes, and said some of the travertine was "heaved . . . because of moisture, condensation coming down in the fall or winter and freezing causing the upheaval mainly through frost through the steel structure."[7]

Four days after the water invasion, Goldsmith, on the witness stand, seemed to deny that such an event could ever have taken place. Absent an unforeseen catastrophe, like vandalism or a fallen tree, Bohrer asked, "Is it possible that any leakage could come into that living room?"

GOLDSMITH: Of water?

BOHRER: Of water or rain.

GOLDSMITH: If it were properly done, no.

BOHRER: Was it properly done?

GOLDSMITH: Insofar as I could ascertain, yes.

BOHRER: Were you not there while these steps were being taken in the construction of this roof?

GOLDSMITH: Pretty nearly all the time, and I inspected it when it was finished.

BOHRER: Was it properly done?

GOLDSMITH: In my opinion, it was.[*]

Two days later, the parties, minus Farnsworth, visited the house to survey the water damage. Mies's eyewitness testimony seemed to be at variance with other accounts of the interior flooding. For instance, when Bohrer asked him if he

---

[*] Goldsmith expressed a different opinion in an oral history interview for the Canadian Centre for Architecture, admitting: "I used a very bad detail at the edge of the roof, which in that famous rain, during the trial, ruined the curtains. . . . I thought I knew quite a bit about construction, but I probably didn't know as much as I thought I knew or we thought I knew."

saw rust spots on the floor, Mies said no. Would you say there were no rust spots? Bohrer pressed. There were some, Mies allowed, on the lower steel beam, and on the windowsill.

Did he see any discoloration on the draperies? No. Spots on the ceiling? No. Indeed, Mies saw some stains at the bottom of the primavera woodwork, "but I thought it was from mopping up the floor."

BOHRER: Was there tar on the windows?

MIES: There was a little spot on one window, just east of the porch.

BOHRER: Did you look at the north wall?

MIES: Oh, the north window, yes.

Bohrer then showed Mies photographs of water damage to the electrical outlets inlaid into the travertine floor. "When I was there I haven't seen that," Mies responded. Presented with pictures of water-stained curtains, Mies said he didn't see those, either.

Along with the other principals, Mies had clambered up a ladder to inspect the alignment of the tar paper and the edge of the leaky roof. "As far as I could see it was in order," he testified. "I didn't see any possibility that rain could come in."[8]

THE ALL-TOO-VISIBLE DISASTER ALLOWED Bohrer to press his point that Mies had no real-world construction skills. "You didn't know how to heat a house, did you?" Mies was asked in a pretrial deposition.

"I don't solve mechanical problems," Mies answered.

Very few architects act as their own heating or plumbing consultants, but this image of Mies as the kind of person who didn't worry about rain gutters stuck.

"Mies was suspicious of mechanical systems," his former associate Fujikawa commented many years later. "I remember Mies saying more than once that the reason the Gothic church is such a great building is because it doesn't have any plumbing." . . . "I don't think he saw mechanical systems as having a great deal to do with architecture," Fujikawa's colleague Duckett responded in a dual interview. "He accepted the fact that you had to have air-conditioning, just like you had to have plumbing fixtures. But, in my opinion, he sort of walked away from it. He thought the heat buildup in a building was a technical problem that the engineers would ultimately solve."

At the Kendall County courthouse, "Her lawyer was after him very aggressively," Goldsmith recalled. "He was, I think, questioned for days, hostilely, and so Mies was in a very big depression at that time. He said that 'I would never get in this again for anything.' I was very depressed."[9]

Although he never complained publicly, Goldsmith himself was harshly treated by Bohrer during his nine days of testimony. A cornerstone of Bohrer's attack on Mies's competence was to assail Goldsmith, his alter ego at the Farnsworth site, as an incompetent lad just out of architecture school. This wasn't true; Goldsmith had graduated from IIT in 1939, then left their postgraduate program to work in private practice and for the U.S. Navy, before joining Mies's office in 1946.[10] Bohrer made much of Goldsmith's one-dollar-an-hour salary, essentially arguing you get what you pay for. (The minimum wage at the time was $0.75 an hour.)

> BOHRER: Did you feel you were worth more [than $1 an hour]?

> GOLDSMITH: Yes, I feel I am worth more than one dollar an hour. . . . People who have been working under me have gone on to other jobs at several times this amount, and at any time I feel I could have left Mr. Van der Rohe if I had wanted to and gotten, oh, three, four, or five times as much for my services.

So why work for peanuts? Bohrer pressed.

"I consider Mr. van der Rohe to be not only the greatest living architect," Goldsmith replied,

> but really one of the significant men of this century. I also like him very much, and I was willing to help contribute to him achieving his work. I believe very much in the work that he is doing and feel that I would do at any time as much as I could to help him in this work.[11]

Bohrer berated Goldsmith for fashioning the $45 andirons from high-cost stainless steel ("Did you know that andirons have been made of wrought iron for many hundreds of years—I am asking if you know that fact?") to match the metal firebox that had to be inserted into the fire-place to preserve the original travertine.

BOHRER: In other words, all these andirons and back was done for aesthetic—I won't forget that word—aesthetic purposes.

GOLDSMITH: No.

Bohrer argued that Mies had sacrificed domestic practicality to chase a vaguely defined "aesthetic" ideal. He accused Mies of favoring the shiny stainless-steel andirons and firebox "in order to take care of the aesthetic values." Faissler jumped in to object "to counsel's argument, and sneering at the witness, and sneering at the word 'aesthetic.'"

Paul Schweikher turned the tables for his friend Mies when he explained on the stand that, even though Mies had not designed Edith's bathroom fixtures, he was responsible for "the aesthetic thought that went into the placement of the fixtures."

"Will you describe the aesthetic beauty of that bathroom?" a bemused Bohrer asked.

"There are certain relationships in all of the arts that have to do with the placement of objects," said Schweikher. "Those spatial relationships were adjusted in such a manner that they would be recognized as similar spatial relationships in other forms of art as producing an aesthetic."[12]

Later, Schweikher remembered that both Goldsmith and Master Nelson told him after the trial, "Your answer was superb."

"It was a desperate answer," Schweikher replied.

And I gave it not knowing whether I was saying anything important or not. But I felt, nevertheless, that it came out as a rather strong feeling. It reflected on the whole profession of architecture. Yes, that may be true, maybe the architect isn't responsible for these places, and to some degree that's undoubtedly true in a certain respect. Sometimes the architect never sees this array of urinals and toilets and so on and he just makes a space for them.

But, in the case of a small house for a woman who's going to live there all by herself and so on, I'm sure that Mies would take great care. He would have taken care, if not for the cosmetics of the room as it were, certainly for the safety of fixtures and so on, so that this would have been always in his mind.[13]

Schweikher was prepared to argue the point further, but Bohrer cut him off. "The idea was that if that were true of the bathroom"—meaning if Mies had paid significant attention to that tiny space—"which was in many ways aesthetically the least important room in the house, then it must be true for the whole house."

Bohrer then attacked Mies on several fronts simultaneously. He not only hammered away at Mies the "aesthete," but also accused him of being a publicity hound:

Q: And you [built] this for the purpose of attaining the attending publicity and honor that would be received as a result of that, isn't that correct?

MIES: Certainly less for this purpose. I don't need much publicity. I have so many [*sic*]. I wanted to build a good house, and I wanted Dr. Farnsworth to get a good house. . . .

Q: Did you take any architects out there?

A: Yes, I did.

Q: How many architects did you take out?

A: I would say about ten.

Q: Was that for the benefit of Dr. Farnsworth?

A: Certainly she became famous with the house.

Q: Did you become famous with the house?

A: I was famous before.[14]

Bohrer repeatedly pointed out that Mies and Goldsmith functioned as their own general contractors for the project, and he repeated Edith's contention that she was never shown a final set of plans. Mies admitted that he hadn't drawn up a full set of plans when he started construction, which he described as "step-by-step work."

"I cannot understand your question," he said to Bohrer, who repeatedly queried the lack of blueprints. "Otherwise—

the house is there. It must have been built according to some drawings and specifications."[15]

We worked on the Farnsworth house much more than we did on any house, and we were so careful, and that is why the house is good. . . . The house is there and everybody knows that it is a top house.

What makes it a top house? Bohrer asked.

I think the house is perfectly constructed, it is perfectly executed. It would be a lot of trouble to find a similar house or house similar to such a careful workmanship, and I think it is an excellent design, too. . . . I think the house speaks for itself.[16]

CHAPTER 11

"I FEEL LIKE A PROWLING ANIMAL, ALWAYS ON THE ALERT."

THE TRIAL WOULD PROVE TO BE THE STORM BEFORE a seemingly endless calm. The Yorkville proceedings adjourned on July 3, 1952, but Master Nelson did not hear final oral arguments from opposing counsel until January 30, 1953. On May 7, close to a year after the trial commenced, Nelson issued his Master's Report, which was overwhelmingly favorable to Mies. For instance, in finding thirty-five of forty-five "findings of fact," Nelson concluded:

> That plaintiff [Mies] did not represent to defendant the cost of the house would not exceed $40,000 or any other specific amount, nor did plaintiff represent to defendant that a house substantially in the likeness of the

model delivered to defendant could be constructed for
a sum not to exceed $40,000.

In other conclusions, Nelson wrote that "plaintiff made no
false representation whatever to the defendant," and "plaintiff
at all times acted in good faith."[1] Nelson ruled that Mies was
entitled to $12,934.30 in unpaid bills and commissions, and that
Edith should also pay for "the costs of this proceeding."

But Nelson's findings were not the final word. A judge
had to approve the findings, and indeed Judge Harry Daniels
held a one-day hearing on Nelson's work prior to ruling on
the case. Daniels then disappeared from view, after expressing his opinion that "it was regrettable that former friends
should litigate." The case was reassigned to a different judge,
who, as Faissler reported to his boss Levinson in a memo,
"made it clear that he was not interested in reading a 3,500-
page record." This judge urged the parties to settle the matter, which they refused to do. Edith's lawyer Bohrer was
making noises about appealing.

So there the matter hung fire, with both sides equally un-
satisfied. Edith professed to be heartsick, even though her
attorney Bohrer had warned her "that a lawsuit is only a
method of settling a quarrel, by no means to be confused
with a way of finding out the truth."

She detested the courtroom experience, and would say so
throughout her life. "As a witness I was disappointing to my
defense," she wrote.

The reduction of my relationship with Mies to a
legal brief looked completely hopeless to me . . . and I

was unable to furnish dates for the few points which could have had some validity in a court of law. Moreover, a sense of profound isolation brought to my mind those multitudes who have tried to defend themselves, their values, their honor and freedom, their lives, in some court, regular or irregular—and plunged me into depression. At the end of the session I took the East-West freeway back to town and work, half-sick with distress.

Edith recalled that, during his ten days on the stand, "It was Mies who took the hardest punishment, not only because of his language limitations but because of his total ignorance of everything that everybody present thought any architect should know." Here she was channeling the braggadocio of the post-litigation Randolph Bohrer. "You can't imagine what an exhibition of ignorance [Mies] put on!" Bohrer said.

He didn't know anything about steel, its properties or its standard dimensions. Not about construction, or high school physics, or just plain common sense. All he knows is that guff about his concept and in the Kendall County courthouse, that doesn't go down. I tell you, we had him sweating blood—he was heard to say afterwards that he would never start another law suit.

But Mies's discomfiture gave Edith little pleasure. "For six mortal weeks those grotesque hearings continued and until at last the records had grown to such proportions that there would be no further doubt that nobody would ever read them," she reported, presciently.

Myron Goldsmith was not alone in expressing his disappointment with Edith's performance on the stand, specifically her silly suggestion that she had not reviewed drawings with him, and her professions of ignorance about costs. While awaiting the verdict, Goldsmith mentioned in a handwritten note to his colleague William Dunlap that he was "very surprised when our friend Edith openly lied on the witness stand about the situation. She still maintains that she never knew until the house was nearly finished that it was to cost more than $40,000."

His colleague Duckett was likewise disappointed by Dr. Farnsworth's lack of candor. He confirmed Edith's recollection that he had helped her with some nephrology graphs, but recalled just as clearly his own photographs of Edith examining drawings for the Plano house: "Some showed Dr. Farnsworth standing there looking at the drawings with the title block, date, and everything. So that knocked out her . . . claim [that she hadn't inspected blueprints]."

"It was a sad day because that was not the kind of woman she was," he concluded. When pressed on the cause of the Mies-Farnsworth dispute, Duckett threw up his hands:

> We don't really know. We assumed it was an emotional thing between the two of them. She perhaps didn't think things were going the way she thought they were supposed to between the two of them. But we didn't think it had a damn thing to do with the house.[2]

In the months after the trial, both sides claimed victory. "The verdict was for Mies. All the way," Paul Schweikher recalled. "And Mies and I, of course as you may guess, had the appropriate martinis to celebrate."

In an extensive oral interview, Schweikher later opined that Mies was observing a "German business arrangement," which in effect made him the project's general contractor.

So he went right ahead with the whole thing and incurred the debts in his own name. When it came to recovering some of this as a part of his fee, which it was to be, Edith was apparently appalled at the costs. Now I don't know whether Mies made these or whether he got these from estimating contractors or not, but I think some of the early estimates were as low as $17,000 and at some point they passed $34,000. This all sounds like peanuts today [1984] but in those days that sudden jump of 100%—I may have all those values wrong, but it was in that general area—made the agreement go haywire.[3]

At one moment during the trial, Mies claimed to Schweikher that he had found a note in which he explained the cost overruns to Edith. "The next day, just before the trial, Mies said to me, 'Paul, I've found my notation with Edith.' The notation was that he had said something to the effect that the estimate was only an estimate and indicated that it might amount to more," Schweikher recalled. "He had found it in one of his German philosopher's books, Nietzsche or someone."

"ALL LIES": A NOTE FOUND IN MIES'S REVIEW
OF EDITH FARNSWORTH'S TESTIMONY

The note never materialized at trial.

The post-trial coverage in the Chicago papers was not fawningly pro-Mies, e.g., "Prof. Ludwige Mise [*sic*] Van der Rohe, world-famed Chicago architect . . . is suing Dr. Edith Farnsworth, famed research physician, also of Chicago." Of course, journalists smirked about the couple's immediate past: "The two were fast friends until recent months." Even the most responsible articles in the *Chicago Tribune* noted that Mies had been working without a contract, which would have raised eyebrows. "Glass House Her Pain," the *Chicago American* headlined, with the subtitle: "NU Prof, Architect in Court Fight; Is It Homey Art?"

"My neighbors tell me they always think of me as that woman slaving away on the glass and steel all weekend,"

Edith told the paper. "Believe me, it's a real job. You work outside with a hose and inside with a squeegee."

The *Chicago Sun-Times* noted that the home "had been the center of a national magazine battle," with one publication calling it "a particularly fine example of a bad modern house."[4]

THE PUBLIC RELATIONS SALVOS annoyed both parties. The bootlicking reviews in the architecture magazines irked Edith, because she thought, with some justification, that they were written by acolytes trying to curry favor with Mies. Neither party liked the newspaper coverage, which treated the foreign-born architect, the spinster kidney researcher, and the curiously designed house as oddities. Mies didn't mind being in the public eye, but he preferred respectful appreciations of his work to wink-wink tittle-tattle about his relations with a female doctor fourteen years his junior.

Quite unexpectedly, Edith acquired a powerful ally in her battle with Mies. Her friend and supporter—although there is no evidence that the two women ever met—was Elizabeth Gordon, the post–World War II editor of Hearst Corporation's successful shelter magazine *House Beautiful*.

Gordon and Farnsworth had a great deal in common. They were roughly the same age, both hailed from the Chicago area, and both had attended the pre-war University of Chicago, a center of liberal arts ferment during the presidency of Robert Maynard Hutchins. Edith was the rare female doctor. Gordon, also tall and handsome, was the rare female pilot and publishing executive. Gordon had married, but chose to live apart from her husband for many years at a time.

Hardworking and ambitious, Gordon cut her teeth writing "home columns" for Joseph Pulitzer's *New York World*, for Hearst's *New York Journal*, and eventually for the *New York Herald-Tribune*. She later switched to advertising, and wrote copy for American Standard at the Blaker agency in New York, and for another client, *House Beautiful*. While working full-time, Gordon also co-authored a book, *More House for Your Money*, intended to help couples "build a better house" by providing them with "facts about how to build, and how to get what you want for what you can pay." Gordon and her co-author saw the homebuilder-client as "a monarch of a small domain . . . guiding the activities of a small army of subjects who are building according to your every wish." Published while Edith Farnsworth was studying medicine, it is not a book Edith was likely to have read.[5]

In the ferocious postwar battle for suzerainty over the greatest consumer explosion in history, Gordon carved out an impressive niche. From 1941 to 1964, she grew *House Beautiful*'s circulation to five hundred thousand, thus rivaling the mainstays of domestic journalism, *Ladies' Home Journal* and *Good Housekeeping*. Gordon held strong opinions, and she wasn't shy about pushing them in stories and editorial letters. She wanted Americans to have nicely designed homes, say, in the manner of Frank Lloyd Wright, whom she cultivated desperately both in and out of the magazine. She liked Wright ("the greatest architect who ever lived") because his style was "organic," because he was American, and because his designs sold magazines.

Wright knew this, and often insisted that magazines devote "exclusives" to his work alone, which made him hard to work with.

Although she regarded her own taste as "modern,"[6] Gordon distinguished between "good modern" (Wright and his disciples) and "bad modern," for example, the International Style. She was nothing if not inconsistent. In September 1947, Gordon included the International Style Adams House in Brookline, Massachusetts, by architects Hugh Stubbins and Royal Barry Wills, among the "12 Best Houses of the Last 12 Years." Yet, at the same time, she scorned internationalists like Mies, Philip Johnson, and Le Corbusier because they belonged to a fancier club than she did. She took the occasional dig at a Museum of Modern Art architecture show or publication, even though it was unlikely that most of her readers knew of or cared about MoMA's taste. She likewise took potshots at *Progressive Architecture* magazine, not much more than a leaflet for a small, indoctrinated clique. Noting that Gordon tossed around adjectives such as *good, humanistic,* and *modern* to describe architecture that she favored, art historian Elizabeth Corbett drily notes that "the terms seem to have little clarity."[7] In her doctoral thesis, "Tilting at Modern," Corbett calls *House Beautiful* "a vehicle for the promotion of a softened modernism in domestic architecture."

Gordon and her magazine trafficked in code words that spoke to her middle-class-and-better audience. She championed "family" houses and family architects. It was common, for instance, for *House Beautiful* to pose an architect, his attractive wife, and their smiling children inside a home of his own creation. She used the term "pacesetter homes" to illustrate the kind of modernism she approved of, which were generally ranchy affairs, nicely arrayed away from the edges of an acre or half-acre lot. What Lewis Mumford called "the Bay Region style," meaning protomodern, postwar home building in the San Francisco area, encapsulated what Gordon liked.[8] Mumford called it "a native and human form of modernism."

"She was enamored with the romantic (and certainly romanticized) picture of suburban California living," her biographer, Monica Penick, wrote. "Happy families living gracious, carefree, leisured lives inside 'worry-free' houses and outside on private backyard patios, all free from pretension."[9]

One could describe Gordon's taste as "Modern but not jarringly so," or "modern like those nice Wright houses in Oak Park, Illinois."

If Le Corbusier talked about dwellings as machines for living, Gordon portrayed them as engines for consumption. She once wrote an article entitled "Americans Want More Windows."[10] Many "pacesetter" homes were stucco-and-stone barns for showcasing appliances and new countertops and floor coverings. "Storage" was a much-repeated code word, because of course people needed to buy things to store.

"Gordon may have been critical of conspicuous consumption, but she happily promoted *continuous* consumption," Penick wrote.[11] She concluded that a key part of Gordon's mission was to urge Americans "to buy new stuff."[12]

While some magazines erected an impermeable barrier between advertising and editorial content, Gordon gleefully plugged her advertisers' products and often asked them to design features around their latest offerings. There were few lines Gordon was unwilling to cross. She once featured her own house in a glossy spread, asserting that it belonged to "Lt. Col. and Mrs. Carol Norcros, of Dobbs Ferry, N.Y."[13] (Gordon's husband was Carl Norcross.) In an article entitled "There Are Two Kinds of Maids," Gordon depicted her own maid, Theresa, modeling a domestic's uniform.[14] She once crafted an essay that one could be forgiven for reading as self-congratulatory: "Nice People Come from Nice Homes."

To be fair, Gordon promoted talented architects like Clifford May, Edward Durell Stone, Craig Ellwood, William Wurster, Joseph Eichler, and, of course, Wright. (She and Wright feuded periodically, because he hated to see his work published alongside that of lesser practitioners.) What she did in showcasing her "pacesetter," or "All American," homes was not far from what John Entenza was doing in California, publishing his famous Case Study House plans in *Arts and Architecture* magazine. Entenza, who also jawboned suppliers into paying for home projects, showcased edgier architects, such as Charles Eames, Eero Saarinen, and Richard Neutra. That said, Entenza's designs flirted with unlivability in the way that much modern architecture did at the time, including the Farnsworth House. Twelve of his thirty-seven designs remained on the drawing board, while versions of Gordon's stylishly bourgeois homes popped up in upscale developments around the country.

———

UNEXPECTEDLY, GORDON PUBLISHED A package of articles in the April 1953 issue of *House Beautiful* under the rubric "The Threat to the Next America." She launched the series of articles with her own lead essay, announcing that "Something is rotten in the state of design."

"There is a well-established movement," Gordon wrote, "in modern architecture, decorating and furnishings, which is promoting the mystical idea that 'less is more.'" Her criticism anticipated the philippics of the John Birch Society, which would appear a few years later:

> Some museums, some professional magazines for architects and decorators, some architectural schools, and some designers . . . *are promoting unlivability, stripped-down emptiness, lack of storage space and therefore lack of possessions. . . .*
>
> No wonder you feel uneasy and repelled!
>
> *These arbiters make such a consistent attack on comfort, convenience and functional values that it becomes, in reality, an attack on reason itself.* [Emphasis in original.]
>
> "Incredible!" you say. "Nobody could seriously sell such nonsense."

Gordon included a handy field guide to the International Style ("Flat roofs," "Walls that look like Mondrian compositions," "Cubist structures on stilts," "Maximum use of glass without any corrective devices for shade or privacy," and so

THE THREAT . . .

forth) and a one-paragraph introduction to the Bauhaus for her unenlightened readers:

> A school of design for poster art, architecture, furniture and the like; started in Weimar, Germany, in 1919 by Walter Gropius. . . . He was replaced as director by Communist architect Hannes Meyer, who gave way in 1930 to Mies van der Rohe. . . . Bauhaus style is part of "International Style." Bauhaus furniture design has a "clinical look": sterile, cold, thin, uncomfortable.

It would be ungracious to note how her views overlapped with those of self-styled architecture critic Adolf Hitler.

In the same guide, Gordon published a picture of the Tugendhat House, which, she claimed, illustrated "The Cult of Austerity . . . the product of Mies van der Rohe's cold, barren design." Then Gordon dropped her bomb: "I have talked to a highly intelligent, now disillusioned, woman who spent more than $70,000 building a one-room house that is nothing but a glass cage on stilts."

Her informant, of course, was Farnsworth, who merited lengthy, special treatment in Gordon's campaign to make American architecture American again. Gordon went on to hail "good" American design of the type practiced by Bernard Maybeck, brothers Charles and Henry Greene, and Frank Lloyd Wright. Leading the reader by the hand, she printed a color plate of a living room by "Edward Wormley for the Dunbar Furniture Company." The room very much conformed to Gordon's ideas of "modern," with gathered gauze curtains, an abstractly patterned rug, and an ovoid glass coffee table.

Gordon spent two more pages deriding the "hair-shirt" school of International Style architecture; it is "perhaps the most unlivable type of home for man since he descended from the tree and entered a cave," she wrote.

You burn up in the summer and freeze in the winter, because nothing must interfere with the "pure" form of their rectangles—no overhanging roofs . . . the bare minimum of gadgets and possessions so as not to spoil the "clean" look . . . no children, no dogs, extremely meager kitchen facilities—nothing human that might disturb the architect's composition.

Gordon also included a brief feature explaining "Cubism and the International Style." "International Stylists are still playing with blocks 30-odd years after Picasso moved on to something else," the unsigned article explained. The article warned yet again that the suspect interlopers van der Rohe and Gropius have come to roost in the United States and offered up yet another example of their sleight-of-handicraft, the United Nations Secretariat Building.

"It is nothing but an over-simplified American grain elevator," *House Beautiful* explained. "Slice the old-fashioned American factory and stretch it skyward and you also have it." Neither Gropius nor Mies had a hand in designing the U.N. building, a collaboration involving a committee of architects that included Brazilian modernist Oscar Niemeyer, Le Corbusier, and the American Wallace Harrison.

Gordon's deputy Joseph Barry functioned as her personal attack dog against the International Style. Barry had worked in Paris for *Newsweek* and *The New York Times,* and wrote a book, *Left Bank, Right Bank,* in which, the magazine reported, he "investigated a much-publicized architect called Le Corbusier by talking to people who lived in Le Corbusier houses," and "reported on their discontent."

Barry contributed an essay called "Report on the American Battle Between Good and Bad Modern Houses." This piece had photos of the Farnsworth House, "a particularly fine example of a bad modern house."

Dr. Edith Farnsworth, a cultured, highly intelligent physician, had gone to Mies van der Rohe for a weekend house. It is, as you can see, a one story, open-plan affair with all four sides made of clear, unshaded glass. It is poised in the middle of a small field like a fishbowl or, better, like an emptied aquarium on a steel stand. It has cost Dr. Farnsworth about $73,000 so far.

Barry cited some breathless reviews of the Farnsworth House in the kind of magazines that *House Beautiful* alternately disdained and competed with. For instance, *House and Garden* reported that the house's "window walls provide a close communion with the outdoors . . . a structure of implacable calm." Then Barry decided to "put questions directly to the owner. Does Dr. Edith Farnsworth feel 'implacable calm' in her Mies van der Rohe house? Is her house working for its owner 'instead of the owner working for the house,' as claimed by one magazine?"

In response, Dr. Farnsworth spoke her mind.

Do I feel "implacable calm"?
The truth is that in this house with its four walls of glass I feel like a prowling animal, always on the alert. I am always restless. Even in the evening, I feel like a sentinel on guard day and night. I can rarely stretch out and relax.

Maintaining the house, she told Barry, was hard work:

The windows steam up in the winter and drive you crazy. You feel as though you are in a car in the rain with a windshield wiper that doesn't work. This great "freedom" Mies's disciples are always talking about has created nothing but great problems for me. Indeed there was no thought of me at any time.

Edith happily recited many of the house's shortcomings. She reported that Mies wanted the wardrobe partition between the living area and bedroom to be five feet high "for reasons of art and proportion."

"Well, I'm six feet tall," she said. "I wanted to be able to change my clothes without my head looking like it was wandering over the top of the partition without a body."

Then there was the fireplace. "Mies wanted the logs to burn directly on the floor itself. But why use the beautiful travertine floor?" Good question. Mies had backed off this scheme and installed a more conventional firebox and chimney. "Another thing," Farnsworth reported,

> I have to watch that my guests don't light the fire when I'm not looking, or we'll have smoke everywhere. This "beautiful" glass cage is so tightly built that you have to open the door in order to get enough air for the draft in the fireplace. In the winter you let more cold in than you get warm air from the fire.
>
> In the summer the air gets very hot and stuffy. The only natural ventilation comes from both ends of the house—there is no ventilation from any of the sides, although they are completely glass. We need an air-filtering system, but there is no longer room in the utility core. . . . The noise is enormous. You hear the furnaces kicking on and off, the blower exhaust going,

everything at work. The costs of heating is incredible. (Mies doesn't believe in thermopane or double glass.)

Farnsworth told Barry that she paid more to heat the Fox River house than she paid to heat her four-bedroom apartment in Chicago.

What else? I don't keep a garbage can under my sink. Do you know why? Because you can see the whole "kitchen" from the road on the way in here and the can would spoil the appearance of the whole house. Mies talks about "free space" but his space is very fixed. Any arrangement of furniture becomes a major problem, because the house is transparent, like an X-ray.

"I wanted to do something 'meaningful,'" Farnsworth told Barry, "and all I got was this glib, false sophistication. The conception of a house as a glass cage suspended in air is ridiculous."

Barry rounded out his article by hailing "good modern" houses, designed by architects on *House Beautiful*'s approved list. "Ease of living, large closet space, rooms properly related to each other, privacy from the outside world," he wrote, are the hallmarks of "good modern." He ended where he began, railing against "the Commissars of Culture" and "the mythmakers of modern architecture" who "are highly vocal (they monopolize the table of contents of many art magazines) and . . . highly placed in some museums and institutions." His dime-store anti-Communism went so far as to accuse Mies & Co. of aggravating women's lot:

> The [modernists'] austerity, far from improving the soul, impoverishes the spirit. They starve themselves in the midst of American plenty. They make life so hard for woman by scoffing at modern aids for her comfort, labor-savers for her time, that one might conclude women are the object of their attack.

A final salvo at Le Corbusier's accursed Unité d'Habitation in Marseille ("no privacy . . . no reason for crowding 1,600 people into one building") and Barry was *almost* done: "There can be no question of the outcome in the current battle between good and bad modern houses, so long as Americans retain their common sense."[15]

But he wasn't quite done. The "architecture of humanism" must conquer the "poverty-stricken clichés of doctrinaire International Stylists with their machine forms and concrete cubes," Barry opined.

> If we choose the barren glass cage of a Mies van der Rohe, we shall suffer the consequences of a loss of privacy and personality. If we crowd collectively in the colossal pigeonholes of a Le Corbusier, we shall set ourselves up for total and authoritarian control. But if we encourage the kinds of homes where the spirit of man can grow and flower, where each can develop in his own peculiar way, we shall ensure *the new democracy of culture*.[16] [Emphasis in original.]

Editors print controversial stories in the hopes of stirring the pot, and Gordon succeeded to a fault. The fancy magazines such as *Architectural Forum* and *Progressive Architecture* attacked her, doubtless raising her spirits. George Howe, who had toured the Farnsworth House with Mies and was now chairman of Yale's architecture department, likewise assailed her. So did some architects she respected and whose work she had showcased, including William Wurster and thirty other practitioners from the factitious Bay Region school. There was one unexpected casualty: Her deputy editor, James Marston Fitch, resigned in protest. "I had argued for months against such an absurd posture," he later wrote, "but realizing that the magazine, as the high-style end of the Hearst empire, would inevitably be drawn into the red-baiting frenzy, I decided that I had no choice but to resign in protest."[17]

Gordon's fans were not shy about putting pen to paper, revealing that she had struck a rich lode of anti-Internationalist feeling. Lewis Mumford congratulated her for highlighting "the irrational nature of so much modern design, and the authoritarian way in which it has been put over." Eliel Saarinen's daughter, Pipsan, voiced the hope that Gordon's article would set off "a general movement against 'the gang.'" A Michigan architect named Roger Allen wrote: "The future of Architecture does not involve the creation of glass tanks which, by moving out a frugal six pieces of furniture and the baby's crib, can be filled with water and rented out to Esther Williams for a retake of *Neptune's Daughter*."

The message that made it all worthwhile was a telegram

from Wright, who hadn't communicated with Gordon in two and a half years:

> SURPRISED AND DELIGHTED,
> DID NOT KNOW YOU HAD IT IN YOU.
> FROM NOW ON AT YOUR SERVICE.

It was signed "Godfather."

Gordon allowed Wright to vent at greater length a few months later, in a prominent feature, "Frank Lloyd Wright Speaks Up." The eighty-eight-year-old Wright attacked the "sterility" and "collectivism" of the International Style's "poverty stricken glass-box architecture" that cast a "communistic shadow . . . over our own [American] tradition." He also blasted away at Mies and Le Corbusier, who "ran from political totalitarianism in Germany to . . . their own totalitarianism in art here in America."

This kind of rhetoric was nothing new from Wright, who could wax nonsensical on political subjects. In a draft of a 1947 letter (never sent) to the Dutch architect Hendrik Wijdeveld, Wright railed about "left wing modernists" such as Mies, Walter Gropius, and Marcel Breuer, whose work he viewed as "distinctly Nazi."[18] Wright evinced zero comprehension of the terms *right* and *left wing,* both of which he condemned with zealous abandon—an odd stance for the only American architect who traveled to Moscow in 1937 to be lionized by the First All-Union Congress of Soviet Architects.

Wright's final salvo to *House Beautiful*: "Old man BOX merely looks different when glassified, that's all. But the more the box is glassed the more it is evident as the box. No new ideas whatever are involved."[19]

Fifteen years earlier, at the Red Lacquer Room in the Palmer House hotel, Wright had had his arm draped around Mies's beefy shoulder, taking credit for bringing him to America.

MIES FOUND THE NEGATIVE publicity irksome. Just a few weeks after Gordon launched her campaign, *Newsweek* weighed in with a full-page story, approvingly citing Gordon and Barry, and quoting Edith at length:

> Under the slogan of simplicity, this theory of architecture has discarded the accumulated wisdom of building. This handsome pavilion I own is almost totally unworkable. There is a certain brutality about having the outside inside . . . the windows steam up in the winter and drive you crazy. You feel as though you are in a car in the rain with a windshield wiper that doesn't work.[20]

Newsweek was an irritant, but Mies worried that the *House Beautiful* attack might cost him business. He consulted his lawyers about suing Gordon's publication, but they advised against tangling with the magazine's formidable owner. While allowing that Gordon's journalism was "not complimentary to say the least," Faissler told Mies that "the magazine is a Hearst publication, so aside from any question of libel there would be a serious question as to the advisability of filing a suit against the magazine."[21] Gordon, it turns out, also had her legal qualms. In a letter to Lewis Mumford, she said Hearst lawyers had made her tone down some of Joseph Barry's anti-Mies sallies: "My legal department says it would be libelous to Mies van der Rohe and that we will have to cut out the juiciest parts of it."[22]

In the background, the lawsuit that had been argued inside the Kendall County courthouse during the summer of 1952 refused to die. Per the convoluted road map dictated by the chancery proceedings (one recalls Charles Dickens's deep loathing of the Chancery Court in *Bleak House*: "Suffer any wrong that can be done you rather than come here!"), Master Nelson's findings were still in search of a judge to approve them. Philip Johnson's factotum Robert Wiley, who was partly responsible for creating this unsightly mess, intervened again. In a letter to Faissler's colleague David Levinson, Wiley noted that Mies "is still brooding somewhat over the 'Farnsworth affair.' He seemed troubled a bit because 1/ nothing seemed to be taking place and 2/ he is not sure 'what goal Mr. Levinson is aiming for.' "

Wiley stated the obvious, which was that it was time to settle the case. He had persuaded Henry-Russell Hitchcock, Johnson's co-author of the influential monograph *The International Style*, to approach Edith about a settlement. Mies had told his lawyers that he, too, was interested in settling, for nothing, if "we could get a promise from the defendant and her attorney to stop slandering him."[23]

Another inconvenient concomitant of the trial and the attendant publicity was an American Institute of Architects ethical inquiry into Mies's behavior vis-à-vis Farnsworth.

"Because of the recent publicity . . . the Executive Committee of the Chicago Chapter has been asked by membership to determine the facts in the case," AIA vice presidents Albert Heino and Philip Will wrote to Mies.

> This publicity pertains, among other charges, to charges of alleged "negligence in the handling of the construction plans" by a Dr. Edith B. Farnsworth. . . .
>
> It is not our purpose to determine legal responsibilities, but to report concerning the professional ethics in this case, and whether or not the American Institute of Architects document No. 330 "Standards of Professional Practice" has been observed.
>
> This task is as distasteful to the undersigned as it must be to you, and we undertake it reluctantly because of our high regard for you. However, we are sure you realize that for the good of the profession, the record must be set straight insofar as any charges of professional ethics are concerned.

The pair requested a meeting with Mies, but there is no further record of this inquiry.

Four years after the trial, Mies's lawyers reached out to Mason Bohrer, Randolph's son, whom they (correctly) viewed as more flexible than his father on matters Farnsworth. The two sides agreed that Edith would pay Mies $2,500, just a fraction of Nelson's suggested reparations, and a sum that completely eliminated payment of an architectural fee and of Mies's legal costs. If it was true that the Bohrers represented Edith pro bono, she got a good deal.

The endless litigation that had blackened all parties and irreconcilably separated once-close friends ended with a whimper, not a bang.

In the course of revising Franz Schulze's 1985 biography of Mies, Edward Windhorst solicited a review of the trial from Chicago attorney James Cooper. Cooper wrote that "there is no question that Mies's team has a stronger hand on the facts, the client and the judge . . . Farnsworth's team had mostly bad facts, an apparently difficult client and seem to lose the Master early on." He opined:

> The big question was whether to bring a case at all. Mies knew he didn't have the written agreements, that he had probably gone over budget and that the record-keeping was sloppy. . . . A corporate client (i.e. a rational economic actor) would not have sued here, instead chalking this one up to experience, and instituting a requirement that arrangements be documented in the future. Mies was clearly not a rational economic actor.

CHAPTER 12

"ARCHITECTS SHOULD KISS THE FEET OF MIES VAN DER ROHE."

THERE IS NO INDICATION THAT, AFTER RECEIVING the $2,500 check that ended their prodigious dispute, Mies ever again communicated with Edith Farnsworth.

Mies was indeed "already famous," as he testified at the Kendall County courthouse, but starting in the 1950s until his death in 1969, he became both famous and successful. Even as the Farnsworth imbroglio was winding down, one of Mies's greatest masterpieces, the apartment building complex at 860/880 Lake Shore Drive, was rising on the Lake Michigan shoreline. In 1957, *Life* magazine featured the Lake Shore Drive towers in a photo essay, "Emergence of a Master Architect."

"Today, at 70," the magazine reported, "after

living inconspicuously in the U.S. for twenty years, Mies is bursting into full, spectacular view."

The unnamed *Life* reporter presented Mies, a "widower [living] a solitary, unpretentious life," as a cigar-smoking architectural oracle, lounging on a "conventional sofa" (not a Barcelona chair) in his "sparsely furnished apartment." For *Life*'s mass readership, Mies spouted Delphic maxims about architecture: "Romanticists don't like my buildings," he told the magazine. "They say they are cold and rigid. But we do not build for fun. We build for a purpose. We are not trying to please people. We are driving to the essence of things. Alone, logic will not make beauty inevitable. But with logic, a beauty shines."

According to *Life*, his buildings—the article included pictures of IIT's just completed Crown Hall, and of the Seagram Building site in Manhattan—"express the simplicity and sturdy nobility of Mies himself."[1]

The magnificent Seagram Building, erected for the Bronfman distillery magnates of Canada, confirmed Mies's status as an international superstar. Selected over architects I. M. Pei, Paul Rudolph, Louis Kahn, Eero Saarinen, and Le Corbusier, Mies delivered one of the most beautiful skyscrapers in Manhattan, boldly set back a hundred feet from Park Avenue, opening sightlines to McKim, Mead, and White's Italian Renaissance Racquet and Tennis Club across the street, and to Gordon Bunshaft's Corbusian Lever House one block to the north. (Mies walked past both buildings every day, from his hotel on Forty-eighth Street on his way to the Seagram offices on Fifty-third.) The *New York Times* architecture critic Hubert Muschamp called it "the Building of the Millennium." Several years later, Muschamp corrected himself. "I now think it is the Building of Two Millenniums," he wrote in 2001, "for it telescopes, within what Mies called his 'almost nothing' aesthetic, everything essential in Western architecture, from the Greeks to the Gothic builders to ourselves."

Waspish to the end—he was in his late eighties when Seagram went up—Frank Lloyd Wright called the project "a whisky bottle on a playing card."

Because Mies didn't have a license to practice in New York, a nominal partnership—"Mies van der Rohe and Philip Johnson, Architects"—became Seagram's designers of record. (In her book *Building Seagram,* Samuel Bronfman's daughter, Phyllis Lambert, who chose the architects, reported that Johnson's eyes welled up when Mies proposed the collaboration.)[2] Despite Johnson's ugly attempts to hog credit for Seagram,* the building is universally ascribed to Mies, with Johnson acknowledged for some of the subtleties of interior design, including the lighting schemes and magnificently appointed Four Seasons restaurant. (Johnson's collaborator on lighting design was Richard Kelly, who did

---

* Biographers Schulze and Windhorst report a colleague asking Mies if it bothered him that Johnson was taking credit for Seagram. "Not especially," Mies replied. "What would bother me would be Johnson claiming that I was chiefly responsible for one of his buildings." Testifying in favor of landmark status for Seagram ("the finest building of a commercial nature of the 20th century") before New York City's Landmarks Preservation Commission in 1988, Johnson "seemed interested in denigrating Mies," Lambert wrote. "Incongruously, he praised me as his 'beloved employer' for many years and avoided mention of Mies."

the splendid work on the Glass House.) Lambert later wrote that "Mies was unquestionably the architect of Seagram." She allowed that "Philip's interest in what one can best call 'atmospheric lighting' would be the source of his major contributions to the building."[3]

The shotgun Seagram collaboration and latent tensions between Mies and Johnson frayed their relationship beyond repair. Mies was more uncommunicative than usual during the Seagram project, and Johnson was chafing in the shadow of the Great Man, who owed his American renown, in part, to Johnson's assiduous pamphleteering. Johnson the creative chameleon would soon cast off his Miesian skin and reinvent himself as an occasionally original, occasionally derivative, postmodernist architect in a career that spanned more than three decades after Mies's death. "I am violently anti-Miesian," he once declared in front of an audience at the Yale School of Architecture. "I think that this is the most natural thing in the world, just as I am not really very fond of my father."

The two men had a famous blow-up, perhaps not accidentally inside Johnson's New Canaan Glass House, while they were working on the Seagram. An inebriated Mies could not refrain from criticizing Johnson's Glass House handiwork, famously copied from the Farnsworth model. "He commenced to belabor Philip," according to Johnson's authorized biographer, Franz Schulze, "not for having copied him but for trying to and failing. . . . The corner, he complained, pointing to one of the four supporting piers, was badly understood and miserably detailed. Obviously, Mies concluded, the designer did not know how to turn a corner."

"Turning the corner," which means addressing the challenges of aligning bricks, girders, windows, or mullions at the corners of buildings, was a famous Mies forte. In their textbook *American Architecture*, Marcus Whiffen and Frederick Koeper praise Mies's "structurally descriptive corner detail" in his IIT buildings, and write that "Mies made every architect corner-conscious; talent became equated with ability to turn a corner—a problem as ancient as the Greek Doric order." Describing the Glass House in a 1950 *Architecture Review* article, Johnson included a section drawing of his corner solution, and admitted that "many details of the house are adapted from Mies's work, especially the corner treatment."

Referring to the storied contretemps, "I just think he felt that my bad copy of his work was extremely unpleasant," Johnson later recalled. "He also deeply resented my inquisitive attitude, making him verbal when he wasn't. He was a groan-and-grunt man, as you may remember."[4] "Mies thought the workmanship was bad, that the design was bad, that it was a bad copy of his Farnsworth House, which had inspired me. He thought I should have understood his work better."[5]

That night, however, Johnson counterpunched, attacking one of Mies's heroes, the Dutch architect Hendrik Berlage:

> I've been meaning to ask you about Berlage and the Stock Exchange he put up in Amsterdam. All that decoration mixed up with masonry and metal . . . in view of your love of pure structure, I am at a loss to comprehend what you see in him or it.

Phyllis Lambert, who was present, knew that Mies revered Berlage's Stock Exchange "for its honesty, fine craftsmanship and clarity of construction. . . . Mies later told me that for Philip to condemn the Berlage in front of me, the client, was wrong, but he clearly sensed that Philip was veering away from the principles of the modern movement."[6] (Lambert also reported Mies's catty remark that Kelly's magnificent night lighting made the Glass House "[look] like a hot dog stand.")

"The blow-up points to the fundamental difference between the two as types of architect," David Holowka observed. "Mies the believer, to whom architecture is a religion based on eternal truths; Johnson the non-ideological style surfer always open to the next new thing."[7]

Mies refused to spend the night on Johnson's property, and his host arranged for him to bed down at the nearby (Johnson-designed) home of his friend Robert Wiley—the man who'd had the bright idea that Mies should file suit against Edith Farnsworth. Johnson would soon discover that Wiley had cheated him out of $250,000 on a building project while posing as a partner of a white-shoe New York law firm. Shamed and exposed, Wiley later committed suicide.

MIES WOULD LIVE ON for another fifteen years, adding to his impressive list of signature buildings, including the Federal Center in Chicago, and the Neue Nationalgalerie—the New National Gallery—in Berlin, where both he and his work were received with special acclaim. Hospitalized for weeks at a time because of arthritis, Mies agonized over the details of the vast, temple-like art museum that stood not far from his own Berlin apartment, which had been razed for one of Albert Speer's never-realized monumental schemes in central Berlin. His New Gallery stood atop a massive granite podium, akin to the classical staging of the nearby Altes Museum of 1830, a masterpiece by one of Mies's heroes, Karl Friedrich Schinkel.

Mies did not live to see the New Gallery completed, but

MIES AT THE NEUE NATIONALGALERIE

he attended a ceremonial roof raising, and delivered some characteristically Miesian remarks:

"It was agreed that nobody would speak more than five minutes. What humbug that was! I want to thank the blokes who worked the steel, and the ones who did the concrete. And when the great roof raised itself up without a sound, I was amazed!"[8]

A starchitect before the term existed, Mies's professional life was not without setbacks. Surprisingly, to him, IIT relieved him of his duties as campus architect. The president who had hired him, Henry Heald, had retired, and the new administration felt that Mies's commercial commissions were diverting his attentions from his campus commitments. They complained that some of his buildings leaked, and they weren't wild about Mies's stark black-steel-and-glass palette; they "liked to have more 'color' in buildings" was an IIT comment relayed to Mies by his associate Fujikawa.[9] John Holabird, one of the architects who helped lure Mies to Chicago, was a huge fan, but later argued that Mies

shouldn't have been doing a campus, because he'd never been to a college himself and he didn't, I think, have the slightest notion of the nice feeling about enclosures in a college, a quadrangle or something or other where you could become at least a little part of a social unit. His layout of IIT, although people brag about it, looks like a chemical or research area, like a pharmaceutical company. The buildings look as if they were ordered for research and not ordered for people to live and have fun in.[10]

Even though most of his campus buildings were already up, Mies was wounded, all the more so because IIT chose Skidmore, Owings and Merrill, the most "Miesian" of the big firms spreading their wings during the post–World War II economic boom, to replace him. (Frank Lloyd Wright called SOM "the Three Blind Mies.")

That was in 1958. A few years later, Jackie Kennedy passed over Mies to choose I. M. Pei to design the Kennedy Library for a harborside site in Boston. Pei himself suggested that "the job should probably go to Mies as the most prominent of the contenders," but Kennedy didn't warm to the seventy-eight-year-old Mies's saturnine personality. He reminded her of "an Egyptian potentate," she later commented, and "conveyed a sense that he didn't really want the job."[11]

Mies didn't live long enough to see his final major design, for Peter Palumbo's Mansion House Square in central London, scuppered by Margaret Thatcher's Conservative government, egged on by self-appointed architecture critic Prince Charles. "It would be a tragedy if the character and skyline of our capital city were to be further ruined and St. Paul's dwarfed by yet another giant glass stump," Charles declared, "better suited to downtown Chicago than the City of London."

Even as other commissions streamed in, Mies's critics were beginning to be heard. "His work got a little repetitious," in the judgment of his admirer Gordon Bunshaft. In his 1981 book, *From Bauhaus to Our House*, Tom Wolfe mocked the line of modernist piles along Manhattan's Sixth Avenue as "Mies van der Row." Writing in *The New Repub-*

lic, critic Wolf von Eckardt verbally carpet-bombed the New Gallery, the capstone of Mies's long career: "Mies, in the end, reduced his Gallery of Twentieth Century Art in Berlin to a roof with four pillars, covering an invisible, glass enclosed space. It is architecture reduced to the absurd, much as Malevich, in his *White on White* canvas, had reduced painting to the absurd."[12]

Mies's biographers Schulze and Windhorst, at the end of a commentary on his later work, conclude: "After the completion of the Farnsworth House and its scaling up for [860/880 Lake Shore Drive], Mies was essentially finished creating."[13] Chicago architect Stanley Tigerman observed that Mies's work had indeed become *Zeitwille*—the will of the epoch—but he didn't intend it as a compliment. "America, Americans, and most of all the image makers of Madison Avenue were thoroughly ready to embrace Mies van der Rohe and his monuments as symbols of the 'spirit of the age,'" Tigerman wrote in 1987.[14]

The starchitect of the *Mad Men* era: Mies van der Row indeed.

Wracked by his arthritis and mostly confined to a wheelchair, Mies devoted a portion of his declining years to the bittersweet job of collecting awards, such as the Medal of Freedom, the gold medal of the American Institute of Architects, the German Pour le Mérite, and others. Architecture historian Fritz Neumeyer found a set of index cards in the Mies archive at the Library of Congress that provided a template for each brief acceptance speech he made at these ceremonies, ideas present in Mies's rhetoric for decades:

1. Search for understanding
2. Learned most from *old buildings*
3. *Architecture must belong to its own time*
4. What is civilization?

And so on, through the familiar appeals of Thomas Aquinas (*"adaequatio rei et intellectus,"* "the intellect must be adequate to the thing") and his oft-invoked Saint Augustine quote: "Beauty is the radiance of truth."[15]

Writing in 1962, seven years before Mies's death, the critic Reyner Banham noted that Miesianism was already falling out of fashion, dismissed as "conservative" by Philip Johnson and others: "Mies is a craftsman of technology," Banham wrote, "and what he has to teach is something that is never very popular—that architectural responsibility is continuous and unremitting and extends down to the smallest detail."

As an octogenarian in the late 1960s, Mies had outlived the heyday of the modernist movement. In 1967, future Pritzker Architecture Prize winner Robert Venturi published the influential postmodernist manifesto *Complexity and Contradiction in Architecture*. Venturi head-butted Mies's "magnificent paradox" *Less is more*. "Less is a bore," Venturi famously declared. "I like complexity and contradiction in architecture." He continued:

Architects can no longer afford to be intimidated by the puritanically moral language of orthodox modern architecture. . . . I am for messy vitality over obvious unity. I include the non sequitur and proclaim the

duality. I am for richness of meaning rather than clarity of meaning.[16]

In 1986, perhaps the high tide line of the postmodern architectural movement, the future Yale School of Architecture dean Robert A. M. Stern unloaded on Mies. "I think he
got bored," Stern declared to director Michael Blackwood in
the documentary *Mies*:

> He sat there with his martinis and his cigars, and
> he's in his nice 1920s apartment, he could look at the
> sculptures he built out on the Chicago lakefront. He
> never had to live in them. To live in them is not to
> enjoy them, at least not for me. He looks out at his
> work on the Chicago skyline, and he talked about St.
> Augustine—it's God, it's got nothing to do with man.
> He made works of man, dreamt of St. Augustine,
> and tempered the split between them with a lot of nice
> martinis.

TODAY, FEW WOULD CHALLENGE the assertion that Mies van
der Rohe was a great architect. In homage to what many
view as his greatest work, in 1986 architects in Barcelona re-
built the Barcelona Pavilion, which disappeared when the
International Exposition closed in 1930. Likewise, the city of
Brno has undertaken a complete rehabilitation of Mies's Tugendhat House, which had fallen into extreme disrepair.
Both sites are must-visit destinations on any architectural
grand tour of Europe.

In 2001, the Museum of Modern Art and the Whitney Museum of American Art collaborated on an unprecedented dual exhibition devoted to Mies's work: *Mies in Berlin*, curated by Terence Riley and Barry Bergdoll, and *Mies in America*, curated by Phyllis Lambert. It would be absurd to suggest that Mies's reputation needed rehabilitation, but the critical reaction was generally euphoric. "These two shows depict Mies as a supervisor of fantasy: an interpreter of the 20th century's deepest dream of itself," Hubert Muschamp wrote in *The New York Times*.[17]

Even Robert Venturi allowed that "of all the things I've said—and I've written and said a lot—I've never wanted to take anything back, except maybe 'Less is a bore.'" In retrospect, he said,

> I was reacting against the dry simplicity of late modern architecture, so it was a rhetorical statement. From our position now there is no doubt that Mies is one of the great masters of the century, and architects should kiss the feet of Mies van der Rohe because of his accomplishments and what we could learn from him.

MIES'S INTIMATE FRIENDSHIP WITH Lora Marx lasted until the end of his life. Why didn't you marry me? she asked him in 1965, four years before his death.

I was a fool, he said. I feared the loss of freedom. It wasn't a valid worry. Shall we marry now?

"No," she replied. "It is rather too late for that; it would only spoil things. I guess I just wanted to know."[18]

When asked by biographer Franz Schulze why she loved
Mies, she answered: "Integrity, honesty; he was the most
honest man I ever knew. Extremely kind. Would not com-
promise. I liked his shyness." Lora's ex-husband, the wealthy
architect and artist Samuel Marx, kept in touch with Mies as
long as Marx lived in Chicago, and invited Mies and Lora to
his legendary birthday bashes at his suburban mansion. "As
always, there will be a staggering amount of good cheer
before dinner, during, and as long as you can stagger thereafter," Marx promised Mies in one invitation.[19]

Mies's daughter Georgia reported a softening in his de-
meanor at the end of his life: "A beautiful, harmonic friendship grew between us which lasted, uninterrupted by
anything or anybody, to his death three years later."[20]

Georgia reported that the elderly Mies dreamed of mov-

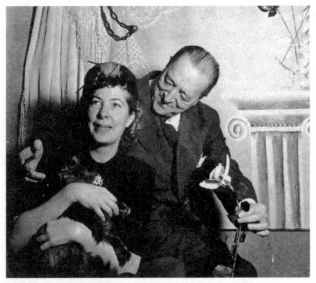

MIES AND LORA MARX

ing to the suburbs. "It would be my dream in Chicago to be able to step out onto the lawn from every room and sit under trees," he told her.

> "But in Chicago I sit like a caged lion in my apartment building and only stare at walls." He told us that he had had the chance to trade a modern house with garden, lawn, and trees in Evanston, a suburb of Chicago, that belonged to an architect friend, for a Picasso painting. But Lora hated the suburbs and for the cook Caroline it was too far. "They won't even let me have the German shepherd that I would so love to have," he complained.[21]

When Mies became very sick, not long before his death, Georgia interviewed him on camera for two hours. After the filming ended, Mies asked that the film lights be turned back on and the camera remounted for a last thought: "You cannot find new architecture every Monday morning. That is a bit naïve. Architecture was always a very serious endeavor, periods were named after it. And that's how it shall remain."[22]

Mies van der Rohe died in August 1969 at age eighty-three, in Chicago. He had been hospitalized following a three-year struggle with esophageal cancer, and passed away with his daughters Marianne and Georgia at his side.

CHAPTER 13

"I REPEAT, MAGIC AND POETRY!"

ER PUBLIC COMPLAINTS NOTWITHSTANDING, Edith Farnsworth fashioned an uneasy peace with her famous glass house. As she lived through her fifties and into her early sixties, she gradually reduced her workload in Chicago and spent more time in Plano. She bought land adjacent to her nine-acre parcel, made friends in the area, and began to turn her attention to what would become her second career: writing and translating poetry.

William Murphy, a young lawyer who worked for the Mies side of the famous litigation, later worked for and befriended Edith. "She had a possession that other people regarded as unique" is how Murphy explained Edith's relationship to her famous house. "I don't think in her heart of hearts Dr.

Farnsworth ever loved the house because it was not what she visualized. And yet it was beautiful."[1]

"She would constantly point out shortcomings of the house," Murphy elaborated. "She didn't care much for the kitchen, she didn't like the lack of privacy in the bedroom, when architecture students would be peering in the glass when she woke up. She didn't like the heat. She didn't like the lack of air-conditioning."

Carl Alving, whose father was a colleague of Edith's, remembers visiting the Plano house during the early 1950s as a little boy. He, too, worried that the glass panels compromised his host's privacy. "Can everybody watch you as you go to the bathroom?" he asked. "She answered me with a chuckle," he recalled. " 'No, those private places are hidden away.' "[2]

"She complained about the house all the time," recalled Parkie Emmons, a friend from Chicago's North Side who also had a second home in Plano. "She complained about the two furnaces, she couldn't get either to work properly. She was very bitter about Mies. He may have created a thing of beauty but it was not a habitation." Neighbor Ellyn Kivitts recalled that Mies's name came up only occasionally. "She talked about him vaguely, but it was not in a kind way."

And yet Edith continued to live there. Her décor became non-Miesian in the extreme. She laid thick-piled North African rugs over the travertine floors and hung family photographs and Chinese prints from the primavera veneer of the house's service core. She favored Danish modern furniture and placed potted plants and flowers around the house, indulging in what might be called normal clutter. A collector of Asian objects, she placed two thigh-high Chinese marble lion statues resembling dogs (sometimes mistakenly called "foo dogs" by Westerners) on the travertine terrace Mies created in his famous approach to her patio. During an epic flood in 1954, Edith demonstrated her characteristic sangfroid. She abandoned the house in a rowboat, rescuing her violin and her beloved poodle, Amy. She spent the night with neighbors who owned houses on higher ground, recalled her friend Neil Emmons. Upon returning to the foul-smelling house, "she was upset that the beautiful raw silk draperies were ruined," he recalled.

Always eager to fill time in the country, Edith offered herself as a language teacher to interested neighbors. Eventually, a tiny knot of local children found their way to the formidable Miss Edith's house for Saturday-morning French lessons. Kelly Simms and Corey Mundwiler, who were in grade school at the time, both remember that "she didn't quite understand children," according to Simms. "She kept saying she wanted to broaden our horizons," Mundwiler remembers. "She thought Kelly should become an interpreter at the United Nations and that I should become a museum curator."

Edith's pedagogy was decidedly old-school. "She would serve us tea on the screened-in porch and just spoke French to us for one or two hours," Simms said. "She told us she would talk to the trees to practice her diction, and she insisted that we speak to the poodle in French, because it was the only language the dog understood. She had this wonderful inspiration to do this but it wasn't very successful."

"She would read us the entire *Rime of the Ancient Mariner*—all ninety-six stanzas—during the break," Mundwiler recalls. "That was her idea of taking a break." Both he and Simms recall the lack of air-conditioning: "It was like a jungle down there in the summer."

Mundwiler, who later became an interior designer, volunteered a portrait of the doctor entering her winter years: "She was a handsome woman, not pretty, and a very hard person to get to know on a personal level. She talked a lot. She was very eloquent, very soft spoken, very wispy in her voice, very lyrical. She loved to pontificate on many different subjects.

"She had a bittersweet relation with the house," he remembered. "She felt it was impractical, but she loved it and she loved being out in the country. In a certain way it was tainted, but she also took great pride in it."

Mundwiler occasionally visited the house on winter nights. "Those evenings were quite amazing," he remembers. "It was always lovely, with the snowy wind blowing outside the windows. She loved to sit by the fire, drink cognac, and smoke incessantly. She would serve honey cake and sometimes play the violin. It was a very special time."

Farnsworth enrolled Mundwiler in an advanced figure drawing class at the Art Institute of Chicago. "I took the train in, or my aunt and uncle would drive in for this Saturday class," Mundwiler remembers. "Edith gave me her Chicago library card, so I could do research for my school papers in their beautiful building. For a little insecure country kid to go into the city, and take this class, it was a great memory, and it was my first exposure to formal art training."

In 1968, the outside world interrupted Edith Farnsworth's pastoral idyll. Kendall County decided to build a new bridge across the Fox River, just downstream from Edith's property. The county was planning to take two acres of Edith's property by eminent domain, but, more troubling, the north-south road between Plano and Millbrook would now pass closer to her house. "[The bridge] will pass within 180 feet of the house," Farnsworth told the *Chicago Tribune*. "Just think, any of those Hell's Angels who seem to be riding around could shoot right into the house—it's all glass."[3]

"She was really out of her mind about that bridge," recalled Kelly Simms, who thought Edith was overreacting to the county's demarche. "She just had to have it her way." Farnsworth enlisted Simms and Mundwiler to stand by the roadside and count passing cars. "She wanted to prove to the county that there wasn't that much traffic on the bridge," Mundwiler said. "We would sit there with clickers and record the traffic."

Farnsworth retained attorney Murphy to propose various resolutions to the bridge dispute. They hired a team of archaeologists who argued that the condemned acres contained Native American artifacts and should not be disturbed. Then Edith offered to deed all of her property to the state, posthumously, if they would cancel the bridge plans. Finally, Edith and Murphy argued that the house was a priceless work of art. Not exactly priceless; she sued for $250,000 in restitution and jawboned the president of the Art Institute to testify on her behalf. All for naught. "The Kendall County jury had no idea what a work of art was," Murphy later commented. Edith received $17,000 for her condemned land, and the bridge was built.

Enter an unlikely savior: Peter Palumbo, a British developer and architecture aficionado, occasionally described as a London playboy. Palumbo happened to be in Chicago visiting Mies, whom he hoped to recruit for a skyscraper project in central London. (Tradition-minded Britons, including Palumbo's former polo teammate Prince Charles, eventually torpedoed the twenty-two-story, modernist Mansion House Square, slated for construction on a plot abutting Sir Christopher Wren's 1679 Church of Saint Stephen Walbrook and Sir Edwin Lutyens's famous 1939 façade for the Midland Bank.) Palumbo says his eye fell upon a small advertisement in that morning's *Chicago Tribune*: " 'For Sale, Farnsworth House, Fox River,' with a phone number underneath—just that—a tiny little box like a visiting card."[4]

Edith now owned sixty acres of land and was selling the house and the property for $250,000.

Palumbo was, arguably, the perfect buyer. The wealthy son of a wealthy property developer, Palumbo said he remembered the Farnsworth House from an architecture lecture at Eton College in 1952, when he was eighteen years old. "I was knocked out by that house," he recalled.[5]

In an interview with British architectural historian Neil Jackson, Palumbo described the house as a "faded beauty":

It had been immensely beautiful and had had the ravages of time and neglect and bitterness applied to it, by her. . . . The western end of the house was completely closed in by mosquito netting. So you came up the steps and through a wire mesh door. . . . There was crazy paving leading up to the house, standard roses growing up on the outside, and motor cars.

The primavera cladding of the service core had been re-peatedly re-veneered, presumably because of water damage. Once a lustrous light brown, it was now "a sort of rusty co-lour, a rusty blackish, reddish colour," Palumbo reported. "The sink was piled high with filthy dishes which obviously hadn't been washed for a day or two or three. It was unkempt and it was dirty. It wasn't pleasant."

"I think old Edith was a very difficult character," Pa-lumbo told Jackson. "The furniture was really a deliberate affront to Mies, doing deliberately what she thought would hurt him most."

Sensing a possible buyer, Edith turned on the charm and invited Palumbo to stay for dinner. "We had a very good chat," he reported, "and she was a very impressive lady." They agreed on the outlines of a deal, and by 1971 Edith had moved to the outskirts of Florence, Italy, and Palumbo owned the house. At the time, Great Britain was enforcing baroque currency-export restrictions, so no one ever ascer-tained exactly how much Palumbo paid. Probably less than Edith's $250,000 asking price and more than the $120,000 sale price officially reported.

Palumbo owned the Farnsworth House for more than thirty years and was an attentive, affectionate, and, most im-portant, affluent owner. He made no pretense of living full-time in the house. London was his primary residence, and in the mid-1980s he added another architectural gem to his portfolio: Kentuck Knob, a Frank Lloyd Wright home in southwestern Pennsylvania. (Palumbo also purchased and restored Le Corbusier's Maisons Jaoul outside of Paris, in 1990, and owned an apartment at Mies's signature 860/880

Lake Shore Drive complex.) Palumbo kept a second home in Plano, a tasteful nineteenth-century Italianate Victorian house, where his family generally overnighted when visiting the Farnsworth House.

"The house needed a lot of TLC," Palumbo recalled in a 2017 interview.

> She was an expensive lady to maintain. It needed new wiring, new drapes, repainting, and the other things. I got rid of the oil fired heating system because it was so dirty, it used to blow oily dirt all over the place. I had electric heat installed instead. The roof was leaking and had to be replaced. All this took some years. Gradually the house responded and it looked beautiful again.

Collaborating on the décor with Mies's grandson, Dirk Lohan, Palumbo furnished the house primarily with Mies-designed furniture, for example, flat-bar steel-frame Brno chairs and Mies's signature glass-and-steel X-framed coffee table. He also included leather-and-steel ottomans originally designed for the 1929 Barcelona Pavilion. Outside, Palumbo hired the landscape architect Lanning Roper to plant a separate orchard and birch grove. Roper also created the setting for a well-stocked sculpture park that featured contemporary works by Henry Moore, Andy Goldsworthy (a site-specific work called *Floodstones*), Alexander Calder, Claes Oldenburg, and others.

During a 1999 visit, *New York Times* architecture writer David Dunlap, the son of Mies's associate William Dunlap, saw more mundane evidence of normal living, for instance, a discreet air-conditioning system to mitigate the worst of the summer heat. Other *objets de vie normale*: a brown leather couch, an antique maple rocking chair, wine bottles on the kitchen counter, family pictures, a Trimline telephone, and neckties hanging inside the teak wardrobe. Palumbo told Dunlap that he kept house more ascetically during his first years of ownership, but that created a problem: "It was becoming a shrine," according to Palumbo. "It was beginning to take itself too seriously. I thought it needed livening up."[6]

Palumbo recalled living in the house as "a wonderful experience."

> The big black sugar maple tree, which no longer exists, was over two hundred years old and used to bend over and sort of caress the house. The leaves and branches used to scratch against the window panes and make patterns on the drapes; it was incredibly serene. It was quite a wonderful place, when it rained or when there was an electric storm it became very exciting. It was like being inside a lotus flower—you could sit in a thunderstorm and never get wet.
>
> It was a therapy in itself to live there. You never quite knew when you pulled back the drapes what you'd find there, or who you'd find there. On one occasion, I found people sitting in a circle on the lower deck of the staircase, in a very reverential way, worshipping at the shrine of Mies.
>
> That was fine, they didn't take any note of me, they didn't do any harm they were just worshippers. It

was really a perfect weekend house for a bachelor though it responded perfectly well to me and the children. I think they enjoyed the austerity, laying out sleeping bags on the floor.

Dunlap, whose father installed the mosquito screens for Edith's west-facing open porch, ended his 1999 appreciation cum travel article with the advice: "Reservations are advised, as is mosquito repellent."

The late architecture critic Martin Pawley described overnighting on the Fox River during Palumbo's tenure. Pawley noticed some Klees hanging inside the bathroom, which had a sign reminding guests to leave the door open, so that condensation wouldn't damage the art. One morning, "the Fox River had overflowed its banks, as it did annually, and . . . he was greeted by the sight of the butler bringing breakfast from the nearby main house (where Palumbo stayed) in a canoe. On that occasion, the terrace did double duty as a boat dock."[7]

Palumbo had his own encounters with the elements. In 1996, the Fox River rose eleven feet, sending a five-foot wall of water rushing through the Farnsworth House. "I remember my wife saying to me, 'Thank God we weren't there, it would have been very interesting.'" Too interesting by half, perhaps:

The force of the water lifted up a very, very heavy teak bed, and spun it around the house. If we had been asleep in the bed, we would have been going round and round near the ceiling. We were very lucky, one of the big glass panels broke and let the water out. If it hadn't, I think the water would have lifted the whole house and sent it downstream—the pressure was enormous. It picked up that teak wardrobe like a feather, and sent it swirling around the room. I lost a bit of stuff, but it could have been worse.

The press gleefully reported that an Andy Warhol silk screen portrait of Elizabeth Taylor was spotted floating downstream to LaSalle County, never to be seen again. "The house could have become a houseboat," Palumbo said. "It could have sailed away down the Fox River. We have to be grateful for the small mercies. It's better to lose an Andy Warhol than to lose a house."

Not for nothing did Mies sink his four-foot-square, two-feet-thick concrete footings four feet below the ground. (One foot below grade, the eight steel columns were bolted to a shaft that rose off the concrete pads.)

In 2000, Palumbo decided to sell the property, precipitating a crisis among architects and preservationists. The state of Illinois initially committed $7.5 million toward the purchase, then backed out after the election of a new governor. Prominent Chicagoans mobilized by arts patron John Bryan tried to buy the house on behalf of the National Trust for Historic Preservation but could not back Palumbo off his $10 million asking price. In 2003, Palumbo said he would auction the house at Sotheby's in New York later that year. Fearing that the house might pass into the hands of an architectural philistine, Mies's friend and patron Phyllis Lambert told *The New York Times*, "I cannot believe that Chicago cannot organize itself to save one of the greatest houses that's ever been. . . . It's putting civilization on the block."

After seven minutes of tense telephone bidding against an unidentified rival, Bryan and the Chicagoans prevailed, and the Farnsworth House became the property of the National Trust for Historic Preservation, for $6.7 million. The house had accrued value like the work of art that it is. The $74,000 construction cost in 1951 would have been $527,000 in 2003, but it sold for more than ten times that amount, thanks in part to Palumbo's stewardship.

"It was one of the proudest moments of my tenure," said Richard Moe, the trust's chairman in 2003. "To have lost it would be unthinkable." But like the other owners, the trust, which opens the house for visitors in collaboration with Illinois's Landmarks Preservation Council, learned that owning the Farnsworth House is a mixed blessing. "We had a three- or four-hundred-year flood very early in the game," Moe said. "We took up the drapes, we lifted everything off the floor, we took the woodwork off the paneling, we opened the doors, so we avoided permanent damage, but there was a lot of cleanup to do. That happened several times early on."

In a 1986 interview for the Canadian Centre for Architecture, Myron Goldsmith offered some second thoughts about the siting of the house:

> Certainly, had we been a little smarter, had I been smarter, because it was finally my responsibility, we could have set it above the highest flood, but there was a little casualness in this because the highest flood was just barely within memory of the old-timers around

there and that it was relatively sudden, comparatively
rare. But if you knew then what we know now, anything is possible.

As part of a $10 million renovation plan, the trust intends
to install hydraulic jacks under the house, to raise it several
feet in the event of a serious flood. Asked to describe the
physical condition of the Farnsworth House, executive director Scott Mehaffey, who also teaches landscape architecture at IIT, replied, "I'd give it an eight." The successive
floods have taken their toll, and some of the outdoor travertine has suffered water and ice damage. Only five of Mies's
original seventeen windowpanes remain in place, in part due
to corrosion of their steel frames, and partly due to normal
aging. Palumbo's rehab work is now over forty years old,
and the house itself is pushing seventy. "What in this world
that is seventy years old doesn't need a little work?" Mehaffey asks.

A capital campaign is on the horizon. Even though the
site has a modest $500,000 annual budget, one-third of that
still comes from the National Trust for Historic Preservation. In a better world, the Farnsworth House would have an
endowment and be able to pay its operating costs. That day
may come, but it is not here yet. The house is open only from
April 1 until December 1 and, at an hour's drive from Chicago, lies well off the better-traveled tourist itineraries. It attracts around ten thousand paying visitors each year, about
one-third of them from overseas, which helps the revenue
stream.

The trust earns some extra cash from programming at the

Farnsworth House, including such events as "Architecture of Asana: Yoga at the Farnsworth House," and "Fox River Flow: Tai Chi at the Farnsworth House."

"There's a Zen feeling there," says trust senior vice president Katherine Malone-France, adding that nighttime events are also popular. "There is no light pollution; you can see every single star." Mindfulness programs use the Farnsworth, and so do bicycle clubs. The house is available for rent, in certain circumstances. Brad Pitt, who has an amateur interest in architecture, filmed a commercial for Japanese blue jean maker Edwin 503 at the house, which also provided a backdrop for country singer Kenny Chesney's 2007 music video "Don't Blink."

The trust often invites artists to "respond" to the house, with varied results. Site-specific chamber music and dance movements have been created for the Farnsworth. You can view Iñigo Manglano-Ovalle's intriguing 1999 video lagniappe "The Kiss" on YouTube. In 2014, the Chicago-based light artists Luftwerk (Petra Bachmaier and Sean Gallero), who had previously created a startling light installation for the seventy-fifth anniversary of Frank Lloyd Wright's Fallingwater, memorably illuminated the Farnsworth House. Using "projection mapping" technology, they bathed the house "in computer-controlled lights in intricate sequences and patterns," according to an admiring *Chicago Reader* reviewer.[8]

Architect Werner Buch, who studied with Mies, would approve of today's cultural programming along the Fox River. "This whole grouping, from the [Barcelona] Pavilion to the Farnsworth House, mediates a new and magical world of space and poetry," he told an interviewer in 1989, at his home in Darmstadt, Germany. "I repeat, magic and poetry! Whoever spoke of Mies as poetry? Usually modern architecture is perceived as cold, boxy, bare-assed, sober, emotionless! But Mies has a way of making a plan that renders architecture poetic."[9]

The producers of *Batman v. Superman: Dawn of Justice* had hoped to use the Farnsworth House as Bruce Wayne's residence, but it lacked a key component: a basement, or underground floor for the Batmobile and other Batcave necessities. In the end they built a near-exact replica of the Farnsworth alongside a lake in rural Michigan, which served double duty in the sequel *Justice League*. Many Miesian details are in evidence, particularly the famous furniture, including the Barcelona X coffee table and Brno chairs from the Tugendhat House. Batman is a darker figure than Edith Farnsworth, so the house is slate gray, not white, and some of the window mullions are painted black. "[Set designer] Patrick Tatopoulos designed Bruce Wayne's house and had it built specifically for filming in order to fit the character of Bruce Wayne—darker, isolated, mysterious, and decidedly masculine in character," according to the Film and Furniture website.

The National Trust also manages Philip Johnson's Glass House in New Canaan, which presents quite a different story. Its attendance is similar to that of the Farnsworth, but New Canaan has become so densely populated that the town and the Trust have agreed to limit the number of visitors. Thanks to cash and art donations by Johnson and his partner David Whitney, the Glass House has a $19 million endowment, compared with the Farnsworth's $835,000. "There was some very smart estate planning by Johnson and Whitney," says Malone-France. "The two houses are resourced in very different ways."

Because of its proximity to New York City, and because Johnson erected other intriguing buildings, including art and sculpture galleries, on his forty-nine-acre property, the Glass House exudes a cosmopolitanism that would be difficult to re-create in Kendall County. Its annual fund-raising Summer Party, loosely inspired by a legendary "country happening" that Johnson hosted in 1967 to raise money for the Merce Cunningham dance troupe (John Cage performed, as did the Velvet Underground; the police came; you had to be there), attracts glamorous sponsors (Taittinger champagne, Swarovski, Tesla) and hipster luminaries of all generations.

"It's one art event where you don't have to wear black," a reveler wearing cherry-red shorts and baby blue shoes explained to a *Wall Street Journal* reporter.[10] Ticket levels range from "Premium Table Captain" ($20,000) to $500, and auction items have included artworks by Josef Albers and Richard Serra, Herb Ritts, and Annie Leibovitz. Plano seems very far away.

The house one now visits in Plano is decorated as Mies intended it to be, with extensive consultation and design work from Mies's grandson, Lohan. Gone are Edith's flowerpots and wicker furniture. Mies's minimalist masterpieces, the Barcelona chairs and the spare dining room table surrounded by MR chairs, again reign supreme. Lohan himself has voiced some doubts about the livability of his grandfather's famous construction:

THE FARNSWORTH HOUSE, DECORATED AS
MIES INTENDED, FACING EAST

[The house] owes its stature as one of the high-
lights of modern architecture to its spiritual rather
than its functional values. The concept, a country retreat from the big city, has been elevated to such a
spiritual abstraction that it demands complete acceptance of its inner logic from the occupant. So unconventional is the house that every move and every
activity in it acquires an aesthetic quality which challenges behavior patterns formed in different surroundings.[11]

The Farnsworth House is not above criticism. Mies's
former student Buch recalled that museum curator John
Zukowsky "asked, 'Tell me, Werner, can you explain to me
why that house was ever built? It is in a hole full of mosqui-

toes, which at times fills up with flood water from the Fox River.'" Buch continued: "In the summer of 1978, my wife and I visited the house with [Mies associate] George Danforth and returned that evening completely covered with mosquito bites. Yet we still sit here today with our photos, completely transfixed by memories of that beautiful day."

Following a 2016 visit to Plano, the Swiss architect Jacques Herzog delivered a withering critique of the house in a staged exchange with the then dean of IIT, Wiel Arets.

Herzog situated the house in the tradition of pavilions or follies planted in parks:

> As such, it's an interesting and instructive statement, containing a lot of things for which Mies became famous . . . but as a house for a woman living here in the wilds, in a wild and isolated piece of nature, it's kind of absurd. . . . It's a home for ghosts.

In the videotaped interview, Herzog waves his hand dismissively at the minimalist fireplace that Edith complained about.

> To me, this is not a fireplace. What does this have to do with fire? Fire would have been a friend of the person living here, but the way this [hearth] is half open like a lavabo or a sink . . . this is not what I expect for such an iconic building. . . . Maybe he was just not that interested in that part, the way it disappears here on the side.

Herzog then points to the broad façades of primavera paneling ("rather generic") flanking the travertine fireplace: "What is this space? The fireplace should be a chapel of warmth. . . . I think this is a disaster." Herzog equally dislikes Mies's beloved travertine: "I especially criticize the travertine floor. I don't know exactly why he uses travertine, it's just a cladding, it's like wallpaper."

"You cannot use this house except as a museum," Herzog says, sitting inside a house that has indeed become a museum. "It's so expensive to maintain; it's like a patient in the hospital, in the emergency clinic."

The Farnsworth House has progeny, perhaps too many to name. Pierre Koenig's much-photographed-and-filmed Stahl House, cantilevered over the Los Angeles skyline, is

CRAIG ELLWOOD'S ROSEN HOUSE, 1961

certainly one. Craig Ellwood's 1961 Rosen House in Brentwood, pictured on the previous page, looks like actionable plagiarism, even more egregious than Johnson's Glass House.

"Those floating steps are really fantastic and so good you can't begrudge another architect using them," says David Holowka, who compiled a list of Farnsworth influences. "They seem to invite you to float up them." Holowka points out that Mies himself used the staircase a second time, at Crown Hall on the IIT campus. But if architectural self-plagiarism were a crime, Frank Lloyd Wright would have spent his life in jail.

Holowka adds Australian Pritzker Prize winner Glenn Murcutt to the list of Farnsworth disciples. Murcutt, who has a reputation as a light-on-the-earth, environmentally friendly builder, said he first learned about the Farnsworth House from his father, a mineral prospector:

My father saw an article about the Farnsworth House. Amongst many issues it discussed the positive issue of ventilation for a single-depth-room house. Once a building is planned for two rooms deep you created ventilation problems, so to make buildings as thin as possible, they would breathe properly. The Farnsworth House did that only in part—it was in a way a roomless house. It was a house that was above the ground, not dissimilar in some ways to houses which Dad had lived in, in Papua New Guinea.

And he said of the Farnsworth House that it was

not only one of the most interesting 20th century
houses, he felt no one could live in it, and therefore [a]
good theoretical exercise. He got me to read this
damned article three or four times—I don't recall how
many—until I could answer every question he posed
to me about that house. I was only thirteen years old
and hadn't shown any signs of interest in architecture.[12]

A few years ago, *The Wall Street Journal*'s "Mansions"
section, a weekly showcase of the architectural lusts of the
upper reaches of America's 1 percent, published a feature
about Florida homes. A Christie's real estate broker, Nelson
Gonzalez, told the newspaper that Miami Beach buyers had
started demolishing the once-popular old Mediterranean-
style houses that lined the city's waterways. "Now, most
buyers want new, modern, lots of glass, lots of light," Gonzalez said.

Edith Farnsworth might counsel: Be careful what you
wish for.

CHAPTER 14

"SHE THEN ABANDONED EVERYTHING FOR POETRY AND ITALY."

N 1959, THE LITERARY MAGAZINE *TRIQUARTERLY* PUBLISHED two poems by Dr. Edith Farnsworth. Soon after, the editors sent an emissary to her office, "to ask her what might be said about poetry by a person who had recently published in a learned journal an article with the formidable title 'The Effect of Hypophysectomy and Adrenalectomy in Nucleoside-Induced Nephrosis in the Rat,'" which appeared in the *Proceedings of the Society for Experimental Biology and Medicine* that fall. The visit generated a brief essay by Edith on the state of contemporary poetry, and eleven new poems.[1]

Edith's short, erudite essay, "The Poet and the Leopards" (she quotes Rilke in the original German, untranslated, as well as Alfred North Whitehead), situates her work in the twentieth century's conventional, lyric tradition. "Human beings have always needed to transcend their immediate experience," she wrote. "But how is the transcending to be done?" She bemoaned "the defection of many of the great themes formerly dependable for a poetic habitat": nature, love, and God. For someone who would later mock Mies's penchant for obscurantist woolgathering, Dr. Farnsworth was no stranger to airy prose:

> When I first went to Germany in 1930, I was struck by the devotion, dogmatic as it was, with which every right-thinking German regarded the *Hochgebirge*. If you didn't climb the mountains on the weekends, you were not the right kind of person. You climbed, you suffered, and you conquered, and it made a hero out of you. You transcended. But now something has happened to nature.

Some poets, she thought, are writing for "shock value and mass communications"—Allen Ginsberg had published *Howl* just two years before—but not Edith. "The purpose of poetry at this time rather than in more culturally stable times, is unquestionably the constant redefinition of beauty and the inspiration of the age." Farnsworth, midwife to an innovative architectural masterpiece, was a cultural conservative where poetry was concerned. Her poems waxed traditional, generally ruminating on nature.

Here is an excerpt from "The Quality Is Lent," an undated poem that seems to have been written about the Plano house:

Silence on mirrored interface
Reflects the limpid notes
Resounds in sun-lit glade

Within these luminous walls
Secluded by reflection
Windowed by solitary calls

—Essences by image heightened,
Image by undulation lightened—
Random light and music play,
Until the end of day.

Or this poem, "Artifact," almost certainly about the famous glass house:

The dawn was close this morning when I woke
To hear some flying creature strike the pane
Of glass beside my bed—strike and flutter
For a moment, strike and beat
Bewildered wings upon the glass.
. . .

The unseen wings are slipping down the pane;
The splintered feathers agonize in vain.
The moments pass
And in the grass
Below, there lies
My hope, and dies.

Edith published several more poems in *TriQuarterly* over the next few years, including what reads like a puckish *réplique* to a long, opaque Wallace Stevens verse, "Extracts of Addresses to the Academy of Fine Ideas." Farnsworth's quick jab was entitled "The Egg-plant of a Prince, Thank You, Mr. Stevens."

Stevens wrote:

> That evil, made magic
> becomes the same as the fruit
> Of an emperor, the egg-plant of a prince.

Prompting Edith's equally-difficult-to-understand, Stevens-esque reply:

> Rotunda his egg-plant his leptoderm
> Mahogany brown to lavender
> By no means a pineapple.

EDITH'S NEXT CAREER WOULD not be as a poet, but as a translator of poetry, which she began working on as she wound down her hospital commitments. Between 1968 and 1971, several events occurred more or less simultaneously: Edith retired from medicine, and in 1969, signed a purchase and sale agreement with Palumbo for the Fox River house. Because of Britain's currency controls, Palumbo had trouble paying Edith, and the sale actually fell through once before the two of them figured out a settlement plan. At the end of the decade, Edith was decamping from the Plano house and packing up her belongings in her Lake Shore Drive apartment.

She did not leave Passavant and the Northwestern University Medical School on good terms. Never one to suffer fools gladly, she occasionally locked horns with the male grandees who ruled the postwar medical world. Her friend James Gerard recalled an incident when Chicago's wealthy McCormick family reached out to Dr. Farnsworth for help:

> Their son had a serious auto accident outside Buffalo (on his way back to Chicago from school) with serious brain damage. (Turned out later to be fatal.) They had a plane waiting at Midway airport and asked Edie who she could recommend to send out to examine the boy. She recommended [Loyal] Davis and called him and asked if he would go.

Davis was a medical legend, nationally renowned for his brilliance in neurosurgery and locally famous as an egomaniac and a ghoul. His former students described him as "not a nice man to work with or for," "a martinet both inside and outside the operating room," and a "tyrant" who "kept an enemies list." Davis did not keep his racist views about African Americans or his misogynous disdain of women in medicine to himself. Each entering class at Northwestern Medical School met with Dr. Davis and encountered his ideology. "He ended the meeting by admonishing the class that if anyone favored socialized medicine they should withdraw immediately," one future doctor recalled.[2]

Aloof and impersonable, Davis took a liking to the young actor who married his stepdaughter, Nancy. It is said that Dr. Davis's reactionary views influenced Ronald Reagan's political metamorphosis from a liberal Democrat to a conservative Republican. Davis was one of the most influential doctors at Passavant Hospital, and not the kind of colleague whom Edith Farnsworth would befriend.

Gerard's story resumes:

> Davis refused (Clearly not a natural born fundraiser) and she got [Dr. Eric] Oldberg (Presbyterian Hospital) to go instead. "I'll never refer another patient to that man again," was her only comment. As you can see, Edie could weave a tale. Enhanced by her dramatic way with a cigarette.[3]

Farnsworth had an unrelated dispute with Passavant administrators that ended her career in medicine. In 1966, a medical board summoned her to explain her management of a case. Details are scanty. The questions arose not from the patient, who had no complaints, but from a colleague or colleagues. Edith appeared before the board, and then seems to have disappeared from Passavant. A memo recorded that she had started treating patients at Illinois Masonic Hospital. A different memo stated that she was thinking of suing Passavant, with no further details. By 1968, Edith was on a temporary "leave of absence," and she asked her colleagues for emeritus status at Passavant and at Northwestern Medical School. They instead proposed making her leave of absence permanent, but not without considerable hand-wringing.

A July 1969 letter between Passavant administrators noted, "Incidentally, the word is that she is worth a fortune. Are we in her will?" A month later, a different doctor offered a bearish assessment: "[Edith Farnsworth] has no family. She lives on Lake Shore Drive and one or two of the Attending Staff members here have indicated at one time or another that she is worth a considerable sum of money." However, given the murky contretemps between Edith and her colleagues, this doctor concluded that "it would be very unusual if we were in Dr. Farnsworth's will."[4] They weren't.

Edith had stopped communicating with Passavant because she was in the process of moving to Italy. Her former French student Corey Mundwiler remembers helping her pack up Chinese jade sculptures and bronze tablets, which she donated to Chicago's Art Institute. The institute still has about a dozen of her bequests, mostly ancient Chinese art objects, as well as two photographs by her friend Harry Callahan. The institute regifted her two sixteenth-century Chinese lion marble sculptures (the misnamed "foo dogs") to the University of Chicago, where they now stand guard outside the university's Cochrane-Woods Art Center.

Edith had decided to move to Italy, where, as a young woman, she had lived for almost two years while studying violin with Corti in Rome. She began house hunting near Florence, and fell in with a top-drawer literary crowd, including the poet, journalist, and critic Eugenio Montale, a future Nobel Prize winner; poets Salvatore Quasimodo and Albino Pierro; their friends, the writer Antonio Pizzuto and the philologist Gianfranco Contini and his wife, Margaret. Elena Croce, the daughter of philosopher Benedetto Croce,

MARBLE LIONS STAND GUARD AT THE WEST END
OF EDITH'S TERRACE.

had written to Montale, suggesting he meet this "very intelligent woman ('this is saying a lot, because it's not something that you find every day')," who "speaks and writes in excellent New England English, and her traditions fascinate me." Croce told Montale that Edith had quit medicine "for reasons of principle" and decided to devote herself to Italian literature.[5]

"Attracted by Italy," according to the Italian critic Giorgio Delia, "chasing the myth (very dear to the Anglo-American culture) of Florence, perennial cradle of the Renaissance, she settled there, in the hope, perhaps in the illusion, of constituting or of becoming part of a coterie of writers and intellectuals."[6]

By the time Edith caught up with the seventy-two-year-old Montale, he was a famous poet entering his twilight years. Contemporary translator Jonathan Galassi called the older Montale a "dry, wry, witty, often acerbic epigrammist" whose later work was "largely an ironic commentary on what came before, the *retrobottega,* or back of the shop, as he called it."[7]

"The front of the shop," Galassi explains, "were the great lyric poems that had made him arguably the greatest and most renowned Italian poet of the century."

Montale had begun collecting honorary degrees from major universities (Milan, Cambridge, Basel), and a presidential appointment as "senator for life" allowed him to stop working as a critic and editor at the Milanese newspaper *Corriere della Sera.* Shuttling between her old home and what was to become her new home, Edith started translating Montale's poetry, and was clearly quite smitten by the gentlemanly poet and scholar (Montale had been director of Florence's famous Gabinetto Vieusseux library before World War II) who was just a few years older than she.

Before leaving Chicago, Farnsworth sought out publisher Henry Regnery—or he her; we have only her reference to "the day when we met at luncheon at the Art Institute (and how beautifully you changed my life!)"[8]—and talked her way into a loosely defined assignment as a freelance literary scout, translator, and entrepreneur for the small Chicago house.

The few surviving letters between Farnsworth and Regnery mostly concern poetry, for example, "Elena Croce called this morning to say that she has decided to write to Montale to urge him to give his benediction to my translations. I don't know whether he has any power of veto but in any case I'd like his blessing." Out of nowhere in 1969 she pitched a book on progressive Czech economist Dr. Ota Sik, one of the luminaries of Alexander Dubček's "Prague Spring." There is no record of a reply.

Several of Edith's Plano friends recalled her tapping away at Montale translations on her green Olivetti, and they likewise remembered her obvious infatuation with him. "I think she was hoping that she and Montale would become an item," Ellyn Kivitts remembered.[9] Parkie Emmons recalled Edith stopping over at her house one day to sip vermouth before lunch and chat about Montale. Emmons said Edith showed her a Montale poem about a house on a river, and claimed that he had written it for her. "He's in love with me, can't you see that?" Edith insisted. "I couldn't see it at all," Emmons later commented.[10]

Farnsworth told a story about inviting Montale to her rented villa in Fiesole, outside of Florence, for the weekend, and its disappointing result. "He came with his housekeeper and all he wanted to do was sit and watch TV," Emmons recalled. "Edith was most put out." A Farnsworth-Montale romance was probably not in the cards. Montale was a widower who had entrusted himself to the care of his housekeeper, and furthermore he blew hot and cold about his feelings for Edith.

Writing to the philologist Contini, Montale complained that "Farnsworth is too remote and rants too much, with much derision (she thinks she is a great violinist)." But in several letters to her, he expressed different emotions: "I always think of you with great affection and nostalgia for Carrot Street [Edith lived on Via Carota] and its dogs and Mugginese hens"; or "I just want to tell you that I CARE DEEPLY FOR YOU and that I am so grateful that you exist and continue (I hope) to live." They read like letters between friends. He discussed the vicissitudes of old age, and in 1975, he groused to her about his freshly awarded Nobel: "It no longer means anything." He told her that he dreaded the trip to Stockholm.

Not for the first time, Edith had feelings for an accomplished, worldly, European man. "Perhaps you are wondering about the adorable Montale," she wrote to her sister, Marion, in 1970. "The days working with him were absolutely lovely, and we continue to exchange poems. Imagine meeting your soul mate at my age!"

Montale did memorialize one of his stays with Farnsworth in the poem "All'Antella" ("At Antella," the name of the neighborhood in Bagno a Ripoli where Edith finally settled down), published under the English title "In an (Italian) Garden"—Edith's villa had a small, manicured Italian garden. In it, the aging Montale compared himself to a three-legged turtle struggling to navigate the hedges and undergrowth of the garden: "The old turtle walks badly, it pitches / because its back foot has been cut off." The venerable animal may be more than half a century old, Montale wrote, and yet its wounds are fresh: "All its wounds are contemporary."

In her only surviving letter to Montale ("Carissimo Eugenio"), Edith mentioned "the turtle [who] is already awake— he came to me the other day on the path, his head was out, his three reptile feet carrying him along at a surprising speed."[11]

Edith published a collection of Montale poems for Regnery in 1970, and a Quasimodo book the following year. Regnery has a few of Edith's letters in its archives, and they read quite like Edith: erudite, amusing, and forthright:

> Perhaps this would be the moment for me to confide in you the indignation and frustration which I felt when I opened our handsome *Provisional Conclusions,* and discovered that [the copy editor] Mihaly had, I think quite unpardonably, meddled rather freely with the translated text. After going over all the poems with Montale, I went over them again with Mihaly when I was in Chicago in April. If he had suggestions, that was the time to make them, not after the galley proofs and unseen by me. Thus I find rhymes, terminal or internal, destroyed, rhythms fouled, meanings bungled, often in such a way as to destroy the sense. You, dear Henry, who know how I feel about that poetry . . . you will easily understand how this hurts and angers me.

IN APRIL 1970, EDITH left Chicago for good. "I finally boarded the Alitalia jet," she wrote to Marion, "with little Miss Amy sitting as good as gold in her traveling container! A smooth crossing, with Amy sitting beside me, and we landed in Roma in broad warm sunlight."

Although she hadn't yet found a place to permanently live, Edith had shipped a car and a container load of artwork, some furniture, and personal possessions to Livorno, on the

Ligurian coast west of Florence. In this April letter, Edith reported that Palumbo's purchase of the Farnsworth House had fallen through, "as the dollar premium for Anglo-American transactions rose to 52%." She mentioned that the state entertained ideas of buying the house, "but they backed down on the Jewel of the Occident."

In her letters, she evinced mixed feelings about Palumbo, as she did about everyone. "I couldn't get rid of the nagging fear that I might be dealing with some high class aristocratic con man," she confided to her sister, "even if he is the polo partner of the Prince Consort . . . [but] Peter is really a charming person, and it will be great fun to see him."[12] In her next letter to Marion, there is news:

> The Plano property has been sold, and I am buying a most beautiful and ancient "casa canonica" up in the hills about 7 km. from the center of Florence.
>
> And here, let me assure you, that there is no question of letting nature in. Nature is definitely outside, in the form of a beautiful view, a large, sloping Italian garden, a "Pratone" and two "boschetti" [groves], plus a number of acres of olives and vines.

The seller was Francesco Carnelutti, a prominent Venetian criminal lawyer who seemed anxious to unload the massive villa—two stories surrounding a courtyard, with a three-story watchtower looming over the Tuscan hilltop. "Not only did he settle all the difficulties so that I can have it for a price well under that which I am getting for the Plano property," she wrote, but he is leaving me a great deal of furniture: dozens of sofas, beds, chairs, a few massive sacristy pieces, the dining room furniture, all the curtains and a flock of lamps. I went up to the villa the other day while he was on a brief visit to Firenze, and we went over the furniture situation.

"Do you like that chest? Do you want that table? Shall I leave the beds? What in the world will you do if I take away all the rugs?" To which I could only say, "Dearest, don't take them all away! I don't need so many, but a few would help."

Edith was clearly ecstatic in her new home, which would be furnished a long way from Barcelona Pavilion chic. "Any ideas of decorating I had acquired have been changed," she wrote her sister. Her new furnishings?

Red satin sofas, Venetian Baroque figures with gilded skirts holding up lamps, mailed arms gripping other lights, massive carved dark wood. I will flourish unrestrained in my ecclesiastical rooms. Two winter parlors and two summer ones, canopied beds. Heavens, you should see!

With ample space, Edith entertained a steady stream of visitors, among them Italian literati, old pals from Chicago, and also Palumbo, who tended to be in the neighborhood. "I went to see her once in Florence, in 1972," Palumbo recalled.

EDITH'S VILLA TODAY

I was there for the Henry Moore retrospective and decided to kill two birds with one stone.

I apologized to Mies when I told him I was going to see her, and all he said was, "Good luck." He never really said anything critical about her, although she started saying rather critical things about him. That stopped because I intervened a little bit. It was clear that the damage had been done.

I had dinner with her in her rather gloomy home overlooking Florence. It was a bit boring, she made me listen while we sat in these immensely high-backed and very uncomfortable chairs while she recited her translation of Montale endlessly. All I wanted was to get back to Henry Moore and the Villa Belvedere and report how the day had gone. I was being read to like a child.

I was treated to this seminar on Montale which I didn't fully understand—it was an interminable thing. Outwardly I appeared interested and unperturbed. She was certainly a very clever person, although I have no idea how well she translated him into English. I was glad to get away, poor old thing. I think she was quite a remote person when she went there.

Edith also entertained *Social Register* companions from Chicago. Her old friend Betsy Straus was much more accommodating than Palumbo about Poetry Nights, Edith reported: "She listened devotedly to every evening of poetry, either original or translated from my Italian poets of the 20th century."

Parkie Emmons visited Bagno and later recalled the villa's frescoed chapel and its extensive olive groves and vineyard. A butler named Vittorio served at meals, wearing white gloves. "Edith really lived in style," Emmons later told an interviewer.

Emmons's daughter Susan also found her way to the Florentine foothills. "I remember that beautiful villa up on the hillside," she said. "It was terraced with olive trees, and she had a pet tortoise rambling around the garden. She had staff there, it was quite lovely." The tortoise—probably *"la vecchia tartaruga"* celebrated in Montale's poem—was named Silvio, Edith wrote to a friend. "Silvio was believed to be a girl, hence Silvia, but more sophisticated friends set me straight and I hastened to change the name to conform."[13]

The sharp-tongued Edith of Chicago and Plano had not mellowed, her visitors recall. One received a dressing-down for confusing a Florentine church dome with a cupola. Mrs. Emmons remembers Edith as being very formal. "She would have commented if my daughter had not sent a thank-you note," she said. "Edith was very particular about such things."

Corey Mundwiler, who had been one of Edith's young French tutees back in Plano, also visited. He was in graduate school in London in 1973 and had contacted her about visiting with his girlfriend.

It was amazing. She lived in this fifteenth century palazzo. She was very much the landlady at the manor. It was the first time we had been served luncheon by white gloved servants; Vittorio the butler came out in a white jacket and presented lunch out in the garden. There was a cook, and an amazing view of the city.

Mundwiler remembered that Edith's villa had a deep well and controlled the water supply for the surrounding countryside. "She was quite paranoid that the Italian Communists were trying to steal her water supply. She thought the American government was full of Communists, too." Edith explained her attempts to assuage the local Reds in a letter to Marion:

I have rather a good system of neighborhood share-cropping which allows me to have what I can use of oil and wine, to keep the property up, thus satisfying the Communist local government and keeping our hill happy. The neighbors are erstwhile peasants and we have a very good relationship. I give them sixty per cent instead of fifty per cent of the produce, and they do lots of little things like dragging out the lemon trees in the spring and putting them back in the fall. . . .

So far, I have given all of them water from my big well, but now they say they wish to share the expense, and, given the cost of electricity, I'm going to let them do so.

Approaching her seventy-fifth year, alone in a drafty villa in a foreign country, Edith did wax paranoid. Vittorio, the butler/factotum, suddenly became impossible. "I nearly go mad with the arterio-sclerotic perversity of Vittorio, who is a dogmatic and manages to frustrate my every hope," she complained to Marion in 1973. Two years later, she reported that her neighbors Dr. and Mrs. Antonini had been selling Vittorio a hundred liters of wine at forty cents a liter. "Since Vittorio is already a deteriorated paranoid schizophrenic stewed in alcohol, I did not take their sub-rosa gesture as the utmost in neighborliness from a colleague."[14] She fired Vittorio soon after.

Two years later, writing to her sister, Marion, Edith woolgathered on the death of civilization:

Whoever would have thought that our generation would witness the crack-up of western civilization to the extent that we now see it! Blessed be the one who goes first, early and not late—the rest of us are like decrepit animals in a jungle!"[15]

"The world is a jungle," Edith cautioned her sister, "and it doesn't do to forget it."

Suffering from osteoporosis, she freely confessed to feelings of decrepitude. "I have been laid up for a number of weeks," she wrote in 1975.

> And am only now getting about a bit. I haven't tried the stairs as yet, but expect to take a few tomorrow. It started with a marked diminution of general strength, which went on to a diffuse inflammation of the left ankle which made it impossible for me to bear any weight on that side. . . . Now I can manage a bit on only one crutch."

How happy she was is anyone's guess. In a letter to Antonio Pizzuto, she talked about "my tired and depressed life."

"I drag myself through the days," she wrote to Montale, "and I abandon myself with relief, even with joy, at night, with the view of the dark hills and the sound of the owls."

Literary friends Montale and Pierro popped in occasionally. She mentioned that Montale had visited to discuss her translation of his 1971 collection *Satura*. "It seemed to me he was happy," Edith reported. "But I have the impression that it will never be published in America." She was right; it would not be published in English in either of their lifetimes. Nor would her comprehensive volume of Giacomo Leopardi translations, nor a volume of her own poems that she had been working on for years.

She described Pierro as "a very strange writer from the remote district of Tursi." Pierro wrote in an archaic Lucanian dialect, "a language outside the course of history, as suitable for speaking to the dead as to the living," according to the critic J. E. Everson. Edith wondered out loud "whether a poet who chooses to write his tales or verses in Lucanian dialect cares very much whether he comes to be read or not."

Pierro came to be read in Edith's translation. In 1976, she published *A Beautiful Story,* a short collection of Pierro's Lucanian poems, with the Milan publishing house All'Insegna del Pesce d'Oro (At the Sign of the Golden Fish). A friend named Felicita Audisio recalled Edith waiting "for the translation of Pierro's poems."

> And she invited me to Antella on the pretext of seeking comfort for her linguistic choices, but in fact for the pleasure to be together, to chat about her translations, to sip a Martini waiting for the sunset in the Italian garden of her villa. She really was an extraordinary woman.

The previous year, Edith reported a visit from John Maxon, vice president in charge of collections at the Art Institute of Chicago: "Every topic tended to begin, 'Oh, how about X? Is he still living?'" she wrote.

> But the height of ghoulishness was reached when John said, "Edith, dear, you should appoint a literary

executor," and intimated that he was just the person for the job. It then developed that he wanted to get control of my memoirs, so that he could modify them toward a reconciliation between "a great architect and a great client."

Edith had been working on her memoirs since her arrival in Italy, and her later recollections of Mies were quite unflattering. "She really hated him," her friend James Gerard recalled. Edith remembered her intellectual exchanges with considerable bitterness:

There was a certain metaphysical vein which enhanced the standard topic of Mies himself. I suppose that it was pretty thoroughly bogus in the sense that it represented only an accouterment to his professional personality and not a true inwardness inevitable in the character of the medieval peasant as I had chosen to see it. . . .

In any case, [his life] was interesting to talk about, or at least to hear Mies talk about it, since nobody among the disciples was disposed to compete with those ponderous reminiscences, whether of modules and dimensions, or of Behrens, van de Velde, van Doesburg, Lilly Reich, the Mayor of Dessau and the last days of the Bauhaus.

Edith recalled being "struck with the force of Mies's preoccupation with death, and it lent a mystic context even to the project of the house by the river, and an undefinable dimension to the personality of Mies." While living in Italy, she spotted a picture of Mies in a London newspaper. It was "the face of a man in the upper eighties, definite and fearful," she wrote.

EDITH FARNSWORTH DIED ON December 4, 1977, at her home, Villa Le Tavernule, outside of Florence. She was seventy-four years old. Gianfranco Contini left an account of her thinly attended funeral, which "was organized by her doctor and neighbor, the gerontologist Francesco Antonini, who had ascertained her death and had had to certify it."

Montale wrote to Contini: "Edith's disappearance grieved me but the fact is that we have seen each other very few times and this deadens the pain. Maybe I am speaking nonsense and I show hardness of heart but at my age nothing remains but to harden."

In an interview some time later, Contini described Edith as "an American woman, who unfortunately died some years ago, who was Montale's best translator, even if no one ever took note." According to Giorgio Delia, Contini, "in declaring Farnsworth's name, specifies that she was 'a great doctor,' that 'she nearly received a Nobel for a clinical discovery, that she then abandoned everything for poetry and Italy,' retreating to a villa in Tuscany."

Edith's brief obituary in the *Chicago Tribune* knew nothing of her poetry, her Italian translations, or her coterie of Florentine intellectuals. The newspaper noted her twenty-seven years of service at Passavant Memorial Hospital and her former ownership of Mies van der Rohe's "world-famous Farnsworth House near Plano . . . a white-painted steel and glass box resting on eight supporting columns."

"Dr. Farnsworth's ashes will be returned to Chicago for interment," the paper reported.

Edith's remains found their final resting place in Chicago's Graceland Cemetery among other members of the extended Brooks family. Her full name was Edith Brooks Farnsworth. Just a few hundred feet away, there is a polished granite headstone marking the grave of Ludwig Mies van der Rohe, 1886–1969.

ACKNOWLEDGMENTS

AM GRATEFUL TO EDWARD WINDHORST, CO-AUTHOR of the University of Chicago Press's definitive biography *Mies van der Rohe,* for his unrelenting, generous assistance in the creation of this book. It was Ed who first drove me to the Farnsworth House in his jazzy red Audi roadster. It was Ed who allowed me to cart the 3,800 pages of the *Van der Rohe v. Farnsworth* trial transcript from his apartment to a downtown Chicago copy shop, and it was Ed and his wife, Carla, who let me spend a week in their Mies-designed apartment at 880 Lake Shore Drive, perhaps the finest address in the city.

This is not the book Ed would have written, but his intelligence and critical input have made it a much better book than it otherwise might have been. He shared many primary sources with me, including but not limited to the many informational interviews he conducted with then-living participants in the Mies-Edith trial. I am deeply grateful.

Ed introduced me to Mies's grandson, the renowned architect Dirk Lohan, who was both courteous and helpful in responding to my various requests.

Few Chicagoans remember Edith well, but fortunately one who does is her nephew, Fairbank Carpenter. Fairbank helped me every way he could, and I am grateful to him for allowing me to quote from his aunt's erudite journal, letters, and groundbreaking translations of Italian poetry.

Corey Mundwiler and Kelly Simms remember Edith as their occasionally captious French teacher in Plano, Illinois, and their recollections enriched this book.

Scott Mehaffey, the executive director of the Farnsworth House, is a promoter and an activist in the best sense of the word, and has yoked together Farnsworthians from all over the world to flesh out a fuller portrait of this intriguing and accomplished woman. Aside from managing the National Trust property in Plano, Scott—and Michelangelo Sabatino, interim dean of the College of Architecture at the Illinois Institute of Technology, Mies's old stomping grounds—have been doing the tough archaeological work of bringing Dr. Farnsworth back to life. *Grazie* also to IIT's Travis Rothe.

At the National Trust for Historic Preservation, I would like to thank Katherine Malone-France, Maurice Parrish, Jennifer Wild-Downing, and Scotty Fleetwood.

Almost all of Edith's writings are at Chicago's Newberry Library, a wonderful place to work that is blessed with a helpful and dedicated staff. I would like to thank D. Bradford

Hunt, Alison Hinderliter, Martha Briggs, Lisa Schoblasky, and Juan Molina Hernández for helping me. Archivist Susan Sacharski at Northwestern Memorial Hospital presides over a trove of documents chronicling Edith's medical career in the Northwestern hospital system. Her help and dedication were invaluable to me.

Paul Galloway, curator of the Museum of Modern Art's extensive and well-catalogued Mies van der Rohe collection, often knew what I needed better than I did. Many thanks.

A small group of Italian scholars have been tending the flame of Edith's poetry translations and chronicling her network of friendships around the Villa Le Tavernule outside Florence. I am grateful to Mario Mignone, director of the Center for Italian Studies at Stony Brook University, for alerting me to the work of Giorgia Delia, an expert on Edith's interactions among the Italian literary elite. Thanks also to Montale expert Jonathan Galassi, who introduced me to Edith's Via Carota neighbor, the unforgettable Thekla Clark.

Edith's former home in Bagno a Ripoli is now a campus of the International School of Florence. Former head Debra Williams allowed me to roam the grounds, in the company of Tanya Bruckner. Thanks also to Patrisha Lauria and to retired teacher Ann Brooks for their help and insights.

Lord Peter Palumbo, Dr. Steven Peitzman, David Dunlap, Mark Lamster, Terence Riley, Richard Press, Christine Cipriani, Carl Alving, Elizabeth Westling, David Holowka, Alice Friedman, Ron Krueck, Richard Moe, Kim Elliman, and Blair Kamin all contributed to my understanding of Edith Farnsworth and of Mies's Fox River masterpiece. Additional thanks to Peter Eisenman, Elizabeth Padjen, Katie

Lansdale, Liz O'Brien, Susan Benjamin, Michael Beam, Markus Placci, and to Kris Wiley and Brian Gramentz of the town of New Ulm, Minnesota.

The MacGillis family of Pittsfield, Massachusetts, and Fratta Todina, in Italy, deserve special thanks for translation assistance. Ingrid translated Mies's daughter's memoir for me, and her daughter Lucy answered my many questions about the Italian language. I am so privileged to have them as friends.

At the Canadian Center for Architecture, I would like to thank Mathieu Pomerleau and Isabelle Huiban. Thanks, too, to Anne Hill Bird, of the Society of Architectural Historians; to Diane Lanigan at Chicago's Graceland Cemetery; Matthew Maschino at Regnery Publishing; Travis Dagenais at Harvard's Graduate School of Design; Carrie Muehle at *Tri-Quarterly* magazine; C. J. Lind at the University of Chicago's Smart Museum of Art; to Marielle Sainvilus and Coleen Mastony at the University of Chicago, and to Teresa Sutter at the Chicago Latin School.

Librarians are the unacknowledged legislators of the universe (though not here!): Heartfelt thanks to Ardys Kozbial at Harvard's Loeb Library, and to her colleague Robert Angilly; to Autumn Mather at the Ryerson & Burnham Libraries in Chicago; the two Aimees—Lind and Calfin—at the Getty Research Library; to Katherine Lattal at Northwestern University's Feinberg School of Medicine; to Nicole Richard, Drawings and Archives Assistant at Columbia University's Avery Architectural & Fine Arts Library; and to Sarah Patton at the Hoover Institution. At the Newton Free Library, Karen Fischer and Jenna Weathers were always ready to help me chase down an elusive book or manuscript. Tom Wolf knows why I am thanking him, too.

It's always nice to have friends to bolster your spirits during a long book project. Mark Feeney, Bill Rawn, and my wife, Kirsten Lundberg, read versions of this manuscript, as did Ed Windhorst. David Warsh, Roger Lowenstein, Paul Brown, David Taylor, Dan Denton, and David Roberts helped see me through. Special thanks to my friend and agent, Michael Carlisle, who found a perfect home for this book at Random House. I am grateful to Renee Loth and Fiona Luis, editors of the Boston Society of Architects' magazine, *ArchitectureBoston,* and to Marjorie Pritchard, op-ed editor of *The Boston Globe,* for getting me started writing about architecture.

Broken Glass became a better book thanks to Random House editors William Murphy, Sam Nicholson, and Caitlin McKenna. Emma Caruso cajoled the manuscript into final form. Barbara Bachman and Anna Bauer created this book's beautiful design. My gratitude, also, to architecture maven/ ace publicist Carrie Neill for tirelessly promoting the book. Thank you also to production editor Nancy Delia, and to my scrupulous and successful copy editor, Michelle Daniel.

NOTES

PROLOGUE: "THIS IS MIES, DARLING."

1. All of Edith Farnsworth's quotes, unless otherwise noted, are taken from her unpublished autobiography in the Edith Farnsworth Papers, 1900–1977, Newberry Library, Chicago.

2. Franz Schulze and Edward Windhorst, *Mies van der Rohe: A Critical Biography*, New and Revised Edition (Chicago: University of Chicago Press, 2012), 49.

3. Katherine Kuh, *My Love Affair with Modern Art* (New York: Arcade Publishing, 2006), 71.

4. *Van der Rohe v. Farnsworth*, van der Rohe deposition, 176.

5. Franz Schulze, "The Farnsworth House," monograph, Lohan Associates, 1997, 6.

6. Schulze and Windhorst, *Mies van der Rohe*, 396.

CHAPTER 1: "I GIVE YOU MY MIES VAN DER ROHE."

1. Schulze and Windhorst, *Mies van der Rohe*, 13.

2. Franz Schulze, *Mies van der Rohe: A Critical Biography* (Chicago: University of Chicago Press, 1985), 80–82.

3. Georgia van der Rohe, *La Donna è Mobile: Mein bedingungsloses Leben* (Berlin: Aufbau Verlag, 2001), 16.

4. Schulze and Windhorst, *Mies van der Rohe*, 36.

5. Ibid., 49.

6.   Ibid., 57.

7.   Marianne Lohan interview with Franz Schulze, November 10, 1981.

8.   Lora Marx interview with Franz Schulze.

9.   Schulze, *Mies van der Rohe*, 71.

10. Fritz Neumeyer, *The Artless Word: Mies van der Rohe on the Building Art* (Cambridge, Mass.: MIT Press, 1991).

11. Philip Johnson interview with Peter Eisenman, July–September 1982, Philip Johnson Papers, Getty Research Institute.

12. Elaine S. Hochman, *Architects of Fortune: Mies van der Rohe and the Third Reich* (New York: Weidenfeld and Nicolson, 1989), 14.

13. Mark Lamster, *The Man in the Glass House: Philip Johnson, Architect of the Modern Century* (New York: Little, Brown, 2018), 179.

14. Martin Filler, "Mies and the Mastodon," *The New Republic*, August 5, 2001.

15. Lohan-Mies interview, MoMA archive, 1968.

16. Hudnut to Conant, September 1936, in Jill Pearlman, *Inventing American Modernism: Joseph Hudnut, Walter Gropius, and the Bauhaus* (Charlottesville: University of Virginia Press, 2007), 67.

17. Ibid., July 21.

18. Phyllis Lambert, ed., *Mies in America* (New York: Harry Abrams, 2001), 134.

19. Ibid., 151.

20. Peter Blake, *The Master Builders* (New York: Knopf, 1960), 214.

21. Hochman, *Architects of Fortune*, 158.

22. Ibid., 306.

23. Georgia van der Rohe, *La Donna è Mobile*, 82.

24. Schulze, *Mies van der Rohe*, 233.

25. Schulze and Windhorst, *Mies van der Rohe*, 244, 385.

26. Schulze, *Mies van der Rohe*, 250.

27. *An Autobiography: Frank Lloyd Wright* (New York: Duell, Sloan and Pearce, 1943), 429.

28. Neumeyer, *Artless Word*, 353.

29. Ibid., 137.

30. William S. Shell, Edward A. Duckett, and Joseph Y. Fujikawa, *Impressions of Mies: An Interview on Mies van der Rohe* (1988), 7.

31. Myron Goldsmith, oral history, Art Institute of Chicago, http://digital-libraries.saic.edu/cdm/ref/collection/caohp/id/4086.   Hereafter cited as "Goldsmith, oral history, AIC."

32. Christian Bjone, *Almost Nothing: 100 Artists Comment on the Work of Mies van der Rohe* (Zurich: Park Books, 2018), 174.

33. Shell, Duckett, and Fujikawa, *Impressions of Mies,* 6.

34. Schulze and Windhorst, *Mies van der Rohe,* 193.

35. Ibid., 191.

CHAPTER 2: "SHE HAD A VERY SHARP TONGUE."

1. Katherine Hathaway to Betsy Warner, June 30, 1942, Schlesinger Library, Radcliffe Institute for Advanced Study, Harvard University.

2. Hathaway papers, SC2, Box 2, Schlesinger Library, Radcliffe Institute for Advanced Study, Harvard University.

3. Letters in Northwestern Medical School archives, November 14, 1937, and October 29, 1937.

4. Ellyn Kivitts, oral history, Farnsworth House, https://farnsworth house.org/oral-histories.

5. Neil and Parkie Emmons, oral history, Farnsworth House, https://farnsworthhouse.org/oral-histories.

CHAPTER 3: "LET THE OUTSIDE IN."

1. *Van der Rohe v. Farnsworth,* transcript, 317.

2. Phyllis Lambert, *Building Seagram* (New Haven, Conn.: Yale University Press, 2013), 103.

3. Trial transcript, 1349.

4. *Fine Homebuilding,* April/May 1988.

5. Shell, Duckett, and Fujikawa, *Impressions of Mies,* 27.

6. Ibid., 26.

7. Alfred Caldwell, oral history, Art Institute of Chicago, http://digital-libraries.saic.edu/cdm/ref/collection/caohp/id/1758.

8. Schulze, *Mies van der Rohe,* 234.

9. Ibid.; Lora Marx interview with Franz Schulze, undated.

10. *The Philip Johnson Tapes: Interviews by Robert A. M. Stern* (New York: Monacelli Press, 2008), 94.

11. Georgia van der Rohe, *La Donna è Mobile,* 140.

12. Ibid.

13. Blake, *Master Builders,* 220.

14. Shell, Duckett, and Fujikawa, *Impressions of Mies,* 5.

15. Stern, *Philip Johnson Tapes,* 139.

16. Schulze, *Mies van der Rohe,* 236.

17. Georgia van der Rohe, *La Donna è Mobile,* 139.

18. Shell, Duckett, and Fujikawa, *Impressions of Mies,* 31.

19. Neumeyer, *Artless Word*, 321.

20. A. James Speyer, "Mies Van Der Rohe," *ArtNews*, September 1947. Edith's authorship emerged on her first day in the witness stand in *Van der Rohe v. Farnsworth*.

21. *Van der Rohe v. Farnsworth*, transcript, 95 actual.

CHAPTER 4: "THE MOST IMPORTANT HOUSE IN THE WORLD"

1. *Van der Rohe v. Farnsworth*, transcript, 1430.

2. *Fine Homebuilding*, April/May 1988, 34.

3. Myron Goldsmith in conversation with Kevin Harrington, May–July 1996, Canadian Center for Architecture. Hereafter cited as "Goldsmith, interview, CCA."

4. *Van der Rohe v. Farnsworth*, transcript, 586.

5. Ibid., 352.

6. Ibid., 522.

7. Ibid., 1671.

8. *Fine Homebuilding*, April/May 1988, 34.

9. Ibid., 384, 570.

10. *Van der Rohe v. Farnsworth*, transcript, 717.

11. Wolf Tegethoff, *Mies van der Rohe: The Villas and Country Houses* (New York: The Museum of Modern Art, 1985), 130.

12. Ibid., 131.

13. Goldsmith, interview, CCA.

14. *Van der Rohe v. Farnsworth*, transcript, 694.

15. Goldsmith, interview, CCA, 75.

16. *Van der Rohe v. Farnsworth*, Edith Farnsworth deposition.

17. Meryle Secrest, *Frank Lloyd Wright: A Biography* (New York: Knopf, 1992), 251.

18. Moises Puente, ed., *Conversations with Mies van der Rohe* (New York: Princeton Architectural Press, 2008), 20.

19. Tegethoff, *Mies van der Rohe*, 96.

20. Ibid., 91.

21. Neumeyer, *Artless Word*, 372, fn. 65.

22. Peter Gay, *Modernism: The Lure of Heresy* (New York: Random House, 2007), 272.

23. *Van der Rohe v. Farnsworth*, Myron Goldsmith deposition, 112.

24. *Van der Rohe v. Farnsworth*, transcript, 552.

25. Blake, *Master Builders*, 229.

26. Goldsmith, oral history, AIC.

27.   *Van der Rohe v. Farnsworth*, transcript, 1510.

28.   Lambert, *Building Seagram*, 103, fn. 6.

29.   Dick Young, oral history, Farnsworth House, https://farnsworth house.org/oral-histories.

CHAPTER 5: "COMPARED TO THE FARNSWORTH HOUSE,
IT'S JUST A TOY."

1.   Robert A. M. Stern, ed., *Philip Johnson: Writings* (Oxford: Oxford University Press, 1979), 227.

2.   Dirk Lohan interview with Mies, summer 1968, Museum of Modern Art, Mies van der Rohe Collection.

3.   Hugh Howard, *Architecture's Odd Couple: Frank Lloyd Wright and Philip Johnson* (New York: Bloomsbury, 2016), 164.

4.   Schulze, *Mies van der Rohe*, 157.

5.   Shell, Duckett, and Fujikawa, *Impressions*, 18.

6.   Columbia School of Architecture Symposium, 1961.

7.   "Walking Tour with Philip Johnson, 1991," Glass House website, http://theglasshouse.org/explore/the-glass-house/.

8.   *Van der Rohe v. Farnsworth*, transcript, 910ff.

9.   "Walking Tour with Philip Johnson, 1991."

10.   Mark Lamster, *The Man in the Glass House: Philip Johnson, Architect of the Modern Century* (New York: Little, Brown, 2018), 228 ff.

11.   Speech, Congress Hall, Berlin, March 1961.

12.   Alice T. Friedman, *Women and the Making of the Modern House: A Social and Architectural History* (New York: Abrams, 1998), 147.

13.   Neil Jackson, *The Modern Steel House* (London: Taylor & Francis), 1996.

14.   "Walking Tour with Philip Johnson, 1991."

15.   Lambert, *Building Seagram*, 133ff.

16.   "Farnsworth House," Mies van der Rohe Archive, MoMA.

17.   Blake, *Master Builders*, 231.

18.   Terence Riley, interview with author, April 6, 2018.

19.   Paul Goldberger, Phyllis Lambert, and Sylvia Lavin, *Modern Views Inspired by the Mies van der Rohe Farnsworth House and the Philip Johnson Glass House* (New York: Assouline, 2010), 47.

20.   Ibid., 19.

21.   David Holowka, "The Farnsworth House, Part One: Whose Less Is More?" *ArchiTakes*, http://www.architakes.com/?p=2097.

22.   *Van der Rohe v. Farnsworth*, transcript, 108.

CHAPTER 6: "YOU GO BACK TO YOUR NEPHRITIS WHERE YOU BELONG."

1. *Chicago Tribune*, September 25, 1949.
2. Goldsmith, oral history, AIC.
3. Goldsmith, interview, CCA.
4. Sibyl Moholy-Nagy, "Hitler's Revenge," *Art in America*, September/October 1968.
5. Undated memo, Mies van der Rohe Archive, MoMA.
6. *Van der Rohe v. Farnsworth*, transcript, 168.
7. Ibid., 1238.
8. Ibid.

CHAPTER 7: "A VIRGILIAN DREAM"

1. "Farnsworth House Dialogue: Jacques Herzog, Pierre de Meuron, Kenneth Frampton, Wiel Arets," IIT Architecture, Chicago, 2014, https://vimeo.com/114609771.
2. Witold Rybczynski, *How Architecture Works* (New York: Farrar, Straus and Giroux, 2013), 91.
3. Philip Johnson to Mies van der Rohe, June 4, 1951, Mies van der Rohe Archive, MoMA.
4. Maritz Vandenberg, *The Farnsworth House: Mies van der Rohe*, Architecture in Detail (London: Phaidon, , 2003), 23.
5. James Ackerman, *The Villa: Form and Ideology of Country Houses* (Princeton, N.J.: Princeton University Press, 1990), 14.
6. Reyner Banham, "The Glass Paradise," in *A Critic Writes* (Berkeley: University of California Press, 1999), 32–38.
7. Michael Pollan, *A Place of My Own: The Education of an Amateur Builder* (New York: Random House, 1997), 250.
8. "Mies van der Rohe and Lilly Reich: Stuttgart, Berlin, Barcelona," Ramon Esteve Studio, March 29, 2017, http://www.ramonesteve.com/en/manufacturing-the-interior/posts/mies-van-der-rohe-y-lilly-reich-stuttgart-berlin-barcelona/.
9. Christian Norberg-Schulz, *A Talk with Mies van der Rohe* (1958), quoted in Neumeyer, *Artless Word*, 339.
10. Vandenberg, *Farnsworth House*, 8.
11. David Holowka, "The Farnsworth House, Part Two: From the Hearth to the Field," *ArchiTakes*, http://www.architakes.com/?p=3266.

12.   http://miessociety.org/mies/bookshelf/.

13.   Reyner Banham, "A Home Is Not a House," *Art in America* 2 (1965): 70–79.

14.   Jacques Herzog and Pierre de Meuron, *Treacherous Transparencies: Thoughts and Observations Triggered by a Visit to the Farnsworth House* (Chicago: ITAC Press, 2016), 37.

15.   Ludwig Mies van der Rohe and Dirk Lohan, *Mies van der Rohe: Farnsworth House, Plano, Illinois, 1945–50,* Global Architecture (Tokyo: ADA Edita Tokyo, 1976), 4.

16.   Schulze, *Mies van der Rohe,* 312.

17.   Ibid., 313.

18.   Witold Rybczynski, *Looking Around: A Journey Through Architecture* (New York: Penguin, 1993), 173.

19.   Schulze and Windhorst, *Mies van der Rohe,* 173.

20.   Rybczynski, *Looking Around,* 240.

21.   Schulze and Windhorst, *Mies van der Rohe,* 308.

22.   Ibid., 309.

23.   Kuh, *My Love Affair with Modern Art,* 76.

24.   Schulze, *Mies van der Rohe,* 248.

25.   *The Glass House: 860–880 Lake Shore Drive, A Home for Gracious Living,* http://860880lakeshoredrive.com/860880lakeshoredrive/wp-content/uploads/2012/05/TheGlassHouseBrochure.pdf.

26.   Schulze, "Farnsworth House" monograph, 19.

27.   *Mies van der Rohe, 1951–52: McCormick House Documentary,* Elmhurst Art Museum, August 18, 2011, https://www.archdaily.com/161232/mies-van-der-rohe-1951-52-mccormick-house-documentary.

28.   Franz Schulze, *Philip Johnson: Life and Work* (Chicago: University of Chicago Press, 1996), 214.

29.   Goldsmith, oral history, AIC, 73–74.

CHAPTER 8: "THE FEAR OF MIES' IMPLACABLE INTENTIONS"

1.   Young, oral history, Farnsworth House.

2.   Kuh, *My Love Affair with Modern Art,* 82.

3.   Paul Schweikher, oral history, Art Institute of Chicago, 109ff, http://digital-libraries.saic.edu/cdm/ref/collection/caohp/id/10266.

4.   David Dunlap, *The New York Times,* June 24, 1999.

5.   Personal communication with the author.

6.   *Van der Rohe v. Farnsworth,* transcript, 2654.

CHAPTER 9: "YOU ARE A GODDAM LIAR."

1. Schulze and Windhorst, *Mies van der Rohe,* 456.
2. Gene Summers, oral history, Art Institute of Chicago, http://digital
-libraries.saic.edu/cdm/ref/collection/caohp/id/10620.
3. Shell, Duckett, and Fujikawa, *Impressions.*
4. Northwestern University Medical Archive, April 28, 1950.
5. Goldsmith, oral history, AIC.
6. Goldsmith, interview, CCA.
7. *Van der Rohe v. Farnsworth,* deposition, 174.
8. Ibid., deposition, 377.
9. Ibid., deposition, 176.
10. Ibid., deposition, 112.
11. *Van der Rohe v. Farnsworth,* transcript, 104.
12. *Van der Rohe v. Farnsworth,* deposition, 274.
13. *Van der Rohe v. Farnsworth,* transcript, 80.
14. Ibid., 104, 108.
15. Ibid., 1449.
16. Ibid., 104.
17. Ibid., 17.
18. Ibid., 238.
19. Ibid., 285ff.
20. Ibid., 301.
21. Ibid., 716.
22. Ibid., 964.
23. Ibid., 794.
24. Ibid., 1199.
25. Ibid., 992.

CHAPTER 10: "I THINK THE HOUSE IS PERFECTLY CONSTRUCTED, IT IS PERFECTLY EXECUTED."

1. *Van der Rohe v. Farnsworth,* transcript, 2862.
2. Ibid., 2961.
3. Ibid., 2623.
4. Ibid., 3227.
5. Ibid., 3245ff.
6. Ibid., 2932.
7. Ibid., 3293.
8. Ibid., 2782–93.

9.   Goldsmith, interview, CCA.

10.   Myron Goldsmith fonds, Canadian Centre for Architecture, https://www.cca.qc.ca/en/search/details/collection/object/261187.

11.   *Van der Rohe v. Farnsworth,* transcript, 2222.

12.   Ibid., 1889.

13.   Schweikher, oral history, AIC.

14.   *Van der Rohe v. Farnsworth,* transcript, 1048.

15.   Ibid., 1158ff.

16.   Ibid., 1177ff.

CHAPTER 11: "I FEEL LIKE A PROWLING ANIMAL, ALWAYS ON THE ALERT."

1.   Schulze and Windhorst, *Mies van der Rohe,* 267.

2.   Shell, Duckett, and Fujikawa, *Impressions,* 27.

3.   Schweikher, oral history, AIC, 200.

4.   *Chicago Sun-Times,* June 9, 1953.

5.   Monica Penick, *Tastemaker: Elizabeth Gordon, "House Beautiful," and the Postwar American Home* (New Haven, Conn.: Yale University Press, 2017), 8.

6.   Ibid., 31.

7.   Elizabeth Corbett, "Tilting at Modern: Elizabeth Gordon's 'The Threat to the Next America'" (PhD diss., University of California, Berkeley, 2010), 48.

8.   Lewis Mumford, *The New Yorker,* October 11, 1947.

9.   Penick, *Tastemaker,* 99.

10.   Corbett, "Tilting at Modern," 26.

11.   Penick, *Tastemaker,* 84.

12.   Ibid., 88.

13.   Corbett, "Tilting at Modern," 47.

14.   Ibid., 39.

15.   "Report on the American Battle Between Good and Bad Modern Houses," *House Beautiful,* May 1953.

16.   Penick, *Tastemaker,* 120.

17.   Corbett, "Tilting at Modern," 101.

18.   Donald Leslie Johnson, *Frank Lloyd Wright Versus America: The 1930s* (Cambridge, Mass.: MIT Press, 1990), 44.

19.   Corbett, "Tilting at Modern," 107.

20.   *Newsweek,* June 8, 1953.

21.   Memo to file, March 19, 1953.

22.   Corbett, "Tilting at Modern," 98.

23.   Faissler-Levinson letter, March 8, 1954.

CHAPTER 12: "ARCHITECTS SHOULD KISS THE FEET OF MIES VAN DER ROHE."

1. *Life* magazine, March 18, 1957.

2. Lambert, *Building Seagram*, 122.

3. Ibid., 9.

4. Ibid., 150.

5. David Whitney and Jeffrey Kipnis, eds., *Philip Johnson: The Glass House* (New York: Pantheon, 1993), 160.

6. Lambert, *Building Seagram*, 9.

7. Holowka, "Farnsworth House, Part One: Whose Less Is More?"

8. Schulze, *Mies van der Rohe*, 310.

9. Schulze and Windhorst, *Mies van der Rohe*, 326.

10. John Holabird, oral history, Art Institute of Chicago, http://digital-libraries.saic.edu/cdm/compoundobject/collection/caohp/id/26885/rec/1.

11. Carter Wiseman, *I. M. Pei: A Profile in American Architecture* (New York: Abrams, 1990), 98ff.

12. Wolf von Eckhardt, "The Death of the Moderns," *The New Republic*, August 6, 1977.

13. Schulze and Windhorst, *Mies van der Rohe*, 381.

14. Thomas Dyja, *The Third Coast: When Chicago Built the American Dream* (New York: Penguin Press), 214.

15. Neumeyer, *Artless Word*, 331.

16. Robert Venturi, *Complexity and Contradiction in Architecture* (New York: Museum of Modern Art, 1967), 16ff.

17. "Mies's Dreams with Windows," *The New York Times*, June 22, 2001.

18. Schulze, *Mies van der Rohe*, 320.

19. "Correspondence," Mies van der Rohe archive, Library of Congress.

20. Georgia van der Rohe, *La Donna è Mobile*, 229.

21. Ibid., 237.

22. Ibid., 245.

CHAPTER 13: "I REPEAT, MAGIC AND POETRY!"

1. William Murphy, oral history, Farnsworth House, https://farnsworthhouse.org/oral-histories/.

2. Interview with author.

3. *Chicago Tribune*, May 2, 1968.

4. Personal communication with the author.

5. *The New York Times*, November 3, 1983.

6. *The New York Times,* June 24, 1999.

7. Rybczynski, *How Architecture Works,* 22.

8. Patrick Sisson, "A New Light Installation Illuminates the Farnsworth House," *Chicago Reader,* October 7, 2014.

9. Werner Buch, oral history, Art Institute of Chicago, http://digital -libraries.saic.edu/cdm/compoundobject/collection/caohp/id/26869/rec/1.

10. *The Wall Street Journal,* June 19, 2015.

11. Van der Rohe and Lohan, *Mies van der Rohe: Farnsworth House, Plano,* 4.

12. David Holowka, "The Farnsworth House, Part Three: The Progeny?" *ArchiTakes,* https://www.architakes.com/?p=3428.

CHAPTER 14: "SHE THEN ABANDONED EVERYTHING FOR POETRY AND ITALY."

1. *Northwestern Tri-Quarterly,* Fall 1960, pp. 6–12.

2. "The Other Man in Nancy Reagan's Life," *Chicago Tribune,* March 8, 2016; "Loyal Davis, Legendary Neurosurgeon," *Hektoen International,* Summer 2018, https://hekint.org/2018/08/16/loyal-davis-legendary-neuro surgeon-1896-1982/.

3. James Gerard, personal communication, August 18, 2002.

4. Northwestern Medical School archives.

5. *Corriere della Serra,* January 23, 2012.

6. Giorgio Delia, "Per Edith Farnsworth," *Forum Italicum; A Journal of Italian Studies* 47, no. 3 (November 2013).

7. Eugenio Montale, *Otherwise: Last and First Poems of Eugenio Montale,* trans. Jonathan Galassi (New York: Random House, 1985); Eugenio Montale, *Montale Collected Poems 1920–1954,* trans. Jonathan Galassi (New York: Farrar, Straus and Giroux, 1999), 417.

8. Farnsworth to Henry Regnery, January 15, 1971, Henry Regnery Papers, Hoover Institution, Stanford, California.

9. Kivitts, oral history, Farnsworth House.

10. Neil and Parkie Emmons, oral history, Farnsworth House.

11. *Corriere della Serra,* January 23, 2012.

12. Farnsworth to Marion Carpenter, letter, April 1, 1971.

13. Letter to Sue Bentley, May 16, 1973.

14. Letters, April 16, 1973; July 24, 1975.

15. Farnsworth to Marion Carpenter, May 8, 1975.

INDEX

ALEX BEAM has written two novels and four works of nonfiction: *American Crucifixion, The Feud, Gracefully Insane,* and *A Great Idea at the Time;* the latter two were *New York Times* Notable Books. Beam has also written for *The Atlantic, Slate,* and *Forbes/FYI.* He lives in Newton, Massachusetts.